Society of Biblical Literature

2003 Seminar Papers

Society of Biblical Literature
Seminar Paper Series

Number 42
Society of Biblical Literature
2003 Seminar Papers

Society of Biblical Literature
2003 Seminar Papers

One Hundred Thirty-Ninth Annual Meeting
November 22–25, 2003
Atlanta Marriott Marquis Hotel
and
Hyatt Regency Atlanta Hotel
Atlanta, Georgia

Society of Biblical Literature
Atlanta

Society of Biblical Literature
2003 Seminar Papers

Copyright © 2003 by the Society of Biblical Literature

All rights reserved. No part of this work may be reproduced or transmitted in any form or by any means, electronic or mechanical, including photocopying and recording, or by means of any information storage or retrieval system, except as may be expressly permitted by the 1976 Copyright Act or in writing from the publisher. Requests for permission should be addressed in writing to the Rights and Permissions Office, Society of Biblical Literature, 825 Houston Mill Road, Atlanta, GA 30329 USA.

Indexed in *Religion Index Two: Multi-Author Works* published by the American Theological Library Association, Evanston, Illinois. Indexing also available in the ATLA Religion Database accessible through Dialog Information Services, Palo Alto, California. Also available for compact-disk searching through ATLA.

ISBN: 1-58983-110-1
ISSN: 0145-2711

Printed in the United States of America on acid-free, recycled paper conforming to ANSI/NISO Z39.48-1992 (R1997) and ISO 9706:1994 standards for paper permanence.

Publisher's Preface

The papers contained in this volume were selected by the leadership of the indicated program units of the Society of Biblical Literature for presentation and discussion in the working sessions of those program units at the 2003 SBL Annual Meeting. By making the full text of these papers available in advance of the Annual Meeting, SBL hopes to facilitate the work of the program units. These papers have been published as submitted to SBL by their individual authors without additional review or editing other than reformatting for typographic consistency. While SBL claims copyright on this volume as a compilation, that claim of copyright is intended only to protect the interests of the individual authors of these papers and is not understood to infringe on the intellectual ownership of their respective work by the individual authors, who retain the right to republish or reuse their work in whole or in part in any other work of their own creation without charge or restriction. These papers may represent the initial stages in the development of an author's work, which will later find formal publication elsewhere in a different form. Consequently, all requests for permission to reproduce material from this volume should be directed to the individual authors.

Contents

African Biblical Hermeneutics Consultation

S22-51   "Surely We Are Not Blind, Are We": An African Theological Reading of the Story of the Healing of the Man Born Blind, John 9:1–41
Ernest M. Ezeogu 1

S22-51   Why Not Postcolonial Biblical Criticism in Southern Africa: Stating the Obvious or Looking for the Impossible?
Jeremy Punt 17

Didache in Context Consultation

S22-61   A New Paradigm for Recovering the Origins and Use of the *Didache*
Aaron Milavec 45

S22-61   The Gathering of the Church in the Kingdom: The Self-Understanding of the *Didache* Community in the Eucharistic Prayers
Huub van de Sandt 69

Theology of the Hebrew Scriptures Section

S22-71   God's Provision for the Well-Being of Living Creatures in Genesis 9
Simon J. De Vries 89

S22-71   Does YHWH *Naḥam*? A Question of Openness
Donald C. Raney II 105

Violence and Representations of Violence among Jews and Christians Consultation

S22-120　(Re)presentations of Violence in Philo
　　　　　Torrey Seland 117

Matthew Section

S23-16　Tradition in Transition, or Antioch versus Sepphoris:
　　　　Rethinking the Matthean Community's Location
　　　　Aaron M. Gale.. 141

Poster Session

S23-65　Blasphemy against the Spirit and the Historical Jesus
　　　　Amy M. Donaldson 167

Biblical Lands and Peoples in Archaeology and Text Section

S24-53　Galilee and Greco-Roman Culture in the Time of
　　　　Jesus: The Neglected Significance of Chronology
　　　　Mark A. Chancey 173

Josephus Seminar

S24-116　Josephus's Caesarian *Acta:* History of a Dossier
　　　　　Claude Eilers 189

Theological Perspectives on the Book of Ezekiel Group

S24-125　When Israel Loses Its Meaning: The Reconstitution
　　　　　of Language and Community in Ezekiel's Prophecy
　　　　　David Casson 215

"Surely We Are Not Blind, Are We": An African Theological Reading of the Story of the Healing of the Man Born Blind, John 9:1–41

Ernest M. Ezeogu
Toronto School of Theology

INTRODUCTION

Among the diversity of approaches to the Fourth Gospel is the so-called political approach, which includes feminist, liberation, postcolonial, African, and other Third World readings. The African theological reading of John 9 that I intend to do in this study belongs with these political readings. One wonders, though, why it is necessary to make such a distinction between *theological* and *political* readings of John. Why are readings from the perspectives of liberation, feminist, and African theologies not described as theological readings alongside other established *theological* readings that are current in theology faculties in Europe and North America? Is that a subtle way of questioning the theological claim of these emergent readings?

Our text, John 9, is generally recognised as a theologically fertile text. It is my proposition that the sort of theology the Fourth Evangelist is advocating in John 9 is, in fact, very close to what mainline theologians call *political* theologies today. John uses the event of Jesus healing a man born blind to present the theological agenda of an emergent *Christian* theology challenging the *Jewish*[1] theological establishment.

An African theological reading of the Bible, simply stated, means reading the Bible with the questions of African theology in mind. More than

---

[1] In the context of first-century religious discourse, "Christian" and "Jewish" refers primarily to a distinction in religious persuasion rather than ethnicity, since most of the players on both sides of the polemical divide would be Jews by ethnicity.

1

many other passages in the Gospels, or in the Fourth Gospel, for that matter, John 9 appears to shed much light on many of the burning issues facing African theology in both areas of theoretical self-understanding and practical engagement. Many interesting aspects of material theology are touched upon in this chapter, such as healing, conversion, faith, salvation, sin, and Christology. My approach in this study is, however, limited to more formal theological questions, such as the task and sources of African theology, predispositions for African theology, legitimation and verification in African theology, individual and institution in African theology, and the like.

It should be understood that we are talking of an approach rather than a specific method different from other established exegetical and hermeneutical methods. The difference between an Africanist reading and other readings lies more in the interests that inform the reading and the preunderstanding that the reader bring to the task. We shall, therefore, be employing the methodological steps of established biblical interpretation while asking questions that arise out of our area of interest, namely, African theology formally understood.

In the more extensive study of which this paper is only a summary, we began, as is normal in New Testament exegesis, with an examination of the Greek text of John 9 to see if there are any major textual variants that might significantly affect the reading. The text we established after such a textual study does not differ significantly from the text of the New Revised Standard Version. We have therefore adopted it as the basic English translation in this study.

We shall now proceed to examine certain expressions in the narrative whose meanings in the Johannine context need to be clarified for a better literary appreciation of the passage. We shall conclude this phase of the study by determining the theme and literal sense of the story. Then, after having determined what the text says as such, we shall proceed with the question of what the text says to us in the African theological context. This rereading of the story from the perspective of the interests and concerns of African theology will bring our study to a conclusion.

Needless to say, this limited study cannot do justice to the highly interesting discussion of the relationship between history and theology or tradition and redaction in the Fourth Gospel that this chapter highlights in a very fascinating manner,[2] nor shall we engage in a detailed narrative study of this captivating and dramatic story, even though this would, no doubt, be a very rewarding exercise.

---

[2] For a landmark study of this illuminating aspect of the Fourth Gospel, the reader is referred to J. Louis Martyn, *History and Theology in the Fouth Gospel* (2d ed.; Nashville: Abingdon, 1979).

A LITERARY READING OF JOHN 9

The search for the literal sense has been described as "the principal task of exegesis."[3] Here the exegete seeks "to define the precise meaning of texts as produced by their authors.... One arrives at this sense by means of a careful analysis of the text, within its literary and historical context."[4] We shall proceed by studying certain terms and expressions in their literary and historical contexts.

"A Man Blind From Birth" (9:1)

There is no instance in the Hebrew Bible of the cure of blindness. One case is recorded in the LXX (Tobit 11:11), but even so the blindness was not congenital. Hebrew prophets believed that opening the eyes of the blind would constitute one of the blessing of the messianic age (Isa 53:5). In the Synoptics, John the Baptist was reminded of this in his uncertainty regarding the messianic identity of Jesus (Matt 11:5). The Synoptics record instances of Jesus healing the blind (Matt 20:29; Mark 8:23; Luke 18:35), but this is the only recorded case where the blindness is said to be from birth.

"Who Sinned, This Man or His Parents, That He Was Born Blind?" (9:2)

Underlying the first alternative is the belief that disease was a divine punishment for personal sin. Though the author of Job had tried to show that this was not always the case, the belief survived well into New Testament times (see John 5:14). Since the man was blind from birth, it would then mean that the sin was prenatal. According to some rabbinical casuists this was a possibility. The feud between Jacob and Esau that began already in the womb had given rise to midrashic speculation on the possibility of prenatal sin.[5]

The second alternative suggest that the blindness could be divine punishment for the sins of the man's parents. This belief is frequently expressed in the Hebrew Bible (Exod 20:5; 34:7; Num 14:18; Pss 79:8; 109:14; Isa 65:6–7). The prophet Ezekiel, however, repudiated this doctrine with the principle, "The person who sins shall die. A child shall not suffer for the iniquity of a parent, nor a parent suffer for the iniquity of a child" (Ezek 18:20).

---

[3] J. L. Houlden, ed., *The Interpretation of the Bible in The Church* (London: SCM, 1995), 79.

[4] Ibid., 79.

[5] Gail R. O'Day, "The Gospel of John," in *The New Interpreter's Bible* (Nashville: Abingdon, 1994), 9:653.

Jesus' rejection of the either-or proposal was a denial of the universal validity of the doctrine of retributive justice that informed the question. Causes do not always have to be located in the past; they could be located in the future, as in this case. The purpose of the man's blindness is that God's works should be manifested in him.

"As Long As I Am in the World, I Am the Light of the World" (9:5)

This is a more nuanced and mitigated version of the universal and exclusivist claim, "I am the light of the world" (8:12). Here the emphatic personal pronoun is omitted; so also is the article before "light." Moreover, the claim here is preceded by an adverbial clause that seems to limit its application to the time of Jesus' earthly ministry. Rudolf Schnackenburg, however, is of the opinion that the adverbial does not limit the claim but merely relates it to the present case.[6] The miracle that follows is a demonstration of this claim. Is that why Jesus did not wait to be asked to do it?

"He Spat on the Ground and Made Mud with the Saliva" (9:6)

That Jesus cured by means of his spittle is found in John (cf. 5:6) and Mark (8:23) but not in Matthew or Luke. Gail O'Day suggests that "Matthew and Luke avoid that detail in their healing stories, probably because of its popular association with magic."[7] There is no doubt that the use of spittle in healing represents the older tradition.

Scholars have wrestled with the question of why Jesus had to use spittle and mud. A pragmatic take on the issue is seen in H. van der Loos, who argues that "Jesus' aim was pedagogic and psychological, viz. the idea had to be aroused in the blind man that Jesus wanted to heal him. The treatment with the clay served as a means of arousing belief, just as going to the pool of Siloam was a means of testing the man."[8] A more symbolic or mythical take on the question is seen in Irenaeus, who compares the use of clay in the cure of the blind man to the creation of humankind out of clay in Gen 2:7. Being blind from birth, he points out, the blind man had virtually *no eyes,* and Jesus *created* new eyes for him out of the clay. That some people who knew the blind man could no longer recognise him after the cure indicates that some plastic-surgical change might have taken place, and so adds credibility to Irenaeus. Sanders and Mastin tend toward

---

[6] Rudolf Schnackenburg, *The Gospel According to St John* (Herder's Theological Commentary on the New Testament; New York: Seabury, 1980 [German original 1971]), 2:242.

[7] O'Day, "John," 9:654.

[8] H. van der Loos, *The Miracles of Jesus* (Supplements to Novum Testamentum 9; Leiden: Brill, 1965), 108.

the same view that "Jesus uses mud to complete the work of creation in the blind man."[9] Be that as it may, most scholars would agree with van der Loos's conclusion that "the laying on of hands and the use of spittle must be regarded here, as elsewhere, against the background of the then methods of healing,"[10] not in light of modern medicine.

"'GO, WASH IN THE POOL OF SILOAM,' WHICH MEANS SENT" (9:7)

The Pool of Siloam, located on the southwestern slope of the old city hill, was fed by the spring of Gihon. King Hezekiah had a tunnel dug from Gihon to the pool and channelled the water of the spring to the pool by an underground route (2 Chr 32:30).

The waters *shiloach* are mentioned in Isa 8:6, and the LXX renders it as "Siloam." The original sense of the Hebrew form (*qal* infinitive) is active, meaning "the sending forth," that is, the duct or channel. It is not a passive participial form, as would be required by John's etymology. Raymond Brown, therefore, thinks that "the evangelist is either following a different reading of the consonants (e.g. *shaluach,* sent) or exercising liberty in adapting the etymology to his purposes."[11] Why would the Fourth Evangelist want to do this? It has been suggested that he was dealing with "the difficulty of Jesus employing gross materials and sending the blind man to the pool when a mere word from him sufficed.... This word is therefore etymologically misinterpreted as 'Sent,' so that, in spite of everything, Jesus turns out to be the healer."[12]

"HE DOES NOT OBSERVE THE SABBATH" (9:16A)

The linking of this cure with the Sabbath seems to be an afterthought on the part of the Evangelist (v. 14). The charge of violating the Sabbath had been made against Jesus on a similar occasion, when he healed the sick man at the pool of Bethzata and told him to carry his pallet away (5:10). According to Brown, Jesus might have contravened the Sabbath observance in more ways than one:

> First, since the man's life was not in danger, Jesus should have waited till another day to heal.... Second, among the thirty-nine works forbidden

---

[9] J. N. Sanders and B. A. Mastin, *A Commentary on the Gospel according to St John* (Black's New Testament Commentaries; London: Adam & Charles Black, 1968), 239.

[10] Loos, *Miracles,* 429.

[11] Raymond E. Brown, *The Gospel according to John* (Anchor Bible; Garden City, New York: Doubleday, 1966), 373.

[12] Ernst Haenchen, *A Commentary on the Gospel of John Chapters 1–6* (trans. R. W. Funk; Hermeneia; (Philadelphia: Fortress, 1984 [German original 1980]), 38.

on the Sabbath ... was kneading, and Jesus kneaded the clay with his spittle to make mud. Third, according to later Jewish tradition ... there was an opinion that it was not permitted to anoint an eye on the Sabbath. Fourth, [according to the Jerusalem Talmud] that one may not put fasting spittle on the eyes on the Sabbath.[13]

Jesus' violation of the Sabbath is seen by some of the Pharisees as evidence that Jesus does not come from God.

"HOW CAN A MAN WHO IS A SINNER PERFORM SUCH SIGNS?" (9:16B)

The principle that a sinner cannot work miracles is not universally attested in biblical tradition. Pharaoh's sorcerers (Exod 7:11) were able to reproduce Aaron's miracle. In Matt 24:24 Jesus warns against false prophets and messiahs who will show great signs and wonders to lead astray even the elect. Yet the overriding principle here, as well as in the Synoptics, seems to be the empirical principle of "by their fruits you will know them." (Matt 7:16–20). "Signs" here would then refer to salutary deeds, deeds of altruism and benevolence. Nowhere in biblical literature are ungodly magicians and sorcerers credited with such signs. All they could perform are signs of "wonder."

"THE JEWS" (9:18)

Brown succeeds in bringing out the strangeness in the Fourth Gospel of Jesus and the Jews around him referring to other Jews simply as "the Jews." "To have the Jewish parents of the blind man in Jerusalem described as being 'afraid of the Jews' (9:22) is just as awkward as having an American living in Washington, DC described as being afraid of 'the Americans'—only a non-American speaks thus of 'the Americans.'"[14] Brown therefore speculates whether this hostile Johannine style of speaking of "the Jews" may not have been borrowed from the Samaritans, on whose lips, as non-Jews, it would have been quite natural.

"The Jews" understood as a people is not always the correct translation of *hoi ioudaioi* in the Fourth Gospel because it refers interchangeably to "the Jews" and to the chief priests and Pharisees (cf. 18:3 and 12; 8:13 and 22). The Fourth Gospel speaks of "the Jews" where the Synoptic Gospels speak of the Sanhedrin (cf. 18:28–31 with Mark 15:1). In John 9:18ff., as in 5:10ff., "the Jews" represent a segment of the Jewish hierarchy that enjoyed the power to excommunicate, namely, the Sanhedrin. Schnackenburg argues convincingly that "with this change from 'Pharisees'

---

[13] Brown, *John*, 373.
[14] Raymond E. Brown, *The Community of the Beloved Disciple* (New York: Paulist, 1979), 41.

to 'Jews' the evangelist certainly intends to indicate the official character of the interrogation ... There are no grounds for taking the change either as an indication of a change of actors or as a sign of a later insertion."[15]

"Put Out of the Synagogue" (9:22)

That anyone who acknowledged Jesus as the Christ was to be "put out of the synagogue" is mentioned again in 12:42 and referred to in 16:2. Certainly some form of excommunication is meant. Brown distinguishes three forms of excommunication practised in first-century Judaism: (1) *nezifah*, the minor ban of about a week's duration; (2) *nidduy* or *shammata*, a more formal banishment lasting thirty days; and (3) *cherem*, the solemn curse or excommunication imposed by Jewish authorities, permanently excluding one from Israel.[16] He concludes that the exclusion of Jewish Christians from the synagogue at the end of the first century would be closest to the last of these three types.

There is virtual unanimity among scholars that exclusion from the synagogue was not a concern at the time of Jesus' ministry but subsequently became so for the community of the Fourth Evangelist. In this way 9:22 becomes a classic example of the two levels on which the Fourth Gospel is meant to be read. "On one level, the story portrays a conflict with the religious authorities in Jesus' own day, but it is told in idioms (e.g., "afraid of the Jews," "be put out of the synagogue") that also communicate directly on the level of the community's own experience of conflict and persecution."[17]

"Do You Also Want to Become his Disciples?" (9:27)

"Not you also" (*me kai humeis*) suggests that it was known that Jesus had made some disciples already and that the Pharisees were aware of it. It could also be seen as the blind man's owning up to the suspicion of the Pharisees that he was in collusion with Jesus as his disciple. Though he had not as yet declared his discipleship, there is no doubt in his mind that, as far as Jesus and himself were concerned, there was no going back. He was already an "anonymous" disciple. Their response accusing him of being a disciple of Jesus (v. 28) lends support to the view that they probably understood what the man said in this light.

"We Do Not Know Where He Comes From" (9:29)

In 7:27 Jesus' authority is questioned precisely because they know where he comes from. Here his authority is questioned because they do

---

15 Schnackenburg, *John,* 2:249.
16 Brown, *John,* 374.
17 O'Day, "John," 9:657.

not know where he comes from. Whereas the former refers to his earthly origin, what is meant here is his divine origin. The Fourth Evangelist here exposes the Pharisees to the ridicule of his readers, who have been informed right from the start (1:1, 14) that Jesus comes from God.

"We Know That God Does Not Listen to Sinners" (9:31)

The man contrasts the lack of knowledge on the part of the Jewish authorities with the common knowledge of believing Jews (*oidamen* "we know") that God does not listen to sinners. On the double level of reading, "the *oidamen* also includes the Christian community, which must have used the same argument as the cured man to counter Jewish attacks."[18] The principle that God does not listen to the prayers of sinners appears frequently in the Hebrew Bible (cf. Job 27:9; Ps 66:18; Isa 1:15; 29:2; Ezek 8:18; Mic 4:4; Zech 7:13). So also does the converse principle that God hears the prayers of the godly (cf. Pss 34:15; 145:19; Prov 15:29; see also James 5:16.) "The argument is clear. God does not hear the prayers of sinners. Miracles are granted in answer to the prayers of a good man. Jesus has worked a miracle. Therefore Jesus is a good man."[19]

"If This Man Were Not from God" (9:33)

The healed man cites the unique character of the miracle as a certain and reliable form of legitimation. This is so because "if this man were not from God, he could do nothing" (v. 33). The principle at work here is the same principle formulated by Nicodemus in 3:2 to the effect that Jesus is legitimated by his miracles: "We know that you are a teacher who has come from God, for no one can do these signs that you are doing unless God is with him."

"And They Drove Him Out" (9:34)

In the story line this does not signify "they excommunicated him" (v. 22); it only means that they put him out of their presence as a way of bringing the interrogation to a close. John uses *ekballein ek* in this sense (see 6:37). Taking into account the two levels of reading the Fourth Gospel that Brown has pointed out, it could, in fact, mean both the one and the other. Excommunication from the synagogue indicates the circumstances of a later period than that of the ministry of Jesus, namely, that of the Evangelist and his community of readers.

---

[18] Schnackenburg, *John,* 2:252.

[19] J. H. Bernard, *A Critical and Exegetical Commenatry on the Gospel according to St. John* (International Critical Commentary; Edinburgh: T&T Clark, 1928), 336.

"Do You Believe in the Son of Man?" (9:35)

Why does Jesus introduce himself to the once-blind man under the title of Son of Man? Two reason are adduced. First, "Son of Man" is a messianic title associated with judgment (12:31–34), and our story ends with the theme of judgment (vv. 39–41). Second, a function of the Johannine Son of Man is to "draw all people to himself" (cf. 12:32). In this verse Jesus takes the initiative to find the man the Jewish authorities had driven away, so as to draw him into fullness of communion with himself.

"And He Worshiped Him" (9:38)

This is the standard reaction to a theophany in the Hebrew Bible (Gen 17:3). The Fourth Evangelist uses *proskunein* (see 4:20; 12:20) to express the worship due to God alone.

"For Judgment I Came into This World" (9:39)

Strictly speaking, this would be the result rather than the purpose of Jesus' mission. Brown explains: "The line of distinction between the result of Jesus' ministry and its purpose is not drawn sharply because of the oversimplified outlook which attributes everything that happens to God's purpose."[20]

By judgment, *krima,* here is meant the result of a *krisis* or act of distinguishing between good and evil, and so of judging. "So the sentence means, 'It is with a view to that ultimate decision which shall distinguish one person from another that I came into this world.'"[21] The supreme test is faith in himself (cf. v. 35; 3:15). This saying is the Johannine equivalent of the Synoptic representation of Jesus as accepting sinners and rejecting the self-justifying, religious people. Blindness is determined not simply by one's physical inability to see but by one's ability to recognize the revelation of God in the person and works of Jesus.

At the end of our semantic-syntactical analysis of the pericope, we shall now try to articulate the literal sense of of John 9. That the theme of John 9 is "Jesus the Light of the World" is fairly clear to all commentators. The Evangelist gives it away both at the beginning (v. 5) and at the end of the narrative (v. 39). It therefore functions as an *inclusio,* a framework for reading the whole story. Brown is right on target when he concludes that "This is a story of how a man who sat in darkness was brought to see the light, not only physically but spiritually. On the other hand, it is also a tale of how those who thought they saw (the Pharisees) were blinding themselves to the light and plunging into darkness."[22]

---

[20] Brown, *John,* 376.
[21] Bernard, *Commenatry,* 339–40.
[22] Brown, *John,* 377.

AN AFRICAN THEOLOGICAL READING OF JOHN 9

The Task of African Theology

What is the task of African theology? What kind of questions and issues should preoccupy African theologians who every day come face to face with the miseries of a weeping continent? There is no gainsaying the fact that Africa is afflicted with a litany of untold miseries and hardships: famine, disease, poverty, illiteracy, war, civil unrest, social instability, economic downturn, and so forth.

In John 9, Jesus and his disciples come face to face with human misery, that of blindness. Blindness, in Hebrew and African experience, is not just the privation of the sense of sight; it is also a condition that hinders one from realizing one's social and economic potentials. The disciples raise a traditional theological question: "Rabbi, who sinned, this man or his parents, that he was born blind?" (v. 2). This is a typical traditional theological question in that it aims at being able to *understand* and explain the situation. For the disciples, the man's congenital blindness is an interesting case for theological investigation. But what does Jesus do? Jesus sees the blindness not as an occasion for curious speculation but as a challenge for practical engagement. For Jesus, the important thing is not to find a theologically satisfactory explanation of the misery but to change, to redeem, and to transform the miserable situation. Ivory-tower theologies, which rationalize the day-to-day, flesh-and-blood concerns of the people, should have no place in African theology.

Sources of African Theology

African theology has been compared to the traditional African tripod. It sands on three feet or three sources, namely, scripture, church tradition, and African cultural experience. The formal education of the African theologian, irrespective of church affiliation, focuses almost entirely on the scriptural and church traditions to the neglect of the African cultural component. This imbalance needs urgent redress because it is only in African cultural tradition that the theologian comes in contact with the lived experience of the people they are called to serve. Moreover, this is the door through which new elements enter into the otherwise stagnant pool of data for theological reflection.

The Pharisees are the professional theologians in the story of John 9. The problem they have with understanding the man who had been blind is that they look to the Bible and Mosaic tradition alone for their answers. When lived experience encounters a new fact and, following that, raises a new question, they find themselves ill-equipped to handle it. If they had made room for lived experience as a source of revelation, and therefore of theological data, they could have handled the issue with more understanding and balance. John 9 shows us the superiority of the theology of the once-blind man to that of the Pharisees, all because the one took experience seriously into account and the other did not.

African theology must seek to build itself from the ground up, not from the top down. This is the only way to construct a theology that is true to lived experience, like that of the once-blind man whose "straightforward theology flowed naturally from his own life experience with Jesus Christ, and not the other way round, as is the case with much of our doctrine today."[23]

PREDISPOSITION FOR AFRICAN THEOLOGY

The traditional understanding of theology as faith seeking understanding, *fides quaerens intellectum*, establishes the premise of faith as a predisposition for theology. Now, theologians have distinguished between objective faith, *fides quae creditur* (faith in the sense of what is to be believed), and subjective faith, *fides qua creditur* (faith in the sense of the personal commitment of the believer). Yet much of traditional theology has focused on objective faith to the almost total exclusion of subjective faith. This imbalance would be corrected if theology began to take account of the fact that the faith that seeks understanding—and that, therefore, is a predisposition for theology—expresses itself in both objective and subjective dimensions

In John 9 we see the Pharisees proficient in objective faith. The blind man, on the other hand, as he recovers his sight, physical and spiritual, can be seen as progressing in subjective faith. His faith commitment in 9:35–38 is to a person ("Do you believe in the Son of Man?" ... "Tell me, so that I may believe in him" [9:35–36]), not an intellectual assent to a proposition. The unnecessary conflict that ensues between them serves as a negative testimony to the complementarity that should exist between these two modes of believing. To avoid such conflicts in African theology, recognition should be given to faith, objective and subjective, as a predisposition for theology.

African theology is a dialogue between two traditions: Judeo-Christian and African. The African theologian should, therefore, as a predisposition, be one who is at home in the two traditions. The model in John 9, apart from Jesus, of course, is the blind man. He is the one who knows and can articulate the Jewish experience ("we know" [9:31]), as well as the new Christian experience ("I know" [9:25]). The Pharisees, on the other hand,

---

[23] Guillermo Cook, "Seeing, Judging and Acting: Evangelism in Jesus' Way: A Biblical Study on Chapter 9 of the Gospel of John," *International Review of Mission* 87, no. 346 (1998): 394.

can speak only for the Jewish tradition ("we know" [9:29]). This is the advantage that the once-blind man has over the Pharisees in John 9. In the same vein, being at home in two traditions should be seen as a predisposition for African theology, since this is the enabling condition for dialogue between the two traditions.

LEGITIMATION IN AFRICAN THEOLOGY

Every system of theology has to deal with the question of what is to be admissible as a legitimate expression of faith seeking understanding. Scientific theology has always had a problem appreciating the various expressions of popular theology, the theology of the generality of believing women and men not educated in formal theology. Because it is not expressed in the thought forms and categories of textbook theology, there is a tendency to depreciate popular theology as not worthy to be called theology. This academic arrogance on the part of formal theology is challenged by a theological reading of John 9 where we see the Pharisees as representing the interests and concerns of traditional formal theology and the blind man as representing those of popular theology.

Between academic and popular theology it is the latter that is closer and more responsive to the actual lived experience of people. The rigorous logic of deductive ratiocination involved in academic theology must, therefore, meet the spontaneous expression of popular theology halfway. This will restrain academic theology from soaring to the ivory tower of irrelevance where it is no longer in touch with real life issues. Everyone agrees that popular theology needs academic theology in order to be fully enlightened. In light of John 9, it is also in order to affirm the corollary, namely, that academic theology needs popular theology in order to remain faithful to its mission of service to the people of God.[24]

The problem of legitimation can also be addressed in the area of encounter between established and developing theologies. This can be seen, for example, in the skepticism with which African, Asian, liberation, feminist, and other new theological expressions have been received by the Euro-American theological establishment. There is often a condescending hesitation on the part of the older theologies to accord the status of theology to these theological newcomers on the ground that they have a line of reasoning that differs from the conventional. We see that in the condescending manner in which the healed man was treated by the Jewish authorities. African theology should avoid this danger by recognising popular theology, or any other brand of theology, for that matter, as complementary rather than adversarial to its theological agenda, since all

---

[24] The term "people of God" is used here in a most inclusive sense.

theologies are fundamentally engaged in the one search for the understanding of faith.

VERIFICATION IN AFRICAN THEOLOGY

Verification differs from legitimation. Legitimation merely demands acceptance of a theological position as a legitimate though perhaps variant expression. It has to do with the formal aspects of the theological process. Verification, on the other hand, is a value judgment. The verifier ends up either endorsing or rejecting the conclusions to be verified. It relates to the material aspects of the theological process. The Jewish authorities might not have been able to verify the blind man's claims, but there is nothing preventing them from leaving him alone as having a legitimate religious experience that is outside their own experience.

The test of Gamaliel comes immediately to mind. Faced with the inability to verify a religious expression, Gamaliel was prepared to grant it at least provisional legitimacy pending ultimate verification: "Keep away from these men and let them alone; because if this plan or this undertaking is of human origin, it will fail; but if it is of God, you will not be able to overthrow them—in that case you may even be found fighting against God" (Acts 5:38–39).

The wisdom of Gamaliel is informed by the fact that theological verification tends to follow the narrow criteria of traditional, canonical theology, which hardly makes room for theological diversity. The test for theological claims needs to be understood in a wider, more redemptive rather than cognitive sense following the gospel (and Gamaliel's) principle of "You will know them by their fruits" (Matt 7:16–20). As Orlando Costas has well said, "The final proof of any theological proposition is not its academic precision but its transforming power."[25]

Guillermo Cook has done a creative analysis of the theological debate among the Pharisees in John 9 in which he discovers the two different criteria for verification at work. Unlike in the case of Gamaliel, however, it is the conservative party that has the day in John 9. "A majority of the religious leaders base their conclusions upon tried and true doctrinal presuppositions ('This man is not from God for he does not keep the Sabbath,' v. 16a). Meanwhile, a minority starts from the fact of the healing and works back inductively to the proposition, 'How can a sinner do such miraculous signs?' (v. 16b)."[26] Here we see that what is going on is the traditional tension between orthodoxy and orthopraxy. His conclusion is our proposal for African theology, namely, that there is need to go beyond the

---

[25] Quoted in Cook, "Seeing, Judging and Acting," 396.
[26] Cook, "Seeing, Judging and Acting," 392.

traditional criteria of orthodoxy and embrace criteria of orthopraxy in the verification of theological claims. This is the only way to avoid the irony of the Jewish authorities in the story acting against their own best interests and avowed purposes.

INDIVIDUAL AND INSTITUTION IN AFRICAN THEOLOGY

Our reading of John 9 will not be complete without touching on the important issue of institutional authority versus the authority of personal experience. In other words, how does the Fourth Evangelist see the relative validity of the Pharisees' claim to sure knowledge ("we know" [9:24, 29]) and the man's appeal to his own lived experience ("I know" [9:25])? The history of Christian theology is replete with waves of the deployment of institutional might against the individual who dares to sing a different theological tune. The inquisitions, heresy trials, and excommunications are, unfortunately, not altogether a thing of the past. When these replace "truth-power" as a means of dialogue and persuasion, the message is that might is right, not that right is might, as we see in John 9. Cook cannot agree more:

> John shows us how an "ordinary" or "common" believer—poor, physically disabled, illiterate and barred from the fellowship of his religion—is capable of judging and confounding the knowledge of sophisticated theologians. This has a lot of significance for us today, when many of our own presuppositions are being challenged by the poor and dispossessed. We are also living in an era when "First World" missions are being called into question by the Two-Thirds World.[27]

Cook reminds us that what we say about individuals in this connection applies not only to singular but also to collective individuals. By a collective individual we mean a community within a community in which the smaller group is perceived to be different on the grounds of religion, ethnicity, gender, or social class. What is it that sometimes blinds the larger community to those realities that seem to be so evident to the smaller group? Cook thinks that it is their preoccupation with preserving their authority and the integrity of their traditions. "The majority faction of the Pharisees, therefore, are not looking at a person who has just been healed. Rather, they perceive a threat to the integrity of the law (their traditions) and to their own authority."[28]

The danger to denigrate the minority viewpoint increases exponentially with the degree of canonical dogmatism with which the dominant

---

[27] Ibid., 389.
[28] Ibid., 392.

theological establishment has been invested. Theologies that hold themselves to possess the truth, all the truth, and nothing but the truth are especially vulnerable in this regard. The dogmatic assurance and certainty of the Jewish authorities in John 9 is enough demonstration of this thesis. Dogmatic orthodoxy is incapable of accepting a fact that contradicts its assured positions, no matter how evident the fact may be.

The precept for African theology here is to espouse the heuristic wisdom of Gamaliel rather than the dogmatic certainties of the Jewish authorities, which ultimately boils down to opposing what the very God has ordained.

CONCLUSION

John 9 ends with the enigmatic words of Jesus: "I came into this world for judgment so that those who do not see may see, and those who do see may become blind" (9:39). The story can, therefore, be read as a dramatic illustration of the Synoptic paradox: "The first shall be the last and the last first" (Matt 20:16; see also Matt 19:30; Mark 9:35; 10:31; Luke 13:30). The agonizingly enigmatic nature of this saying consists in this, that whenever we think we have the equation right, that could be precisely the moment when we could be surprised by the truth. More than anything, therefore, John 9 is an invitation to theological humility and inclusivity. It is an invitation to the African theologian, and to all theologians, for that matter, to eschew above all a theological better-than-thou attitude toward the people of God whom we are called to serve in our vocation as theologians. Their lived experiences should serve as sounding board for the theories and postulates of the speculative theologian.

More than that, theologians should see the people of God as companions in the journey of faith seeking understanding. Theologians should recognise that, in spite of their formal training, they are still as blind as anyone else before the mystery of divinity. Wherein then lies the expertise of the theologian? I can find no better answer than this: "In the profound words of D. T. Niles, they [should] recognise themselves as 'beggars who show other beggars where together they can find bread.'"[29] This is an imperative for African theology, for this is the only way to escape the lot of the Pharisaic theologians whose blindness remains because they believe that they have access to a privileged vision of truth from which the men and women of their time are excluded.

---

[29] Ibid., 396.

Why Not Postcolonial Biblical Criticism in Southern Africa: Stating the Obvious or Looking for the Impossible?

Jeremy Punt
University of Fort Hare

1. SETTING THE SCENE: THEOLOGY AND HERMENEUTICS IN AFRICA

It is important to situate the question about the role and place of postcolonial biblical criticism in Southern Africa in the context of the two broad modes of theologising in Africa:[1] African theology with its strong inculturationist interest, and Black theology characterised by a liberationist agenda.[2] While not constituting entirely different epistemological

---

* First draft of a paper to be read at the Annual Meeting of the Society of Biblical Literature, to be held in Atlanta, Georgia, 22–25 November 2003.

[1] Although a functional distinction (cf., e.g., also in Hastings 1989: 32, 90–91; Maluleke 1996b: 36–38; Mushete 1994: 13–24), the validity of the perception of two, separate "theological schools" is contested; recently cf., e.g., Maimela (1994b: vii–ix; 1994c: 1–17); Martey (1993); Parratt (1995: 195); Pato (1997: 40–46) and Young (1986); and much earlier of course Cone (1993: 393–403) and Tutu (1993: 385–92)— the latter two references are to reprinted essays. Others argue for an integrated "African theology" since the concerns for indigenisation and liberation are not exclusive but mutually informing, even two sides of the same coin. For further references to this discussion, cf. Punt (1997: 133, esp. n. 35). Nyamiti (1994: 35–36) distinguishes between South African Black theology and African liberation theology, the latter of which approaches the integration of the two streams as mentioned above.

[2] For other typologies of theologies in Africa cf. De Gruchy (1991: 217–23) and Maluleke (1996b: 33–60; 2001: 169–75). However, in Africa the theological arena is still dominated by these two theological streams, both statistically as far as published theology goes and by providing the launching pad, or more, for more recent theological developments (e.g., the links between African theology and the gospel-translatability theologies of Bediako and Sanneh, and the relation of feminist/womanist theology to Black theology). However, "mission theology" with its

frameworks, they do operationalise two essentially different frames of reference as well as interpretative paradigms. Not surprisingly, two different hermeneutics, a hermeneutics of resonance and a hermeneutics of liberation, respectively, inform African and Black theology readings of the Bible (Levison and Pope-Levison 1995: 336–39).[3] Concerning perceptions about the nature and role of the Bible, and still in general terms, the former is appreciative of the Bible and sees it as informing African theology, while Black theology has increasingly implicated both the interpretation of the Bible and the biblical documents as such in a wide range of injustices, often culminating in the purging of certain text and even calls to *rewrite* Scripture.

Without inordinate insistence on such generalised distinctions between African and Black theologies, the typology does show African theology's stress on the appropriation of the full canonical use of the Bible, compared to Black theology's demarcation of biblical texts perceived as exhibiting "liberative" moments.[4]

> [W]hereas inculturationists are obsessed with finding continuities and discontinuities between the Bible and African cultural life and thought, black liberationists acknowledge the ambiguity of scripture and therefore contend that the Bible can be used as a force for liberation and oppression. (Martey 1993: 106)

---

emphasis on the salvation of souls and continuing (increasing?) impact on the landscape of African Christianity is probably exercising more influence on believers in general than what theologians allow themselves to admit (cf. Mushete 1994: 13–16).

[3] Although a comparison with readings of the Bible in the Black Diaspora proves interesting and valuable, it will not be dealt with here because of obvious constraints. For brief historical overviews, cf., however, Wimbush (1991: 81–97; 1993: 130–32). Yorke's (1997: 149–57) typology applied to the two different appropriations of the Bible in the Black Diaspora context fails to convince. Some "liberationist/sociopolitical" readings are equally "literalist" if not "magical" and vice versa—is it simply a matter of inadequate terminology amid valid distinctions, or are the latter flawed as well?

[4] Cf. EATWOT (1994: 169). For one example of each theological school's relationship with the Bible, cf., e.g., Mbiti (1986: 43), who states almost categorically that "African Christianity is based on and is using the *entire Bible*" (emphasis added), compared to Maimela's emphasis on a liberatory "biblical theological vision" (Maimela 1994a: 190–92, 195). Martey (1993: 131, 137) who attempts to integrate the inculturationist and liberationist emphases—"(a) relevant, contextual and authentic theology for Africa must have a unitary perception of inculturation and liberation"—pleads for a rereading of the Bible within the ambit of a hermeneutics of suspicion, a task he identifies as crucial. Differences in hermeneutical approach and methodology will have to be addressed elsewhere.

Discussions on biblical hermeneutics in Africa ultimately have to take these different appropriations of the biblical texts into account, as well as the difference in status accorded to these texts, within the broad categories of African and Black theology. From a postcolonial perspective, it is important to acknowledge that Black theology implicates the biblical texts themselves as the products of the wider power struggle between the powerful and the oppressed that necessitates a selective, liberatory hermeneutic. On the other, however, it is not as easy as claiming that African theologians simply subscribe to biblical authority whereas Black theologians subordinate the Bible to other matters such as sociopolitical and economic experiences. African culture and especially African traditional religion often determines the use of the Bible in African theology, as much as the political agenda of Black theology remains to a large extent biblically enscribed and justified.[5] Statements that

> [t]he Bible is an essential source for all Christian theologians. Little, then, need to be said of African theologians' use of the Bible but that their engagement in the study of African traditional religion is subject to its authority (Young 1986: 62)

are perhaps too simplistic to adequately account for the evaluation of the Bible in the African context. However, this distinction is helpful to some degree in considering the appropriation of the Bible in Africa, showing not only two options in a inculturationist or liberationist agenda[6] but calling also for hermeneutical (and theological) strategies to penetrate and bridge the divide.

Postcolonial biblical interpretation can assist in breaking through the impasse that often appears in the discussions around different interpretive paradigms in African biblical studies by reposing the question about hermeneutics in general and hermeneutical privilege in particular. It may even find itself eminently suitable for providing a framework to link the

---

[5] Such generalisation is not intended to deny that African theology is plural, effectively consisting of a range of African theologies, allowing a variety of typologies such as denominational or confessional and others (Hastings 1989: 86–87), each of which would ascribe a particular level of value to the biblical texts. However, the "issue-orientated approach to theology" common to African *theologies* (Hastings) provides justification for some cautious generalisation, without deleting necessary distinctions.

[6] Although the Black theological agenda is replacing the African one "at the cutting edge of Christian intellectual activity," according to Hastings (1989: 32). His presupposition, however, is clear: "A healthy culture today ... is a justice-conscious culture; an unhealthy culture is a culture-conscious culture" (Hastings 1989: 35).

different emphases in African and Black theology and their derivative hermeneutical strategies. Before considering possible reasons why postcolonial biblical studies has not really caught on in Africa, either to connect the two hermeneutical-theological streams or in a general sense, a short description of postcolonial criticism in biblical studies is appropriate.

2. POSTCOLONIALISM AND BIBLICAL HERMENEUTICS

The postcolonial discourse seems to have so much potential for biblical studies in Africa, yet postcolonial biblical criticism has until now been less than eagerly embraced.[7] This is strange, since the inclusion of postcolonial discourse in mainstream biblical studies offers another opportunity for biblical studies to move beyond its ghetto-like existence of a narrow religious sphere. It also creates space for considering the Bible's legacy in our cultural heritage, where it has continued to be a "book for life" in the sense of an identity cultural marker (Brenner 2000: 11).

Postcolonial studies of texts can, in short, be described as a variety of hermeneutical approaches characterised by their political nature and ideological agenda, the textual politics of which ultimately concerns both a hermeneutic of suspicion and a hermeneutic of retrieval or restoration. It interacts with colonial history and its aftermath, where a history of repression and repudiation is foregrounded, but since it also deals with exposé, restoration and transformation are part of the repertoire of a postcolonial overture. As a form of ideology criticism, it considers the sociopolitical context and the interpreter's stand within it of primary importance. At the same time, postcolonialism is about more than ideology criticism. It specifically addresses the silencing of the Other through the colonial strategy of posing the colonised as the inverse of the coloniser, and so emptying the colonised world of meaning (Gandhi 1998: 15),[8] and often vilifying the

---

[7] Scholars who have pursued postcolonial biblical studies in Africa include notably, e.g., Dube (1996a; 2000). However, even a cursory investigation of recent scholarly writing in Southern Africa reveals little sustained interest in postcolonial biblical studies; cf. the articles in Kinoti and Waliggo (1997); Getui, Maluleke, and Ukpong (2001); and West and Dube (2001).

[8] Postcolonial studies illustrate how coloniser and colonised were (are) linked to one another, although the interaction was hardly on equal terms. It attempts to "analyze the major mistakes of the past" while building "bridges for future dialogue" (Dube 1996b: 248–49). But how is "coloniser and colonised" to be defined? Can one simply rely on past configurations and/or experiences in a postmodern world with its many manifestations of manipulative, oppressive, excessive forms and practices of power? May one man's liberating experience not be another woman's encounter with hegemony?

colonised Other: the savage versus the civilised, the emotional/stupid versus the rational/intelligent, the heathen versus the religiously committed. Location is an important, heuristic, political matter,[9] and time, distance, and space are categories of prime significance, and so is the autobiographical,[10] all of which is of great importance in getting to grips with imperialist and hegemonic structures of oppression.

Often other hegemonic and contemporary contexts are included in its purview. Postcolonial studies is a synecdoche (a *part that represents the whole,* or inversely the whole that represents a part) for imperialist-(post)colonial studies[11] and is "ideological reflection on the discourse and practice of imperialism and colonialism from the vantage point of a situation where imperialism and colonialism have come—by and large but by no means altogether so—to a formal end but remain very much at work in practice, as neoimperialism and neocolonialism" (Segovia 1998: 51 n. 3). Imperialism and colonialism, respectively, exhibit many faces, register conflicting impacts on human lives and society, and are experienced in a variety of different ways. However, both phenomena are intimately related to structures of political power and ideology, economic structures and practices, and social-cultural configurations and experiences.[12] A postcolonial study concerns itself with social formation and analysis as well as cultural production, and it is therefore an attempt to rewrite history. More than but not excluding the attempt at rewriting history, postcolonialism

---

[9] The production and promotion of New Testament texts during the period of imperial formation are considered as more than merely an important setting or "background." The imperial context is seen as constitutive for the development and production of New Testament texts. But equally so does the location and practices of interpretation—the politics of biblical interpretation—assume a significance beyond being the tools of the trade and the locations where the trade is practiced.

[10] Autobiographical criticism often resists the personal, with the emphasis on political, economical, or social/cultural systems, local or global, which cause inequitable power relations and downright oppression. My own social location is that of a white, male, South African biblical scholar at a historical disadvantaged (black) higher education institution and a part-time minister in a rural, coloured and black church, while my investigation is naturally informed by the broader South African and global context.

[11] One commentator goes further in arguing that it is a "classic and confusing study of synecdoche," opting rather for "Imperial/Colonial Studies" (Segovia 2000b: 14 n. 1).

[12] Used more loosely, colonialism refers to "any relation of structural domination which relies upon a self-serving suppression of 'the heterogeneity of the subject(s) in question'" (Gandhi 1998: 85, referring to Talpade Mohanty).

posits a reflective modality that allows for a critical rethinking[13] (thinking "through" and therefore "out of") of historical imbalances and cultural inequalities that were established by colonialism (Gandhi 1998: 176). And the postcolonial label is therefore both historical and based on a political position (Gallagher 1994: 3).

Postcolonial studies is intrinsically tied to hermeneutics and represents a shift in emphasis, a particular strategy of reading, an attempt to point out what was missing in previous analyses, to rewrite and correct, although its politics of textuality has already come under fire for its lack of political action. However, the culture-critical call by Robert Scholes that "textual studies must be pushed beyond the discrete boundaries of the page and the book into institutional practices and social structures" (Leitch 1994: 281) necessarily becomes integral to postcolonial biblical studies and interpretation.[14] The engaged political and literary interventionist strategy of postcolonial criticism notwithstanding, such approaches to the Bible cannot be separated from other debates on the contemporary practice of biblical studies. In fact, such debates can often most aptly be described with reference to the postcolonial condition, especially if the latter is perceived to include both the colonial or suppressed and the imperial or hegemonic.

The urge toward decolonisation is often represented in a wide spectrum of stances and practices, emerging with the awareness of imperial forces and accompanying domination strategies. In biblical studies they include strategies for resisting the latter, while exploring alternative positions and practices to foster "liberating interdependence" between nations, races, genders, economics, and cultures (Dube 1996a: 38). Postcolonial biblical interpretation is not intended either as a monolithic approach devoted only to the geopolitical scene of historical colonisation or modern superpower activity, nor can it afford to aspire to become an all-encompassing and replacement master narrative. Postcolonial studies generally focus on "nations" and political power formation (Gugelberger 1994: 582), and issues concerning race, gender, sexual orientation, and others are increasingly put on its agenda. "Pioneers of postcolonial criticism are from the outset also

---

[13] "Post" should not conjure up the ideas of amnesia or repetition, but rather "a procedure in 'ana-', including analysis, anamnesis, anagogy and anamorphosis which elaborates an 'initial forgetting'" (Lyotard in Gandhi 1998: 174).

[14] So, e.g., Segovia claims that besides a biblical critic and even a constructive theologian, he is also a cultural critic, a task that includes a focus on issues of construction, representation, and power through an investment in contextual and ideological analysis as found in the accumulation of studies referred to as "cultural studies." The task includes the investigation of various other dimensions of the biblical interpreter's social context besides the socioreligious (1998: 51 n. 2; 2000c: 59).

seeking to make alliances with those subjected to and seeking liberation from sexual, racial, colonial, and class domination" (Horsley 2000: 10).[15]

This does not mean that a postcolonial approach champions the "ideal of a cosmopolitics," an ultimate and all-inclusive oppositional front,[16] a "new optic" characterised by an accommodating nature (within its own perceived paradigm, of course). Amid the dialectic of colonial and imperial experience, projects of resistance and emancipation are disparate rather than harmonious, diverse rather than uniform, "given the diverse nature of domination and oppression"—in other words, "there is no self-evident project of resistance and emancipation for all in the periphery."[17] It is both important and required that "the differences among the various discourses of resistance and emancipation are to be emphasized as much as the similarities" (Segovia 2000a: 140–41).[18] Postcolonial biblical criticism could therefore not try to be everything to everybody or attempt to replace or co-opt, for example, feminism[19] or Marxism, since postcolonial criticism

---

[15] It is interesting that "religion" as a hegemonic category is but for Dube still under-investigated.

[16] The danger of "postmodern colonization of the postcolonial" relates to the tendency to assimilate, incorporate, and in the end homogenise everything, including the "oppositional other," into the "Western post(al) network." In order to avoid such homogenisation while allowing for the unitary sense of the multifarious network of postcolonial studies, Gugelberger proposes to take "postcolonial" to refer to "the cultures affected by the imperial process." But similarly, the use of postcolonial as a catch-all can make it impervious to addressing the specifics of the past and present and so become an imperialist metanarrative itself. "The ahistorical, universalizing, homogenizing effects of postcolonial theory ... may not provide a politically useful analysis for those cast as Others in a specific time and place" (Gallagher 1996: 232).

[17] Postcolonial study insists on transgressing disciplinary boundaries in its advocacy of an interdisciplinarity and a multicultural curriculum. Postcolonial studies is not reducible to a specific "field" or "core" within such a field, as much as it cannot be disconnected from previous disciplines. Cultural and postcolonial studies are deliberately not disciplinary but rather inquisitive activities that question the inherent problems of disciplinary studies; they "discipline the disciplines" (Gugelberger 1994: 582).

[18] From a postmodern vantage point, Segovia stresses that a multidimensional and conflicted conception of resistance and emancipation is not debilitating but liberating by adding to the relativising power of diversity in a context of domination or oppression. Not disavowing the ideal of a cosmopolitics, he recognises that it can only be advanced and even defined as a common task of all groups in question, "a most challenging and demanding task" (2000a: 141).

[19] Schüssler Fiorenza argues that the combination of a rhetorical emphasis with feminist theory will enable the "full-turn" of biblical studies, although a paradigm

addresses a different context and sets of relationships. Rather, a postcolonial approach to biblical studies "takes competing modes of discourse for granted, renounces the idea of any master narrative as in itself a construct, and looks for truly global interaction" (Segovia 2000a: 33).

Postcolonial biblical criticism functions as an anamneutic and heuristic framework within which to engage the biblical texts.[20] It challenges scholars who find more value in other hermeneutic frameworks, and even its detractors, to ensure that their work does not produce or contribute to readings that will perpetuate colonialist, imperialist, or hegemonic interpretations of the texts of the Bible or its nature and status.

3. WHY NOT POSTCOLONIAL BIBLICAL CRITICISM IN SOUTHERN AFRICA?

Why is it, then, that despite the obvious and many possibilities for the fruitful use of the postcolonial discourse, it has not caught on in biblical studies in Southern Africa? A postcolonial approach is eminently suitable to articulate the desire of subjugated people regarding their sense(s) of identity and self-determination and offer strategies to pose a counteroffensive against political, economic, and cultural forms of imperialism (cf. Carusi 1991: 95–96), including issues of gender, sexuality, and ethnicity in the process. Is it simply the strong influence of the traditional or conventional, and largely religious, setting pertaining in the subcontinent of Southern Africa that rules out cultural studies in biblical studies? Is the power of spiritual-devotional readings as popular style of biblical reading and the historico-grammatical readings of the academy simply too overwhelming? It may be that the term "postcolonial" is not only slippery but in the South African context notoriously influenced by linguistic and racial position, at least.[21]

---

shift in biblical studies has so far stayed out due to the inability of rhetoric to link up with feminist, liberationist, and postcolonial studies (1999: 13). Attention to rhetoric and especially to its epistemic status is certainly important, but it may in the end be postcolonial studies that offers the theory and practice for exposing configurations of center and margin, empire and colonised, hegemony and powerlessness. Postcolonial studies is liberatory in nature, and without eschewing the gender component, or indeed issues of race, sexual orientation, class, and social status, it offers a framework that is not predisposed toward creating, anew, an insider-outsider rhetoric based on such components.

[20] Probably more than this, in the sense of retrieving both subjugated voices and unacknowledged voices, but this was spelled out above in detail.

[21] The term *colonial* is disputed on both sides of the historical Apartheid divide, but Carusi (1991: 96) suggests that the term "neo-imperialism" is more than apt for the contemporary South African society.

This essay seeks to advance a number of possible reasons for the neglect of the postcolonial paradigm in Southern African biblical studies and intends to do so with a somewhat broader scope.

3.1. Hermeneutics in Service to the Church or the Academy

The answer to the question why postcolonial biblical studies has not yet caught on should be searched for beyond the strained relationship between academic and ecclesial-popular readings, the strong pietist context in which the Bible is read in Southern Africa, and the dominance of the traditional. And, in Southern Africa the problem lies deeper and is more profound than that of political and cultural relationship. Power relations are important; they need to be acknowledged, and, therefore, everyone in biblical studies but especially those in influential positions and with great resources should strive for equitable arrangements in biblical studies. But it is also about inherent contradictions and dichotomies in and of biblical studies. For example, trained, academic-intellectual readings of the Bible as literary document as part of full-time, professional careers are often opposed to "ordinary," religious-devotional readings of the Bible as sacred text, readings for moral, mystical, or ritual purposes.

The power-play distinctions are thus not exclusively borne out by male/female or Western/African orientation or Two-Thirds world/Western world binaries, but also by the different purposes of reading. The situation is exacerbated by specialisation in the field of biblical studies and its inevitable spin-off, fragmentation. Issues of commercial value of research and publishing projects, academic and scientific merit, and the concomitant status and power positions of scholars are underwritten by a philosophical and ideological frame of reference. Given this situation, will African biblical scholars eventually have a relationship to African Bible readers different from that of their Western counterparts in Europe and the United States of America?[22] Would such a claim be based on scholarly acumen or personal, hermeneutical privilege? And to what extent can these two in any case be divorced from each other?

3.2. Textual Politics, and Real Readers—in Real Locations

As a counter-force, the biblical studies guild can benefit from postcolonialism's ability to loosen the grip by which Western cultural disciplines control intellectual practices around the world and in Southern Africa, in order to conform to their endorsed designs. Aligning itself with marginalised and excluded voices, postcolonial criticism can point out the

---

[22] Space does not allow for introducing and participation in the Eurocentric-Afrocentric debate here!

cultural hegemonies and relations of domination as well as the neo-imperial designs that veil or hide them away. Accordingly, postcolonial biblical criticism can provide the ground for political challenges to reigning forms of hegemony (Horsley 1998: 170–72). Imperial power relations that during the time of the New Testament become more subtle and reliant upon imperial images rather than the exercise of (military) force, especially in the wake of crumbling cultural and political resistance, reminds of the neo-imperial impact of global capital. Behind the subterfuge of images, global capital in decentralised format asserts its presence in the modern world.[23]

One of the most important and valuable elements of postcolonial biblical interpretation is its movement beyond the Enlightenment quest for the universal, rational reader.[24] It encourages biblical scholars to own up to their gender, culture, and social location and in the process develops models of interpretation that can empower all readers of the Bible within their particular contexts (Brett 1998: 306). Postcolonialism's reach extends to the global *academic* world, providing "an ethical paradigm for a systematic critique of institutional suffering" (Gandhi 1998: 1/4). However, postcolonial biblical criticism can in its literary focus on the biblical texts become restrictive, and an emphasis on the sociocultural can exclude the political aspect of the study of the Bible. Beyond biblical studies, "decolonising cultural resistance" (Said) has been castigated for its cultural focus that generally excluded political engagement, although it is admitted that cultural and political aspects cannot be detached.

As a discourse of resistance and emancipation, postcolonial hermeneutics operates from the perspective of the "geopolitical relationship between center and periphery, the imperial and the colonial." The investigation and analysis of this relationship extends to the interpretation of texts as much as it does to the practice of interpretation itself. The postcolonial hermeneutical privilege extends to the periphery rather than the center and the colonial rather than the imperial and therefore highlights an agenda of liberation and emancipation (Segovia 2000a: 140). A postcolonial reading is socially located and acknowledges differences related to race, gender, religion, nation, environment, and values while admitting that difference does not equal eficiency. As a multicultural reading,[25] it

---

[23] And caution is advised, since "postcoloniality is just another name for the globalisation of cultures and histories" (Gandhi 1998: 126).

[24] Or the "scientific reader," as Segovia (1998: 52) refers to the same construct based on universality, objectiveness, and impartiality, fully decontextualised and nonideological.

[25] It is appropriate, therefore, to envisage postcolonial studies as multidimensional, multiperspectival, and multidisciplinary (Segovia 2000b: 11–12).

perceives of no one religion, race, gender or nation as superior to another (Dube 1996: 249).

Postcolonial biblical criticism requires of scholars to address questions of positionality (Ghandi 1998: 59) and the politics of representation (Kwok 1996: 215) and makes it imperative for them to announce and acknowledge their social location(s). But does it indeed contribute to the scholarly work, and who can justifiably claim to represent the postcolonial others? And more practical, how are postcolonial readings to be incorporated into mainstream academy, without placing such a focus on its marginal status that the very act of inclusion becomes, ironically, exclusion by default, effected through romanticisation of the margin? How does one ensure that postcolonial readings indeed become more than technical exercises but rather moral acts of commitment (Berquist 1996: 32) capable of reshaping social, historical, and literary insights in our discipline?[26]

If the maxim "The worth and credibility of postcolonial criticism will be judged by how it orchestrates the unique and fragile and imagined claims of one community against another" (Sugirtharajah 1998a: 24) is applied to postcolonial biblical studies, the notions of its valuation and comparative value need to be maintained. Clearly, the value of postcolonial biblical criticism is not determined by some essentialist notion of truth, scientific rigour, or methodological consistency, as espoused in the Cartesian-Enlightenment scientific models. Rather, postcolonial biblical criticism will remain contested, at least in part, since it requires value-judgments and ethical considerations, evaluation and critique (Segovia 2000c: 80–81) and furthermore has to deal with the relevancy question more directly than many traditional (read, historical-critical, literary and socioscientific) hermeneutical paradigms and methodologies ever tended to do!

3.3. A Different Status for the Bible

It is ironic, but also useful, that attention to postcolonial criticism of *current* political-economic and cultural relations allows for the identification of layers in the *ancient* biblical literature, as the products of an emerging struggle for domination and authority (Horsley 2000: 153). Investigation of the influence of colonising elements during the texts' production (Berquist 1996: 32–33; Kwok 1996: 213; Tamez 1996: 204), the status of the texts and the nature of the Bible as authoritative or authorising document, and the ambivalence of the biblical texts all form part of a

---

[26] Postcolonial biblical criticism allows us to rethink biblical interpretation, increasingly characterised by globalisation, diverse forms of neocolonialism, devaluing and commercialisation of human life, ongoing violent and armed conflicts—so many of the latter which have a religious subtext.

postcolonial agenda. Postcolonial investigation of the formation of the biblical texts and ultimately the biblical canon requires more than just an investigation and analysis of the historically layered development of the text as found in historical approaches and has to deal with the importance of cultural materialist assumptions. Such assumptions include that "texts are implicated in their economic and political contexts" and that "all literature is symptomatic of, and responsive to, historical conditions of repression and recuperation" (Gandhi 1998: 141–42).

The status and the nature of the Bible as a literary as well as a cultural product (cf. Kwok 1996: 212), and its complicity in the colonial and imperial projects of the past as reflected in its texts, deserve as much attention as its later profitable use in legitimising colonisation. In its texts, the Bible gives evidence of its agency in its own embodiment and sanctioning of imperialist intent, as well as being the casualty of the imperialism of others. "[C]olonialism dominates and determines the interest of the biblical texts, and we could reasonably describe the Bible as a colonial document" (Sugirtharajah 1998a: 19; cf. Tamez 1996: 203–5).[27] At least three distinct but related areas of investigation present themselves. A postcolonial study of the history of the formation of the texts, and ultimately the canon as imperialist construct, would concern itself with their layered nature, relating these to the contemporary dominant interests. But secondly, a focus on the history of the presentation of the texts and that ultimate symbol, *the Bible,* in the Southern African context will lead to the investigation of the ways in which and the reasons why it soon attained authoritative status.[28] A valuable and informative framework for such studies is provided when the text is seen as Other (e.g., Segovia; McDonald) and when this framework is heuristically combined with views of the canon as prototype rather than archetype (e.g., Schüssler Fiorenza) or even as "diasporic adventure" (Kwok).[29] And finally, postcolonial biblical studies have to cross the boundaries of the canon, leading to a transversal look at the biblical text (Tamez 1996: 205). Multiscripturality demands not only the discovery and

---

[27] So, for example, Peskowitz argues that the Bible "cannot be separated from an imperial history and its attendant occupations and displacements, its degradations and pain" (1996: 192). And, "[a]lthough the Bible's democratization was greatly enhanced by translations into vernaculars, it remained confined in elite secrecy" (Brenner 2000: 11).

[28] Studies on the "Word-of-God" theologies in Africa already point in this direction. Cf the debate on the Bible as "Word of God" in the African context (e.g., Punt 1998: esp. 272–76); Kwok (1996: 213) on the "apolitical reification" of the Bible as Word of God.

[29] Where the canon and texts are no longer "fixed, stable and privileged points of origin" (Kwok 1996: 213).

creation of different texts but also coming to terms with other religious texts on different levels (cf. Punt 2001).

However, if in the framing of postcolonial hermeneutics it is in the final instance not concerned with the "truth of the text" but rather with the central issue of the texts' promotion of colonial ideology (Sugirtharajah 1998a: 19), its usefulness on the African continent, where the Bible is still highly valued for many reasons, becomes a concern. If the Bible is studied only for identifying intrinsic textual elements that provide colonial codes, and when the value of studying these texts for their own sakes or for theological (and spiritual) inspiration are secondary at best, it remains a question whether postcolonial hermeneutics is not short-circuiting *itself,* in Africa but also elsewhere.[30] Given the complicity of religion and, in particular, Christianity in the discourse and practices of Western colonialism and imperialism, and the powerful role accorded to the Bible in all this, the focus on colonial codes in texts is necessary. But should the rehabilitation of biblical texts relevant to a reading practice shaped by interlocking concerns such as self-determination, ethnicity, migration, and other such themes not also include a rereading on theological level, in light of past and remaining imperial tendencies in this regard?

3.4. The Role of Tradition(s) of Interpretation

Postcolonial interpretation requires investigation and explanation of the influence of interpretive histories not only in as far as the hermeneutics and readerly strategies of trained readers are concerned but equally so with hermeneutical and other traditions of influence operative in the ordinary, thematic reading style. It includes traditions that run in a general sense across both popular and trained readings such as the spiritual and individualised interpretation of Paul, as well as more particular and locally formatted readings, for example, an emphasis related to either an African liberationist or African cultural approach. But the analysis of the influence of traditions of interpretation also includes, and extends beyond, the differences in hermeneutical position and method, or spiritual-meditative versus socially engaged readings.[31]

---

[30] Whereas postcolonial biblical studies indeed intends to address, among others, the gulf between the academic study of the Bible and "the needs of Christians around the world" (Warrior 1996: 207).

[31] The role of ecclesial and educational programmes as dispensers of Western-oriented, Enlightenment-style paradigm of biblical studies in Southern Africa has to be accounted for as well. Similarly, the powerful and monetary influence of communities often characterised by their devout if conservative/fundamentalist tendencies on institutions and their programmes of learning in theology and biblical studies often ensure the continuation of traditional hermeneutical practices.

3.4.1. Western (Scientific) Discourse

Biblical studies as it exists today is largely characterised by its Western origins and resultant discourses, as it appears in theological, hermeneutical, and other enterprises. Biblical scholars are not unlike other academics and intellectuals when they defend existing discursive formations, construct elaborate defenses and apologies, and otherwise extol the virtue of their and their predecessors' contributions. Scholars, however, are not only primary role players in discourses that are "heavily policed cognitive systems" but have until recently and with the exception of a few been unwilling to admit to what extent scholarly discourses "control and delimit both the mode and the means of *representation* in a given society" (Gandhi 1998: 77). On the other hand, and emerging from debates along the lines of vernacular hermeneutics and the politics of identity and exclusion, strong postmodern sentiments were in the past expressed against the notion of representing others and their particular identities, concluding that it amounts to nothing more than the futile search for the comfort of origins (Brett 1996: 222).

In fact, a post-Apartheid reading in South Africa finds it in the unenviable position that in its attempt to define itself it has to contend with its own subjection to cultural and epistemic imperialism, while internalisation of Western discursive formations already shows up in its terminology and intellectual categories. When strong nationalist discursive strategies reappraise the difference of Africa, some colonialist or imperial tendencies take a second bow. For example, emphasising oppositionality to the extent of reaffirming the binary oppositions of Western thought leads to a contrast between a collective African spirit and the individual Western consciousness, communal ownership in Africa versus capitalism and its inherent greed, and sexual expression in Africa unencumbered by "guilt-producing oedipalizing mechanisms" and Western sexual pathologies.

> This type of oppositionality can occur only where Western epistemic systems have become so powerful that they achieve universal value, to the extent that the colonized body identifies its difference in terms of the imperialist's binaries. (Carusi 1991: 97–98)

The classic response of indigenous authors is to embark upon a self-defense and reinvestment of culture[32] and the past with value. "Calls for a

---

[32] Ironically, at the time when anthropological theory divests itself from "culture" for its excessive coherence and orderliness, as well as restrictedness and totality (Brett 1996: 220). Brett explores the distinction between culture and ethnic identity or people groups, holding to culturally permeable nature of people groups but also pointing out that people are the moral agents and not culture.

return to pre-colonial identity[33] based upon ... a [Marxist] view of consciousness are evidently self-contradictory,[34] since they construct identity precisely in the same terms as the bourgeois imperialist subject, cloaked however in a disclosure of return and recovery" (Carusi 1991: 99).

3.4.2. Beyond Humanism: Roots and Continuing Legacies

The link between postcolonialism and poststructuralism is based not merely on temporal contingency, although postcolonialism might have gained institutional ascendancy in this way,[35] especially through poststructuralism's "clear and confidently theorised proposition for a Western critique of Western civilisation" that proceeds beyond Marxist, economic paradigms. Poststructuralist theory understands Western domination as the manifestation of an injurious association between power and knowledge and thus "diagnose[s] the material effects and implications of colonialism as an epistemological malaise at the heart of Western rationality" (Gandhi 1998: 25–26). The intellectual theory of postcolonial studies is informed by the dialectic between Marxism, and poststructuralism and postmodernism. "While the poststructuralist critique of Western epistemology[36] and

---

[33] "But original African culture, which would include perhaps a mode of subject-specification different from Western culture, has been eradicated and hybridized to a virtually irrecoverable degree" (Carusi 1991: 99–100). In the end, any claim to an authentic indigenity may in the contemporary world prove self-defeating.

[34] A particular problem for Third-World liberation-focused hermeneutics and theologies were (are) their shared assumptions with metropolitan, academic culture, availing themselves of the same intellectual structure and modernist assumptions, mobilising the same Western theories and methodologies, using an overly Christocentric framework, and in the process were absorbed by the West (Sugirtharajah 1999b: 11–12).

[35] Viewed from the vantage point of social activity and political processes, the rise of postcolonial studies can be connected to three politically identifiable events: the failure of communism, the rise of capitalism, and the loss of political momentum by the nonaligned movement. For a broader positioning, cf. Gugelberger's (1994: 581) references to the end of France's involvement in Indochina; the Algerian war; the Mau Mau uprisings in Kenya and the dethroning of Egypt's King Farouk; on the literary front Satre broke with Camus on the Algerian issue, Castro delivered his "History shall absolve me" speech, Fanon published his "Black skin, white masks." In 1950 Alfred Sauvy invented the term "Third World," generally seen as pejorative in the English-speaking world but widely used in the French-, German-, and Spanish-speaking worlds and by Marxists generally (Gugelberger 1994: 853).

[36] As propounded in the classic ideals of the Enlightenment: "all knowledge as science; the scientific method as applicable to all areas of inquiry; nature or facts as neutral and knowable; research as a search for truth involving value-free

theorisation of cultural alterity/difference is indispensable to postcolonial theory, materialist philosophies, such as Marxism, seem to supply the most compelling basis for postcolonial *politics*" (Gandhi 1998: ix).[37] While postmodernism depicts both a crisis of legitimation and a crisis of rationality,[38] poststructuralism in a similar vein evidences a celebration of difference,[39] with deconstructive différance incapable of much more than the recognition of alternatives.[40] Poststructuralist alternatives are open textual traces, which always allow and in fact invite other, different readings. Rationality is destabilised as much as Truth is subverted, and assuming a political position is both indefensible and unreasonable. To perceive of poststructuralism as originally a critique on and contestation of bourgeois structures therefore goes beyond Derridean deconstruction to include also criticism of humanism, as is evident in the work of Kristeva and Barthes.

But it is the specific form of its critique of humanism[41]—and Western metaphysics and rationality—that renders poststructuralism politically

---

observation and recovery of facts; and the researcher as a champion of reason who surveys the facts with disinterested eyes" (Segovia 2000a: 38).

[37] This is of course not to ignore the ongoing debate between Marxist critics and postcolonial critics. The latter are accused of succumbing to late capitalism or "capitalist modernity" (Ahmad), in addressing the "superstructure of imperialism" while ignoring its material base: social formation is neglected and unaffected, and cultural production remains at the level of capitalism. Marxist critics, on the other hand, are charged by their postcolonial counterparts for failing to direct a comprehensive critique against colonial history and ideology and neglecting to consider the historical, cultural, and political alterity or difference of the colonised world and being blinded by socioeconomic class to such an extent that they fail to perceive any other social difference and ultimately succumb to the ideology of racism embedded in Western life and thought (cf. Gandhi 1998: 24; Segovia 2000a: 136–37). Said also reminds us of Marx's argument that the benefits of British colonialism more than counteracted its violence and injustices (Gandhi 1998: 33).

[38] Postmodernism invokes the notion of co-existing social and cultural narratives, presupposing a utopia of equality, and so questions both the effectiveness and in particular the desirability of political intervention (Carusi 1991: 101).

[39] Lacan offers a fragmented and split subject, shifting the emphasis from fullness to lack; Kristeva focus on significance that "overflows and subverts the limits of the Logos"; Derrida proposes différance where Meaning is reduced to a trace of absence/presence; and Deleuze launches an attack on the underpinnings of Rational action through desiring mechanisms (Carusi 1991: 100–101).

[40] It is therefore understandable that Habermas consigned both poststructuralism and postmodernism to a neoconservative domain (Carusi 1991: 101).

[41] A contentious term, as evidenced by other configurations upon which this term has been bestowed upon in the past, e.g., Christianity and the critique of Christianity, science and antiscience, Marxism, existentialism, personalism, National Socialism, and Stalinism (Bernhauer and Mahon in Gandhi 1998: 27).

inoperative. "The post-structuralist project can in many ways be seen as the affirmation of difference as pure negativity, giving way to an infinite pluralism or dispersion: the index of its failure is the point at which it erupts into a positivity" (Carusi 1991: 100–101). While poststructuralism might have initiated its own inability to transform itself, its emphasis on antihumanism is nevertheless important and can be useful in theorising postcolonialism. Poststructuralism nevertheless found sustained engagement in a positive political agenda difficult, since its theoretical position promotes the recognition of endless alternatives even when, to be sure, it emphasises antihumanism and transformation.

Poststructuralism reacts against an Enlightenment humanism(s)[42] that postulates that beyond the diversity of human experience it is possible to distinguish a universal and given human nature, and—equally important— that its discernment can be evidenced in the common language of rationality. Poststructuralist critics attack the notion of the possibility of rational and universal consensus toward conceptualising a humane, liberal, and just society, arguing that such universal (and thus normative) postulation of rational unanimity is totalitarian and hostile to the challenges of otherness and difference. In fact, since "rationality" and "human nature" are historical constructions, they are subject to historical interests and conditions (Gandhi 1998: 27).

Poststructuralist antihumanism challenges the human sciences discourse, calling a self-present Rationality and Enlightenment into question primarily through the "empirico-transcendental doublet" (Foucault). The infinite duality of the subject-object relation refers to a person being at once the knowing subject and the object of knowledge, positing finitude as both the condition for and the limitation of knowledge.[43] But this very

---

[42] Which accommodates the theory of subjectivity, rationality, and knowledge first theorised by Bacon, Descartes, and Locke and scientifically corroborated by Galileo and Newton—"scientific humanism," where humanity described the way people know. Renaissance Italy's cultural and educational programme of humanism, better described as "literary humanism," is humanity described by the "curricular content of knowledge." Both forms of humanism, though, have a subtle subtext that insists upon the superiority of certain human beings, either because of superior learning or cognitive facilities (Gandhi 1998: 28–29).

[43] In addition, continuing the debate with Marxist theory that insists upon dialogue to achieve cross-cultural consensus, poststructuralists argue that ethico-political dialogue partners are generally not equal and mostly not equally represented in the final consensus. In the debate on humanism, it leaves the latter insisting upon the impossibility of a universal human nature, and Marxists on the impossibility of a politics lacking the principle of "solidarity" (Gandhi 1998: 28).

discourse becomes the aporia of poststructuralism,[44] since the closure of the subject-object relation, as well as the attempts to account for it, eventually leads to the conjecture of what approximates a reservoir of the inexpressible[45] and in the final instance the impossibility of breaking with Western systems of thought.[46]

3.4.3. Colonial Mimicry: More of the Same?

Postcolonial interpretation accepts with postmodernism that truth is mapped, constructed, and negotiated and rejects the notion of objective and neutral truth as expressions of political, religious, and scholarly power. As far as the Bible is concerned, it is also no longer the meaning of the text that is sought after, as a multiplicity of meanings are acknowledged from the outset. This includes the revaluing of the little traditions (Meeks), the hidden transcripts (Scott) of the disadvantaged, marginalised, and displaced, in other words, the Other embodied in women and minorities. A move beyond an essentialist notion of text vis-à-vis meaning is required, since it is not texts that contain meaning, waiting to be discovered, but meaning is properly viewed as being constructed in the text-reader interaction.

---

[44] Drawing upon poststructuralist theory, a postcolonial commitment to the subaltern as the subject of his or her history requires both a new historicism and recognition of heterogeneity that ascribes value to difference although it cannot always be named—knowing and valuing difference in and for itself. Firstly, rather than searching for origins, historicism has to investigate present and future conditions while acknowledging the sociohistorical embeddedness of the subject-effects, "which allows for an understanding of the materiality of a "body," traversed by plural and sometimes contradictory lines of determination, which constitute a subject capable of action in those sociohistorical configurations. And, secondly, heterogeneity in the postcolonial context needed to posit the colonised body as the subject of history, but moreover, to recognise the Other as an effect and not a positivity: it is "irretrievable, unlocatable, refractory and by definition unnameable." "Consciousness is here only an effect, with strategic usefulness, of a plural and hybrid subject in a position eminently suited to appropriation of different discursive strategies, and therefore to turning each against itself" (Carusi 1991: 104).

[45] "[T]he otherness of the Other, which is by definition nothing in itself, but simply all we project onto it, the repository of our desires" (Foucault in Carusi 1991: 102).

[46] This explains poststructuralism's ability to explain imperialism but its inability to account for anticolonialism of the kind that does not protest in the terms and discourse of the oppressor (Carusi 1991: 103). Postcolonial discourse is often distinguished in its use of "so-called natural language," posing a particularity foreign to Western terminology and collapsing the theory of différance through the encounter with the untranslatable.

The readings of postcolonial critics are generally illustrative of "colonial mimicry,"[47] firstly in the sense of appearing to avail themselves of the "political and semantic imperatives of colonial discourse," which in biblical studies would mean using the stock-in-trade hermeneutical tools of the established (read: imperial) academy. To some extent, postcolonial biblical studies and commentary is not about the construction of new methodologies as much as about reinventing the tools of the trade, while abrogating their hegemonic elements. However, some traditional approaches in biblical studies might have to be consigned to the past or alternatively might have to be so fundamentally altered as to no longer resemble their original vantage point, reasoning, and format. Remaining claims to these approaches might serve only a final defiant, hegemonic purpose of claiming academic validity on their perceived institutional status—in other words, retaining and maintaining academic privilege and power. This would of course apply in particular to such hermeneutical paradigms and models that are reliant upon a Cartesian model of truth and reason. In the second place, colonial mimicry is also, and simultaneously, present among postcolonial biblical critics through recurrent attempts to "systematically [misrepresent] the foundational assumptions of this discourse by articulating it ... 'syntagmatically with a range of differential knowledges and positionalities that both estrange its "identity" and produce new forms of knowledge, new modes of differentiation, new sites of power'" (Bhabha in Gandhi 1998: 150).[48]

Mimicry is about the indispensable and many-sided hermeneutical and translational activities through which the transition from colonial vocabulary to its anticolonial use is achieved, exemplified in postcolonial biblical

---

[47] A concept which at once indicates "the ethical gap between the normative vision of post-Enlightenment civility and its distorted colonial (mis)imitation" and also becomes the "sly weapon of anti-colonial civility, and ambivalent mixture of deference and disobedience." Gandhi suggests that traces of Harold Bloom's (literary) notion of the anxiety of influence, where the "beginning poet" struggles in Oedipal fashion against the "crippling influence of powerful literary 'forefathers'" (and the gender specification is intended), are found in Bhabha's use of colonial mimicry (Gandhi 1998: 149).

[48] Some postcolonial literary critics refuse the syncretism and hybridity inherent to mimicry, and Ngugi wa Thiong'o therefore decided to write only in his native Gikuyu. Ngugi's approach is often compared to that of Raja Rao, who continues to use English in his work and so subverts the supremacy of imperial textuality while simultaneously denying any invocation of an authentic or essential nativism (in his case, Indian-ness). Rao's approach is not without danger, since from without the anticolonial writer is co-opted for a critique of "third world cultural nationalism" (Gandhi 1998: 151).

studies by the rereadings that invert the traditional readings and understandings and recognise the suppressed voices in and around the texts. Mimicry is not postcolonial revenge, epistemological and cultural revenge of previously excluded or marginal voices, but postcolonial approaches readjust its target to "diversify its mode of address and learn to speak more adequately to the world which its speaks for" and to "acquire the capacity to facilitate a democratic colloquium between the antagonistic inheritors of the colonial aftermath" (cf. Gandhi 1998: x). Postcolonial studies along with other liberatory approaches will, of course, want to avoid the accusation of enacting the mimetic desire of empire.

3.5. HYBRIDITY CONFRONTS THE NATIONALIST AGENDA

A proper romantic modality might just be what postcolonial literature needs: "a willingness to critique, ameliorate and build upon the compositions of the colonial aftermath" (Gandhi 1998: 166). This requires reevaluation of the "militancy or the battle-cry for freedom," "the revaluation of humanism and especially African humanism," and "the position of Marxist discourse" (cf. Carusi 1991: 97),[49] as Southern African readings of the Bible cannot ignore these thrusts in biblical—and wider literary—discourse. Building rather on Bhabha's notion of hybridity, which formulates the colonial presence as ambivalent, and divided between "its appearance as original and authoritative and its articulation as repetition and difference" (Bhabha in Wan 2000: 110), hybridity allows for staking out common ground and the ability to foster a universal[50] discourse in the postcolonial setting. Cultural hybridity cannot easily be unpacked or lead to a quest for true origins, since it is never merely the aggregation of pre-given

---

[49] The usefulness of materialist (Marxist) criticism in reading the Bible probably needs renewed attention, with the vast majority of South African citizens from the working class and its overwhelming black racial composition matched as the most significant distinguishing factor by having been the victims of Apartheid. But the Marxist paradigm is also limiting in South Africa since while racial oppression can be functionally described with reference to the proletariat but is not exhausted by such ascription. It is prevalent also in the social and cultural arena, given the quest for cultural dominance and the formation of a national identity. The value of Marxism's notion of consciousness and the accompanying conscientisation and mobilisation is at stake when, because of its subject's dependence on humanism, it may reintroduce an imperialist subject. Such subservience to positivist essentialism amounts to the introduction of a new ideology to replace an older one (Carusi 1991: 99).

[50] Which is of course not equivalent to reestablishing (the pretension of) universalism, since the latter often amounts to no less than the dominant cultural values and hierarchy made universal (cf. Wan 2000: 109).

identities or essences (Bhabha in Brett 1996: 226), but identities which are, rather, strategically claimed and exerted performatively. Cultural hybridity, then, emphasises the many diverse and at times contradictory but never hierarchically arranged identities of the postcolonial subject and goes beyond the simple coloniser/colonised contrast (Gallagher 1996: 235). Avoiding the trap of affirming a particular culture and therefore reinstating the prejudices embodied in the unconditional affirmation of European culture, "[n]ational consciousness [and not the different variant, nationalism] ought to prepare for the emergence of an ethically and politically enlightened global community." This will facilitate "getting beyond vengeful sorrows and lamentations over our colonial histories, necessary and therapeutic as they have been in our coming to terms with our colonial past and present postcolonial identities, and towards entering a new forum of equality in which we participate as confident dialogic partners" (Wan 2000: 111).

The postcolonial maxim that "the reversed scramble for cultural primacy only serves to reinforce the old binaries which secured the performance of colonial ideology in the first place" (Gandhi 1998: 147) might have become commonplace, but its note of caution is still applicable. The idealisation of indigenous culture, its endowment with redemptive properties, and its "portrayal as vehicle of deliverance from our entire hermeneutical malaise" is not a real option for vernacular hermeneutics, even if it allows and stimulates cultural contact with and credibility between interpreters and their indigenous audiences. Vernacular hermeneutics questions the missionary condemnation of indigenous culture, affirming the presence of religious truths in such cultures before the advent or introduction of Christianity. But vernacular hermeneutics cannot ignore that "indigenous cultures carry along with their enlivening aspects a baggage of feudal, patriarchal and anti-egalitarian traditions" (Sugirtharajah 1999a: 106-7; cf. West 1999: 41).

If in hermeneutics the prevailing danger is one of viewing all Western or colonial texts as repressive while all postcolonial texts are taken as being infused with subversive qualities (Gandhi 1998: 154), it means that postcolonial criticism cannot claim hermeneutical privilege. What Sugirtharajah claims for a postcolonial Indian context holds true in the South African post-Apartheid context, as well.

> The notion that everyone who writes in one of our regional languages and utilizes autochthonous idioms, symbols and ceremonies is always free, emancipated and represents true India, and that those who write in English and use contemporary western modes of interpretation are by contrast always conniving with Anglo-American or Sanskritic imperialism, is too simplistic. (Sugirtharajah 1999: 108)

It suggests that biblical scholars plying their trade against the backdrop of colonial and Apartheid South Africa, reaching toward postcolonial times, should avoid being aggressively self-assured about as much as being solemnly dismissive of indigenous cultures.

Explicit and covert attempts to read the Bible beyond or at least outside traditional denominational and ecclesial boundaries as well as other established sociocultural perimeters already function as symbolic forms of dissent and resistance and resemble the postcolonial urge to let the subaltern speak. Such readings ultimately provide a challenge to social and ecclesial consensus, normalisation, and ideology, through displacement of the texts and its traditional hermeneutics.[51]

Therefore, applying Bhabha's notion of postcolonial literature's "colonial mimicry" to postcolonial biblical studies would entail dealing with the ambivalent mixture of deference and disobedience in the latter. It can also serve to dispel the notion that academic integrity and scientific rigour, elements valued so highly in the academy, are no longer deemed worthy. Indeed, the resultant postcolonial critic becomes a Janus-faced creature, with a split consciousness of double vision. The impossibility of a return to or rediscovery of "an absolute pre-colonial cultural purity" is accompanied by the impossibility of creating "national or regional formations entirely independent of their historical implication in the European colonial enterprise" (Ashcroft et al. 1989: 195–96). The implications of moving toward postcolonial biblical interpretation as hybridical reading in Southern Africa still need to be established, but the scars of South African Apartheid might still lie to shallow to allow this in the true sense of the word.

4. CONCLUSION

Postcolonial biblical studies confirms that biblical interpretation is always influenced by reigning and dominant cultural values and that all

---

[51] In cultural studies the phenomenon of challenge to social consensus through displacement as symbolic forms of dissent and resistance has been argued with reference to, e.g., formations among English working-class youths such as skinheads, rockers, punks, and so on (Leitch 1994: 281). The "PC" of postcolonial biblical criticism can therefore not afford to covet the status of being or becoming PC (politically correct) or to replicate a Hollywood-simulated underdog-becomes-hero style. All romantic(ised) versions of claiming moral justification for attaining or maintaining power or control over people are up for scrutiny, and anticolonial nationalism can easily become a refuge from facing "internal orthodoxies and injustices." From another angle, Said registers his concern that anticolonial critique might come to replace anticolonial resistance and in this way inscribe and eventually subscribe to the chauvinism and authoritarianism of the postcolonial nation-state, "itself a conformity-producing prison-house which reverses, and so merely replicates, the old colonial divisions of racial consciousness" (in Gandhi 1998: 81).

interpretation subscribes to cultural codes, thought patterns, and the social location of its interpreter.[52] "[W]ithout conscious and committed attention to the entangling of biblical studies and colonial culture, Biblical Studies continues with these foundations, and continues within its colonial legacy" (Peskowitz 1996: 180). Like postcolonial studies, postcolonial biblical hermeneutics cannot be content merely to fit into the hegemonic discourses of "the academy" but has to initiate change in structure and content, if not also epistemology.[53] "[P]ostcolonialism will continue to challenge the context and contours of biblical interpretation, and the existing notions and preconceptions of professional guilds and academics" (Sugirtharajah 1998b: 21).

When the focus shifts from an emphasis on nationalism to affirming national consciousness, a number of possibilities present themselves to be explored. For example, can postcolonial biblical criticism allow for the integration of the liberation (Black theologies) and cultural (African theologies) foci in approaches to the Bible (and theology) in Africa, to accommodate both suspicion and retrieval, the local/vernacular and global/metropolitan, the indigenous and diaspora, and so on? Can it not also shift the mangled debate about the possibility, advisabilty, and nature of a (to-be-developed) authentic African hermeneutic, toward the search for elements to be incorporated into an African-infused hermeneutic?

Reading the Bible in Southern Africa in a way that allows the voices of the marginalised to be heard while stimulating hybridical interpretations can guard against falling prey to the unfortunate consequence of those readings against the grain, whose counter-discourse preserves the binary opposition and reestablishes a privileged reading while it seeks to subvert the basis of discriminatory polarity (Sharrad in Berquist 1996: 33). Postcolonial biblical criticism as operational framework for reading the Bible in Southern Africa can easily be perceived as ambivalent and even ambiguous. Employing vernacular hermeneutics that is context-sensitive, local language and culture, celebrates in a postmodern way the local while subverting prevailing foreign theories and practice in postcolonial fashion

---

[52] Cf. the interesting examples from eighth-century Saxon poetry (Germanic chieftainship and Christology) and the more familiar examples of Anselm's atonement theology (with a medieval peasant's insult of the king as the reference), Luther's reinterpretation of justification by faith (in the era of emerging individualism), and Bultmann's existentialist interpretation (reacting to Heideggerian existentialism) (Sugirtharajah 1999: 104–5).

[53] In order to counter the epistemic violence of colonisation. But, "[g]iven its poststructuralist inheritance, recent postcolonial critique tends to favour those varieties of counter-hegemonic anti-colonialisms which subvert rather than reverse the chronic oppositions of colonial discourse" (Gandhi 1998: 112).

(Sugirtharajah 1999b: 12).[54] But at the same time it is the postcolonial inclination that will caution vernacular hermeneutics to avoid both the danger of romaticising or idealising the contribution of the marginalised, as well as the danger of minimising and rationalising their contribution to biblical reading. Like all other flesh-and-blood readers they and their readings too are local, perspectival, and interested and thus contextualised and ideological (Segovia 1998: 52). Postcolonial biblical criticism is neither the obvious nor the impossible choice in Southern Africa but does require more sustained attention than the traces that are currently found on the scene of local biblical interpretation.

WORKS CITED

Ashcroft, B., G. Griffiths, and H. Tiffin. 1989. *The Empire Writes Back: Theory and Practice in Post-colonial Literature.* New York: Routledge.

Banana, C. S. 1993. The Case for a New Bible. Pages 17–32 in *"Rewriting" the Bible: The Real Issues. Perspectives from with Biblical and Religious Studies in Zimbabwe.* Edited by I. Mukonyora, J. L. Cox and F. J. Verstraelen. Religious and Theological Series 1. Gweru: Mambo.

Berquist, J. L. 1996. Postcolonialism and the Imperial Motives for Canonization. *Semeia* 75:15–35.

Brenner, A. 2000. Foreword. Pages 7–12 in *Culture, Entertainment and the Bible.* Edited by G. Aichele. JSOTSup 309. Sheffield: Sheffield Academic Press.

Brett, M. G. 1996. The Ethics of Postcolonial Criticism. *Semeia* 75:219–28.

———. 1998. Locating Readers: A Response to Frank Moloney. *Pacifica* 11:303–15.

Carusi, A. 1991. Post, Post and Post. Or, Where Is South African Literature in All This? Pages 95–108 in *Past the Last Post: Theorizing Post-Colonialism and Post-Modernism.* Edited by I. Adam and H. Tiffin. New York: Harvester Wheatsheaf.

Cone, J. H. 1993. A Black American Perspective on the Future of African Theology. Pages 393–403 in Cone and Wilmore.

Cone, J. H., and G. S. Wilmore, eds. 1993. *Black Theology: A Documentary History. Vol. 1: 1966–1979.* 2d ed. Maryknoll: Orbis.

---

[54] Vernacular hermeneutics is naturally characterised and defined by its context(s), since what is vernacular depends on context (Sugirtharajah 1999a: 95ff.). Especially when indigenes engage in vernacular readings, and since their "ground rules" are different from the academic norms and standards, these efforts would often go unappreciated or even unnoticed (cf. Sugirtharajah 1999b: 12).

De Gruchy, J. W. 1991. South African Theology Comes of Age. *RSR* 17(3): 217–23.
Dube, M. W. 1996a. Reading for Decolonialization (John 4:1-42). *Semeia* 75:37–59.
———. 1996b. "Woman, What Have I to Do with You?" A Post–colonial Feminist Theological Reflection on the Role of Christianity in Development, Peace and Reconstruction in Africa. Pages 244–58 in *The Role of Christianity in Development, Peace and Reconstruction*. Edited by I. A. Phiri, K. R. Ross, and J. L. Cox. Nairobi: All Africa Conference of Churches.
———. 2000. *Postcolonial Feminist Interpretation of the Bible*. St Louis: Chalice.
EATWOT. 1994. Final Statement of the EATWOT Pan African Theological Conference. Pages 165–69 in Maimela 1994d.
Gallagher, S. V. 1996. Mapping the Hybrid World: Three Postcolonial Motifs. *Semeia* 75:229–40.
Gandhi, L. 1998. *Postcolonial Theory. A Critical Introduction*. New York: Columbia University Press.
Getui, M., T. S. Maluleke, and J. Ukpong, eds. 2001. *Interpreting the New Testament in Africa*. Nairobi: Acton.
Gibellini, R., ed. 1994. *Paths of African Theology*. London: SCM.
Green, J. B. 1995. *Hearing the New Testament. Strategies for Interpretation*. Grand Rapids: Eerdmans; Carlisle: Paternoster.
Groden, M., and M. Kreiswirth, eds. 1994. *The Johns Hopkins Guide to Literary Theory and Criticism*. Baltimore: Johns Hopkins University Press.
Gugelberger, G. M. 1994. Postcolonial Cultural Studies. Pages 581–85 in Groden and Kreiswirth.
Hastings, A. 1989. *African Catholicism: Essays in Discovery*. London: SCM.
Horsley, R. A. 1998. Submerged Biblical Histories and Imperial Biblical Studies. Pages 152–73 in *The Postcolonial Bible*. Edited by R. S. Sugirtharajah. Bible and Postcolonialism 1. Sheffield: Sheffield Academic Press.
———. 2000. Introduction: Krister Stendahl's Challenge to Pauline Studies. Pages 1–16 in *Paul and Politics: Ekklesia, Israel, Imperium, Interpretation. Essays in Honour of Krister Stendahl*. Edited by R. A. Horsley. Harrisburg: Trinity Press International.
Kinoti, H. W., and J. M. Waliggo, eds. 1997. *The Bible in African Christianity: Essays in Biblical Theology*. African Christianity Series. Nairobi: Acton.
Kwok, Pui-Lan. 1996. Response to the Semeia Volume on Postcolonial Criticism. *Semeia* 75:211–17.
Leitch, V. B. 1994. Cultural Studies. 2. United States. Pages 179–82 in *The Johns Hopkins Guide to Literary Theory and Criticism*. Edited

by M. Groden and M. Kreiswirth. Baltimore: Johns Hopkins University Press.
Levison, J. R., and P. Pope-Levison. 1995. Global perspectives on New Testament Interpretation. Pages 329–48 in Green.
Maimela, S. S. 1994a. Black Theology of Liberation. Pages 182–95 in Gibellini.
———. 1994b. Preface. Pages vii–ix in Maimela 1994d.
———. 1994c. Religion and Culture: Blessings or Curses? Pages 1–17 in Maimela 1994d.
Maimela, S. S., ed. 1994d. *Culture, Religion and Liberation: Proceedings of the EATWOT Pan African Theological Conference, Harare, Zimbabwe, January 6–11, 1991*. African Challenges Series (AACC). Pretoria: Penrose.
Maluleke, T. S. 1996a. Black and African Theologies in the New World Order: A Time to Drink from Our Own Wells. *JTSA* 96:3–19.
———. 1996b. Recent Developments in the Christian Theologies of Africa. Towards the Twenty-First Century. *Journal of Constructive Theology* 2(2):33–60.
———. 2000. The Bible among African Christians: A Missiological Perspective. Pages 87-112 in *To Cast Fire upon the Earth: Bible and Mission Collaborating in Today's Multicultural Global Context*. Edited by T. Okure. Pietermaritzburg: Cluster.
———. 2001. The Bible and African theologies. Pages 165-176 in Getui, Maluleke, and Ukpong.
Martey, E. 1993. *African Theology: Inculturation and Liberation*. Maryknoll, N.Y.: Orbis.
Mbiti, J. S. 1986. *Bible and Theology in African Christianity*. Nairobi: Oxford University Press.
Mushete, A. N. 1994. An Overview of African Theology. Pages 9–26 in Gibellini.
Nyamiti, C. 1994. Contemporary African Christologies: Assessment and Practical Suggestions. Pages 62–77 in Gibellini.
Parratt, J. 1995. *Reinventing Christianity: African Theology Today*. Grand Rapids: Eerdmans; Trenton: Africa World.
Pato, L. L. 1997. Indigenisation and Liberation: A Challenge to Theology in the Southern African Context. *JTSA* 99:40–46.
Peskowitz, M. 1996. Tropes of Travail. *Semeia* 75:177–96.
Punt, J. 1997. Reading the Bible in Africa: On Strategies and Ownership. *R&T* 4(2):124–54.
Punt, J. 1998. The Bible, Its Status and African Christian Theologies: Foundational Document or Stumbling Block? *R&T* 5(3): 265–310.
Schüssler Fiorenza, E. 1999. *Rhetoric and Ethic: The Politics of Biblical Studies*. Minneapolis: Fortress.

Segovia, F. F. 1998. Biblical Criticism and Postcolonial Studies: Towards a Postcolonial Optic. Pages 49–65 in Sugirtharajah 1999c.

———. 2000a. *Decolonizing Biblical Studies: A View from the Margins.* Maryknoll, N.Y.: Orbis.

———. 2000b. Interpreting beyond Borders: Postcolonial Studies and Diasporic Studies in Biblical Criticism. Pages 11–34 in Segovia 2000d.

———. 2000c. Reading–across: Intercultural Criticism and Textual Posture. Pages 59–83 in Segovia 2000d.

———, ed. 2000d. *Interpreting beyond Borders.* The Bible and Postcolonialism 3. Sheffield: Sheffield Academic Press.

Sugirtharajah, R. S. 1998a. *Asian Biblical Hermeneutics and Postcolonialism: Contesting the Interpretations.* Bible and Liberation. Maryknoll, N.Y.: Orbis.

———. 1998b. Biblical Studies after the Empire: From a Colonial to a Postcolonial Mode of Interpretation. Pages 12–22 in *The Postcolonial Bible*. Edited by R. S. Sugirtharajah. Bible and Postcolonialism 1. Sheffield: Sheffield Academic Press.

———. 1999a. Thinking about Vernacular Hermeneutics Sitting in a Metropolitan setting. Pages 92–115 in Sugirtharajah 1999c.

———. 1999b. Vernacular Resurrections: An Introduction. Pages 11–17 in Sugirtharajah 1999c.

———, ed. 1999c. *Vernacular Hermeneutics.* Bible and Postcolonialism 2. Sheffield: Sheffield Academic Press.

Tamez, E. 1996. The Hermeneutical Leap of Today. *Semeia* 75:203–5.

Tutu, D. M. 1993. Black Theology/African Theology * Soul Mates or Antagonists? Pages 385–92 in Cone and Wilmore.

Wan, S. 2000. Does Diaspora Identity Imply Some Sort of Universality? An Asian-American Reading of Galatians. Pages 107–31 in Segovia 2002d.

Warrior, R. A. 1996. Response. *Semeia* 75:207–9.

West, G. O. 1999. Local is Lekker, but Ubuntu Is Best: Indigenous Reading Resources from a South African Perspective. Pages 37–51 in Sugirtharajah 1999c.

West, G. O., and M. W. Dube, eds. 2001. *The Bible in Africa: Transactions, Trajectories, and Trends.* Ledien: Brill.

Wimbush, V. L. 1991. The Bible and African Americans: An Outline of an Interpretive History. Pages 81–97 in *Stony the Road We Trod: African American Biblical Interpretation.* Edited by C. H. Felder. Minneapolis: Fortress.

———. 1993. Reading Texts through Worlds, Worlds through Texts. *Semeia* 62:129–39.

Young, J. U. 1986. *Black and African Theologies: Siblings or Distant Cousins?* The Bishop Henry McNeal Turner Studies in North American Black Theology 2. Maryknoll, N.Y.: Orbis.

Yorke, G. L. O. R. 1997. The Bible and the Black Diaspora. Pages 145–64 in Kinoti and Waliggo.

A New Paradigm for Recovering the Origins and Use of the *Didache*

Aaron Milavec
Center for the Study of Religion and Society

My ideas regarding the *Didache* have changed many times in the course of the last fifteen years. During this period, three convictions have emerged that have guided my studies.

1. Unity of the *Didache*—Up to this point, a unified reading of the Didache has been impossible because the prevailing assumption has been that the Didache was created in stages with the compiler splicing together preexisting documents with only a minimum of editing. The end result, therefore, was a complex (or even a haphazard) collage that joined together bits and pieces of traditional material coming from unidentified communities and unknown authors. Thanks to the impact of Jacob Neusner during our 1988 summer seminar on "Religious Systems," I have slowly come to the conviction that the Didache has a intentional unity from beginning to end that, up to this point, has gone unnoticed.

2. Independence of the *Didache* from the Gospels—The *Didache* has been widely understood as citing either Matthew's Gospel or some combination of the Matthean or Lukan traditions. From this vantage point, it followed that the date of composition had to be set beyond the 80s and that the Synoptic material could be used to help interpret and understand the *Didache*. Thanks to my work with Willy Rordorf during the summers of 1990 and 1992, I came to an early appreciation of the possibility that the *Didache* might have been created without any dependence upon any known Gospel. My extensive study of this issue demonstrates that the internal logic, theological orientation, and pastoral practice of the *Didache* runs decisively counter to what one finds within the received Gospels.[1]

---

[1] Aaron Milavec, *The Didache: Faith, Hope, and Life of the Earliest Christian Communities* (New York: Paulist, 2003), 693–740; idem, "Synoptic Tradition in the Didache Revisited," *Journal of Early Christian Studies* 10/3 (2003): forthcoming.

The repercussions of this conclusion are enormous: I am encouraged to return to a mid-first-century dating for the *Didache,* and I am prohibited from using Matthew's Gospel to clarify the intent of the *Didache.*

3. The *Didache*'s Oral Character—Given the manifest clues of orality[2] within the *Didache* itself, one can be quite certain that it was originally

---

[2] Within the *Didache,* the vocabulary and the linguistic structure itself displays a one-sided preference for orality. Thus the *Didache* defines the Way of Life and immediately goes on to specify the "training" required for the assimilation "of these *words*" (1:3). The novice is told to honor "the one *speaking* to you the *word* of God" (4:1), thereby signaling that oral training was presupposed. Moreover, the novice trembles "at the *words* that you have *heard*" (3:8).

In every instance where the *Didache* cites specific mandates from the Hebrew Scriptures, the oral aspect (as opposed to the written) is highlighted: "It has been *said*" (1:6); "The Lord has likewise *said*" (9:5); "This is the thing having been *said* by the Lord" (14:3); "As it has been *said*" (16:7). The same thing can be presumed to hold true when citing the "good news" (8:2; 11:3; 15:3, 4; see #11e). Accordingly, the *Didache* gives full attention to speaking rightly (1:3b; 2:3,:5; 4:8b, 14; 15:3b) and entirely neglects false or empty writing. At the baptism, the novice is immersed in water "having *said* all these things beforehand" (7:1). Thus, when the novice is warned to watch out for those who "might make you wander from this way of training" (6:1), one surmises that defective words rather than defective texts are implied. The same holds true, when later in the *Didache,* the baptized are warned only to receive him or her who "should train you in all the things *said* beforehand" (11:1), indicating that even the *Didache* was being heard. Finally, faced with the end time, each one is alerted to the importance of frequently being "gathered together" (16:2). This enforces an earlier admonition to "seek every day the presence of the saint in order that you may rest upon their *words*" (4:2)—thereby signaling once again how verbal exchange was paramount when "seeking the things pertaining to your souls" (16:2). The one misbehaving, accordingly, was reproved "not in anger [i.e., angry words], but in peace" (15:3). Those unable to abide by the reproof received were cut off from hearing or being discussed by community members: "Let no one *speak* to him or her, nor let anyone *hear* from you about him or her until he or she should repent" (15:3).

From beginning to end, therefore, the vocabulary and linguistic structure of the *Didache* reinforce oral performance. The literary world of seeing, reading, writing, and editing are entirely passed over in silence. Accordingly, the *Didache* was created, transmitted, interpreted, and transformed in "a culture of high residual orality which nevertheless communicated significantly by means of literary creations" (Paul J. Achtemeier, "*Omne verbum sonat:* The New Testament and the Oral Environment of Late Western Antiquity," *JBL* 109 [1990]: 9–19, 26–27). See Jonathan Draper, "Confessional Western Text-Centered Biblical Interpretation and an Oral or Residual-Oral Context," *Semeia* 73 (1996): 61–80; Ian H. Henderson, "*Didache* and Orality in Synoptic Comparison," *JBL* 111 (1992): 295–99; and Milavec, *Didache,* 715–25.

composed orally and that it circulated on the lips of the members of this community for many years before any occasion arose that called for a scribe to prepare a textual version. The Didache was created in "a culture of high residual orality"[3] wherein "oral sources" attached to respected persons were routinely given greater weight and were immeasurably more serviceable than "written sources."[4] Furthermore, recent studies have demonstrated that oral repetition has a measure of socially maintained stability but not the frozen rigidity of a written text.[5] As such, any methodology circumscribed by the bias of textuality and ignorant of orality can no longer be relied upon to explain the origin, the internal structures, and the use of the *Didache*.

RECOVERING THE ORALITY OF THE *DIDACHE*

To test this "orality" on the part of the *Didache*, I decided some dozen years ago to memorize it. Linda Bartholomew and other members of the National Organization of Biblical Storytellers gave me some practical hints on how to do this. For my part, I was skeptical. Let's face it, I had become thoroughly habituated to making, consulting, and relying upon written records—in everything from analyzing texts to shopping for groceries. Once I began, however, I surprised myself. By abandoning the norms of linear logic that structure written texts, I gradually found that I was able to intuit the oral logic that structured the *Didache*. Once this happened, I memorized the *Didache* with great ease.

Once the whole of the *Didache* was in my bones, I took every opportunity to perform it—before my students, before my faculty, at regional meetings of learned societies. As word got around, I was even invited to perform it before a Jewish audience. With each performance, I was adjusting my translation and expanding my understanding of the narrative until, in gradual steps, I finally felt assured that my narrative performance revealed the flow of topics and the marvelous unity hidden below the surface from beginning to end. The suspicion that overcame me, therefore, was that I had recovered the same thread that those who originally recited the *Didache* relied upon for ordering their recitation. My participating in the orality of the *Didache* consequently served to reveal to me the flawless progression and unity of the *Didache* taken as a whole.[6]

---

[3] Achtemeier, "*Omne verbum sonat*," 3.
[4] Ibid., 9–11, and Walter Ong, *The Presence of the Word* (Minneapolis: University of Minnesota Press, 1967), 52–53.
[5] Achtemeier, "*Omne verbum sonat*," 27; Ong, *Presence of the Word*, 231–34.
[6] In my seminars, consequently, I perform segments of the *Didache* so that participants can take in the oral feel before they read it on the page. I furthermore

THE ORGANIZATIONAL UNITY OF THE *DIDACHE* IN A NUTSHELL

The object of my thousand-page commentary[7] is to reconstruct the pastoral genius of the framers of the *Didache*. In a nutshell, this pastoral genius consisted in establishing a comprehensive, step-by-step program of formation that would transform the settled habits of perceiving and of judging of Gentile candidates seeking perfection in their new religious movement. Throughout the framers of the *Didache* gave detailed norms and practical descriptions of what was to be done. Behind these particulars, however, lie the concerns and the anxieties, the experience and the successes of senior mentors who, over a period of time, worked with candidates and fashioned a training program that transmitted, in measured and gradual steps, the operative values and theological underpinnings that knit together their individual and collective lives. Undoubtedly the framers of the *Didache* were well aware that any community that did not effectively pass on its values, its rites, its way of life would flounder and eventually perish from the face of the earth. The *Didache* was the insurance policy that this was not going to happen to them!

Within the next twenty minutes, I will reconstruct some of the hidden dynamics of this training program in order to allow you to glimpse something of its organic unity. I will also reflect upon the key importance of selecting and testing an origination hypothesis by way of resolving the perplexing question of why the *Didache* was created and how it was used. Finally, I will reflect on how date and provenance of the *Didache* shift once one establishes its independence from Matthew's Gospel.

THE WAY OF LIFE AS IMPLYING AN APPRENTICESHIP

After defining the Way of Life, the *Didache* turns its attention to "the training [required for the assimilation] of these words" (1:3). The Greek word *didachê* makes reference to the training that a master-trainer (*didaskalos*) imparts to apprentices or disciples. In classical Greek, basket weaving, hunting with a bow, and pottery making represent typical skills transmitted under the term *didachê* (*TDNT* 3:135). For our purposes here, it is significant to note that the verb *didaskein*, customarily translated as

---

invite participants to make a tape of the *Didache* that they can listen to as they go to sleep at night or as they travel back and forth in their cars. For those hesitant to create their own oral recording, *EasyGreek Software* has reproduced, at a nominal cost, my oral presentation (20 min.) and, on the reverse side, has recorded a feminist adaptation by Deborah Rose-Milavec. Portions of this cassette might even find a suitable use in the classroom. See www.Didache.info for details.

[7] Milavec, *Didache*.

"to teach," was normally used to refer to a prolonged apprenticeship under the direction of a master:

> Thus, *didaskein* is the word used more especially for the imparting of practical or theoretical knowledge when there is a continued activity with a view to a gradual, systematic, and therefore all the more fundamental assimilation. (*TDNT* 3:135)

This usage finds confirmation from modern studies of how the rudiments of a scientific, artistic, or religious tradition are passed on from one generation to the next. Michael Polanyi, more especially, has noted that all deep knowing implies a way of being in one's body and a way of being in the world that cannot be transmitted by a mere telling in words.[8] For an adult to learn the ways of a master, a novice has to submit to a prolonged apprenticeship. Polanyi notes that, even during an apprenticeship, learning depends upon a certain sympathy that exists between the novice and the master. This sympathy begins in the spontaneous admiration that prompts the novice to establish a master-apprentice relationship in the first place. This sympathy operates throughout the apprenticeship itself, giving the novice the means to enter into and to assimilate the performance skills exhibited by his or her trusted master.[9]

---

[8] Polanyi repudiates the ideal of critical, detached knowing as unrealized and unrealizable (both in science as well as in religion), and Polanyi explains that this is so by virtue of the fact that all knowledge is embodied knowledge relying upon tacit skills: "If we know a great deal that we cannot tell, and if even that which we know and can tell is accepted by us as true only in view of its bearing on a reality beyond it...; if indeed we recognize a great discovery, or else a great personality, as most real, owing to the wide range of its yet unknown future manifestations: then the idea of knowledge based on wholly identifiable grounds collapse, and we must conclude that *the transmission of knowledge from one generation to the other must be predominantly tacit*" (Polanyi, *The Tacit Dimension* [Garden City, N.Y.: Doubleday, 1966], 61). Given the tacit character of all deep knowing, Polanyi insists that no scientific, artistic, or religious enterprise can be entirely analyzed, dissected, and expressed in plain language such that a detached observer could discern and affirm the foundational principles involved and, through progressive steps in clear logic, arrive at the same tacit skills presupposed by the master.

[9] Michael Polanyi notes that the success of any given master-apprentice relationship either succeeds or falters on the basis of the quality of the sustained admiration and sympathy operative within the apprenticeship itself: "The pupil must presume that a teaching which appears meaningless to start with has in fact a meaning which can be discovered by hitting on the same kind of indwelling as the teacher is practicing. Such an effort is based upon accepting the teacher's authority" (Polanyi, *Tacit Dimension,* 61). Authority within the context of an

The authority of a master, consequently, is directed toward progressively enlarging the performance skills of novices such that they, in the end, demonstrate that they understand his or her words because they share the way of being and doing that is upheld and prized by the community to which they belong.

REMEMBERING ONE'S MENTOR, THE PRESENCE OF THE LORD, AND "TREMBLING"

The internal clues of the *Didache* demonstrate that the Way of Life was not received as mere information. Mentors understood themselves as "speaking to you the word of God" (4:1); hence, they were honored "as the Lord for where the dominion of the Lord is spoken of, there the Lord is" (4:1). Faced with this realization, the *Didache* notes in passing that the novice became someone "trembling through all time at the words that you have heard" (3:8). This was the way that Israel originally experienced the word of the Lord from Mount Sinai (Exod 19:16) and the way that the prophets came to discover the transforming power of their own callings (e.g., Ezra 9:4; Isa 66:2; Hab 3:16).

The temptation might exist to trivialize "trembling" and to imagine that here one finds only a pious metaphor. On the other hand, those of you who have studied the phenomenology of scientific knowing by Michael Polanyi[10] or those of you who have firsthand experience of being

---

apprenticeship is not to be confused with authoritarianism. The master of a craft does not intend to accept the compliance and admiration of disciples in order to rule over them but rather to transform them into skilled performers. The authority of a master, consequently, is directed toward progressively enlarging the performance skills of novices such that they, in the end, demonstrate that they understand his or her words because they share the way of being and doing that is upheld and prized by the community to which they belong. Applying this to the *Didache*, it becomes clear that novices were not intent upon entering an authoritarian system where they were simply told what to do and what not to do. Rather, novices came forward intent upon achieving for themselves the way of being and of doing (the wisdom) exemplified by those mentors whom they admired. This demanded an interior transformation that could only be achieved due to trusting person-to-person contacts over an extended period of time in what Polanyi would describe as an apprenticeship.

[10] Michael Polanyi, *Personal Knowledge* (Chicago: University of Chicago Press, 1958). Polanyi insisted that the ideal of objective knowing based upon facts and experimentation alone was a misleading ideal that could never be put into practice. As suggested earlier, the personal calling of a scientist followed by long years of apprenticeship under admired masters reveals the personal dynamics that make all deep and transformative learning possible. Even later, those collaborating within a

transformed by an apprenticeship under the direction of a beloved mentor might well imagine that this is the stuff of which the *Didache* speaks.

Consider, for example, the case of Malcolm X. In his autobiography, Malcolm recalls how he trembled at reading Elijah Mohammed's words during his time in prison.[11] This was so, not because someone had told him to do so, but because the words of his spiritual master were liberating him from his former way of death and opening him up to embrace his true destiny and calling as a Black Muslim.

> I went to bed every night ever more awed. If not Allah, who else could have put such wisdom into that little humble lamb of a man from the Georgia fourth grade and sawmills and cotton patches.... My adoration of Mr. Muhammad grew.... My worship of him was so awesome that he was the first man whom I had ever feared—not fear such as of a man with a gun, but the fear such as one has of the power of the sun. (210, 211, 212)[12]

This is what the *Didache* means when it speaks of "remember[ing] night and day the one speaking to you the word of God" (4:1) and "trembling at all times at the words that you have received" (3:8). This same phenomenology existed among the classical rabbis, where it was commonplace to find disciples listening to their masters "with awe and fear, with trembling and trepidation" (*b. Berakhot* 22a).

WHETHER EACH NOVICE HAD A SINGLE SPIRITUAL MENTOR

The *Didache* offers evidence suggesting that each novice was paired with a single spiritual master. The principal clue for this is the fact that the entire training program (save for 1:3) addresses a single novice using the

---

research program continue to be guided by the tacit skills and overarching ideals learned from their mentors: "The riches of mental companionship between two equals can be released only if they share a convivial passion for others greater than themselves, within a like-minded community—the partners must belong to each other by participating in a reverence for a common superior knowledge" (378). All this applies, with even a greater force, to the bonds within the *Didache* communities.

[11] *Autobiography of Malcolm X* (New York: Ballentine, 1965), 170.

[12] Elijah Mohammed represented a way of life that powerfully attracted Malcolm. Through letters, and later, through personal contacts, Malcolm gradually discovered his own calling "to remove the blinders from the eyes of the black man [and woman] in the wilderness of North America" (210). This calling emerged for Malcolm within the spontaneous awe and fear that he felt for his teacher. For more details, see Milavec, *Didache,* box #1h.

second-person singular. If, under normal circumstances, a single spiritual master were assigned the training of many or all the novices within a community, one would have expected that the second-person plural would have been used throughout. Furthermore, within the Way of Life training program, the novice is instructed to actively remember and mull over the life and the training of "the one speaking to you the word of God" (4:1). This use of the singular here points in the direction of each novice having a single master. So, too, when regulations are put forward for choosing the water for baptism (7:2–3) and for ordering "the one being baptized to fast beforehand" (7:4), in each case the singular is used—again confirming the expectation that each candidate was baptized individually by a single individual—presumably the one who was the spiritual mentor and parent.

Since women in the ancient world were accustomed to be trained by other women (#1g, #2b),[13] and since it would have been a source of scandal for a man to be alone for prolonged periods with a woman unrelated to him, it would be presumed that, save for special circumstances, women were appointed to train female candidates, and men were appointed to train male candidates.

FIRST RULE: PRAYING FOR ENEMIES AND TURNING THE OTHER CHEEK

Seen from the vantage point of an orderly progressive of topics, the initial section dealing with praying for enemies and turning the other cheek would appear to be placed at the head of the training program because new recruits had to be immediately prepared to receive abusive treatment (1:3–4). When examined in detail, the "enemies" envisioned by the *Didache* were not highway robbers or Roman soldiers but relatives and friends who had become antagonists due to the candidate's new religious convictions.[14] Thus, praying and fasting (#4c) for such "enemies"

---

[13] In Milavec, *Didache,* one finds over three hundred extended discussions bearing upon particular aspects of the social, historical, and religious world in which the *Didache* communities took shape. These discussions provide information and sources that are placed in boxes (defined by shaded areas) that are scattered throughout the book. For purposes of brevity, these sources will be henceforth presented in the text in abbreviated form. Thus #1g refers to box g in chapter 1 of Milavec, *Didache,* while #2b refers to box b in chapter 2.

[14] Aaron Milavec, "The Social Setting of 'Turning the Other Cheek' and 'Loving One's Enemies' in Light of the *Didache,*" *BTB* 25/2 (1995): 131–43. Kloppenborg, in his paper in this volume, continues to think of the *Didache* as using Luke 6:29–30 and imagining the social setting of a robbery. In the Synoptic Gospels, meanwhile, one finds what John Dominic Crossan refers to as a "an almost savage

functioned to sustain a nonviolent surrender to the abusive family situations[15] hinted at in *Did.* 1:4.

THE GREAT DIFFERENCE BETWEEN THE TWO RULES OF GIVING

Within the training program, the issue of giving is taken up at the very beginning and, again, near the very end. The first giving (1:4) is presented in the present imperative and represents the kind of giving the candidate was expected to practice immediately upon entering upon his or her apprenticeship. The second section on giving (4:5–8), however, is much more than a reinforcement of the earlier giving. Now everything (save for 4:5) is presented in the future tense, and the focus is on the routine "taking and giving" and the much more extensive "partnering" of all one's resources "with your brother [or sister]" (4:8; #2m, #2o). The future tense used here could function as a mild imperative (as in English), but then this would leave the awkward situation whereby two diverse rules of giving are provided and no attempt is made to harmonize them. On the other hand, if one examines the second set of rules for giving, one discovers that this later giving involves sharing one's resources with members of the community—a situation that would prevail only after the time the candidate had gained admittance as a full member of the movement through baptism.

Consider the character of the first kind of giving (1:5). The novice is taught to yield "to anyone asking you for anything" simply because "the Father wishes to give these things from his own free gifts" (1:5). This is the first instance where the fatherhood of God is introduced within the pragmatic theology of *imitatio dei* ("the imitation of God"). God gives freely; hence, in imitation of the one who has blessed the novice with the necessities of life, the novice acts in a parallel fashion.[16] Acting as a faithful

---

attack on family values" (*Jesus: A Revolutionary Biography* [San Francisco: Harper, 1994], 58). Sayings such as "I have come to set a man against his father" (Matt 10:35–36) and "Call no one your father on earth" (Matt 23:9) serve to illustrate how intergenerational strife arose as parents endeavored to use their authority to block the conversion of their adult children. See note 34 below for further illustrations.

[15] Among other things, the abusive family situation envisioned the forcible seizure of the novice's goods (1:4). The candidate was instructed to yield completely to such hostile acts and, at the same time, to surrender his or her goods to beggars (1:5), not due to any compulsion, but simply because his or her "Father" wished it. What emerges here is the contrast between a natural father seizing assets and the Father in heaven who generously gives to everyone in need and invites imitation. The text will return to this shortly.

[16] The *Didache* is the oldest known Christian document that makes it clear that, in the act of giving, what is given has been freely received from the Father. This

steward or broker, the novice dispenses not his own resources but the Father's "free gifts." In so doing, the novice is prohibited from feeling proud or generous in the act of giving since whatever he or she gives belongs to the Father to begin with. The one receiving, meanwhile, need not feel humiliated or indebted to the one giving (namely, "do not ask for it back") since, in point of fact, the recipient is receiving what belongs to the Father.[17]

Roman society placed great emphasis upon the inviolability of private ownership and upon economizing; hence, Romans felt no moral or civic obligation to come to the aid of the poor or destitute.[18] There were public benefactors, to be sure, who erected monuments, subsidized festivals, and provided short-term relief in the face of emergencies. Such persons, however, did so with the motive of promoting themselves and their families as "benefactors." In contrast, the rule of giving advanced by the *Didache* is calculated to break down and replace these very instincts. To enforce this, the novice is further prevented from even examining the worthiness or honesty of the one asking (1:5). This final examination is left in God's hands. Thus, by this rule of action, the former stubborn instincts governing possessions are broken down and replaced by the notion of stewardship, gratitude, and *imitatio dei*. Those incapable of implementing the rule of *Did.* 1:5 would have to be sent away since, in the end, such persons would be incapable of practicing a lifelong responsiveness to the needs of "brothers" and "sisters" within the community they aspired to join. The opening rule of giving, consequently, now appears as the absolutely indispensable training grounds for the economic partnership that comes later. And this is only the first of eight pragmatic reasons accounting for this rule.[19]

---

evaluation of personal possessions finds clear expression in other Christian and Jewish documents as well (see #2d).

[17] The *Derek Eres Zuta*, a third-century training manual for rabbinic students, echoes this same theology: "If you did a great favor [for someone], regard it as small, and do not say, 'I did this good act with my own [money].' ... Rather it was [from what God] had graciously given you, and you should offer thanks to Heaven" (2:10).

[18] G. E. M. de Sainte Croix, *The Class Struggle in the Ancient Greek World from the Archaic Age to the Arab Conquests* (Ithaca, N.Y.: Cornell University Press, 1981), 194–97; Gildas Hamel, *Poverty and Charity in Roman Palestine: First Three Centuries CE* (Berkeley and Los Angeles: University of California Press, 1990), 219; J. S. Reid, "Charity, Almsgiving (Roman)," *Encyclopedia of Religion and Ethics* (ed. James Hastings; Edinburgh: T&T Clark, 1922), 3:391–92.

[19] Milavec, *Didache*, 190–98. The eight effects of implementing the rule of 1:5 are as follows: (1) preparing for a lifetime of sharing everything with one's brothers; (2) breaking addiction to increased economic productivity; (3) developing the

THE PROGRESSIVE TRAINING IN THE TWO WAYS SCHEMA

When one examines how material respecting vices and virtues is set out in the Way of Life, one discovers that a progressive training is implied. Notice, for example, that the negative prohibitions (2:2–7) come first. Then, once this foundation is in place, "fences" (3:1–6) can be introduced by way of supplying a framework whereby grave infractions are prevented by avoiding minor infractions. Finally, once minor infractions are checked, then positive virtues can be cultivated (3:7–10). Any mentor who would scramble this propaedeutic order would clearly be building on sand and risking disaster.

THE ART OF RECONCILIATION REVEALED BY DEGREES

From 4:2 onward, everything is framed in the simple future tense. Herein one hears the novice being trained for future eventualities that will emerge only after baptism when community life becomes a possibility. The *Didache* first holds out the future promise of finding "rest" among the "saints" (4:2), and then it addresses the darker side of community life: "dissention" and "fighting" (4:3). The novice is trained to anticipate the obligation of intervening in these latter instances. The details of this intervention, however, are kept for later when the practice of "reproving" and "shunning" are spelled out in detail (15:3). From this case, one can learn that the ordering of materials does not stop with the end of the Way of Life but continues throughout the whole of the *Didache*. One might suspect, therefore, that whenever the same issue shows up in two places, this might have been done deliberately in order to respect the condition of the candidate and to implement the principle of gradualism.

As another instance of this, consider the confession of failings. Training in the Way of Life closes with the injunction that "in church [i.e., in the assembly], you will confess your failings" (4:14). The novice is thus alerted that all the particulars of the Way of Life would be used for an examination of conscience and a public admission of failures. For the moment, the candidate is entirely unfamiliar with the eucharistic meal; hence, neither the time, place, nor the character of this confession are presented. This will

---

habit of acting in imitation of God; (4) relieving the debt of gratitude for the knowledge and life received; (5) tasting the benefit of almsgiving as ransoming one's sins; (6) beginning a prophetic witness to God's future designs; (7) preparing to publicly account for one's new commitments; and (8) breaking down the bond between the candidate and his biological family.

come later at *Did.* 14:1–3. It suffices that the novice be forewarned that a confession will take place so that "you will not go to your prayer with a bad conscience" (4:14). This general rubric suffices and, in due course, will give way to a theology of sacrifice once the Eucharist is experienced. Again, the condition of the candidate is respected and the principle of gradualism prevails.

THE MYSTERIOUS PLACEMENT OF THE FOOD PROHIBITIONS

The absolute prohibition against eating "the food sacrificed to idols" (6:3) occurs at the beginning of what has frequently been accepted as the beginning of the "liturgical section." How or why this would be the initial topic in a "liturgical section" never made sense to me.[20] On the other hand, it is possible that the placement of this important and absolute injunction may have evolved in order to address a very practical purpose. As long as candidates were in training, they were obliged to refrain from attending the sacred community meals (9:5). This we know. Of necessity, therefore, most candidates would have been constrained to take part in family and community meals wherein, either regularly or periodically, offerings were made to the household gods as part of the meal or some portion of the meats served had been previously offered at a public altar.[21] Only with

---

[20] Nearly all scholars have attempted to demonstrate that the *Didache* was composed by an editor who slightly altered and connected preexisting documents. The *Didache* thus appears as a kind of literary collage that was composed by cutting and pasting together literary units that were already at hand and that served purposes foreign to the *Didache.* Willy Rordorf, for instance, characterizes the *Didache* as follows: "Such as it presents itself in the Jerusalem manuscript, the *Didache* is devoid of literary unity.... In effect, it is composed of many parts of unequal length which belong to different genres" (*La doctrine,* 17). From this vantage point, it is impossible to imagine that the progression of topics flows from one section to the next following a deliberate plan. Thus, in what Rordorf calls the "liturgical section" (18) of the *Didache* (7:1–10:7), he does not anticipate that there is any rhythm or reason why this section should go from baptism to fasting, from fasting to daily prayer, from daily prayer to the Eucharist. Nor does it appear strange that the repeated use of *peri de* in the "liturgical section" actually begins with the instruction regarding permitted foods (6:3). Because this instruction is in the singular and because refraining from eating certain foods is not what one would expect to initiate a "liturgical section," Rordorf regards it as "a transition between the first and second part of the book" (17 n. 2). Why this "transition" is used and not another appears to need no explanation.

[21] A novice would be expected to receive invitations from friends and extended family members to give thanks to the gods on the occasion of important moments in their lives: the birth, coming of age, or marriage of a child; success in business,

New Paradigm for Recovering the Origins and Use of the Didache 57

baptism a few days away, therefore, could the candidate be bound by this final rule.

THE KEY SIGNIFICANCE OF PREBAPTISMAL FASTING

Baptism marked a turning point. Social bonds were being broken, and new ones were being forged. Following baptism, every day would be spent visiting the saints and "rest[ing] upon their words" (4:2). Prior to baptism, however, most candidates probably felt the keen anticipation of entering into their new way of life along with the anxiety attendant upon the irreversible step that would cut them off from most of their family and friends.[22] During these few days, it is no accident that the candidate was

---

returning safe from a long voyage, and the like. Such meals were not, in and of themselves, pagan rites. Nor was there necessarily any notion that eating of the food constituted some sort of sacramental union with a god (Wendel Lee Willis, *Idol Meat in Corinth: The Pauline Argument in 1 Corinthians 8 and 10* [Chico, Calif.: Scholars Press, 1985], 21–62 with reference to 1 Cor 10:20). The *Didache*, after all, regarded the gods as "dead" (6:3). Nonetheless, those who joined in the meal would be expected to tacitly acknowledge that the feast was being celebrated in thanksgiving for a particular blessing received from a particular god (Willis, *Idol Meat in Corinth*, 39–42). Thus, eating any meal offered to idols constituted a denial that "apart from [the true] God, nothing happens" (3:10). Hence, such food was off limits.

[22] Anticipation and anxiety the desire to eat (#3f). Paul, for example, following his unsettling experience on the road to Damascus, "was without sight, and neither ate nor drank" (Acts 9:9) for three days. More pointedly, the book of *Joseph and Aseneth* (100 B.C.E.) describes how Aseneth, the beautiful and virtuous daughter of an Egyptian priest, converted to Judaism and went on to become the fitting bride of Joseph, who had gained great favor with the pharaoh in Egypt. The narrator describes how, upon first encountering Joseph, "she wept bitterly, and she repented of her gods she used to worship" (9:2). As a result, "she was listless and wept until sunset: she ate no bread and drank no water" (10:2). After passing the entire night "groaning and weeping" (10:7), Aseneth "took all her innumerable gold and silver gods and broke them up into little pieces and threw them out of the window for the poor and needy" (10:13). Later she took her royal dinner "and all the sacrifices for her gods and the wine-vessels for their libations; and she threw them all out of the window as food for the dogs" (10:14). Then, for seven nights and days, she remained utterly alone, without food or drink, weeping bitterly and groaning. On the eighth day, "she stretched her hands out toward the east, and her eyes looked up to the heaven" (12:1), and she expressed for the first time her plight:

"To you, O Lord ..., will I cry:
Deliver me from my persecutors, for to you I have fled,
Like a child to her father and her mother.

told to fast (7:4), and it is no accident that the one baptizing and able members of the community fasted in solidarity with the candidate (7:4). During this period, all "the food sacrificed to idols" eaten by the candidates was being expelled, and they were prepared to eat only the pure and sacred food at the homes of "brothers and sisters" since the communion meals binding them to ancestral gods would now be forever forbidden to them. The fasting, therefore, which was propaedeutic for the biweekly practice of fasting, hardly needed an expressed theology.

The fasting prior to baptism led to feasting. While the *Didache* gives no strict chronology as to how much time expired between baptism and the first Eucharist, one can read between the lines. If the candidate was meeting his or her "new family" for the first time at baptism, it is difficult to imagine that the newly baptized did not celebrate immediately thereafter. Given the eschatological significance of the Eucharist, it is improbable that this celebratory meal would not have been the weekly Eucharist. Without going into the details, therefore, I would propose that the *Didache* signals this sequence of events:

1. community gathers in the place of baptism (many have been fasting one or two days);
2. candidates are led in by their spiritual mentors and all grow silent;
3. mentors recite the Way of Life and Way of Death with the appropriate refrains;
4. each candidate is immersed, dried off, and reclothed in a dry tunic;

O Lord, stretch forth your hands over me,
As a father who loves his children and is tenderly affectionate,
And snatch me from the hands of the enemy....
The gods of the Egyptians whom I have abandoned and destroyed
And their father the Devil are trying to destroy me....
Save me, O Lord, deserted as I am,
For my father and mother denied me,
Because I destroyed and shattered their gods;
And now I am an orphan and deserted,
And I have no other hope save in you, O Lord.
                (12:8–9, 11; grammar corrected).

This prayer vividly portrays the distress of a convert abandoned by her parents and defenseless against the gods whom she has betrayed. Aseneth's fasting and weeping, consequently, portray the force of the terrors associated with her conversion. One might expect that many Gentiles embracing the Way of Life were similarly situated.

5. new members are embraced and kissed (same sex only) by their new family;
6. Lord's Prayer is prayed together for the first time (facing east);
7. all retire to the home where the fast-breaking Eucharist has been prepared.

TESTING VARIOUS ORIGINATION HYPOTHESES: THE PLACEMENT OF *DIDACHE* 14

When contending origination hypotheses examine the peculiarities of the *Didache,* they necessarily act like lenses that force their users to see things quite differently. Consider, for example, an easily recognized peculiarity of the text: *Did.* 9–10 presents what the text calls "the Eucharist" (9:1), and, four chapters later, the confession of failings is described as taking place prior to the Eucharist (14:1). One may wonder why the compiler did not place *Did.* 14 just prior to *Did.* 9–10 and thereby retain a topical and chronological unity to his finished text. Jean-Paul Audet takes this problem up as follows:

> The author returns to the subject [in *Did.* 14] not because he is a bad writer, or because he had, oddly enough, forgotten something, or because he is compiling his materials at random, or because someone else had created a subsequent interpolation of 14:1–3, but simply because experience has demonstrated, in the meantime, the inadequacy of the instructions in 9–10.[23]

Audet's unwarranted assumption here is that the *Didache* was composed in writing. The author comes back with a fresh idea, the confession of failings, but there are no blank spaces prior to the eucharistic section to place it. Hence, he was forced to put it where he left off writing the last time (i.e., after 13:7).

Kurt Niederwimmer, for his part, imagined that the compiler of the *Didache* was "a respected and influential bishop" who "quotes existing, sometimes archaic rules and seeks both to preserve what has been inherited and at the same time to accommodate that heritage to his own time [turn of the second century]."[24] Niederwimmer was uneasy with Rordorf's[25]

---

[23] Jean-Paul Audet, *La Didache: Instructions des apôtres* (Paris: Gabalda, 1958), 460. Here and elsewhere I have translated the French into English.
[24] Kurt Niederwimmer, *The Didache* (trans. Linda M. Maloney; Minneapolis: Fortress, 1998 [German original 1989]), 228.
[25] Willy Rordorf, *La doctrine des douze apôtres* (trans. of Greek and critical notes by A. Tuilier; Paris: Cerf, 1978), 49–50; 226–28 in 1998 revision of the same work.

hypothesis to the effect that *Did.* 14 was added later by a second compiler. He was also put off by Audet's thesis that the original writer returned to his document at a later time in order to supplement what he had written earlier. Rather, Niederwimmer tried to discern the internal logic ordering the text. Here is what he found: "in chaps. 11–13, the Didachist had, in a sense, looked outward (toward the arriving guests of the community), in chaps. 14–15 he looks inward (at the relationships within the community itself)."[26] Thus, according to Niederwimmer, the eucharistic prayers (9–10) came early because they were grouped with the prayer section (8:1–10:7); the confession of failings comes later because it is grouped in the "internal relationships" section (14–15). Beyond this grouping of materials, Niederwimmer did not look for or expect to find any reason why one grouping should come before or after another. In a word, given the lenses used by Niederwimmer, he did not see nor hear any sequential plan in the *Didache.*

Georg Schöllgen supplies us with an origination hypothesis much different from that of Niederwimmer. For him, the author "simply provides an authoritative regulation on controversial points."[27] Thus, *Did.* 9–10 responds to the problem of having "an aberrant or insufficient" or "no fixed formula"[28] for the Eucharist. *Didache* 14, on the other hand, is directed toward resolving the author's concern for "the purity" of those eating the eucharistic meal.[29] Two topics; two places. Seemingly the author takes up controversial points in the idiosyncratic order that they occur to him. The origination hypothesis of Schöllgen does not lead him to anticipate finding any progression or ordering of topics beyond this. Schöllgen is neither surprised nor disappointed that no order exists. His theories teaches him how to look and what to look for. Schöllgen, not surprisingly, embraces an origination hypothesis that is entirely blind to any ordering or chronology of the topics.

My own origination hypothesis, on the contrary, leads me to anticipate a closely worked out progression of topics that follows the ordering of training and the experiences given to new members. Thus my hypothesis leads me to look for something that, for the moment, is hidden within the clues of the narrative:

---

[26] Niederwimmer, *Didache,* 199.

[27] Georg Schöllgen, "The *Didache* As a Church Order: An Examination of the Purpose for the Composition of the *Didache* and Its Consequences for Its Interpretation," in *The Didache in Modern Research* (ed. Jonathan A. Draper; Leiden: Brill, 1996), 63. Translated and reprinted as, "Die *Didache* als Kirchenordnung," *Jahrbuch für Antike und Christentum* 29 (1986): 5–26.

[28] Schöllgen, "The *Didache* As a Church Order," 50.

[29] Ibid., 59.

Under ordinary circumstances, the *Didache* informs us that a confession of failings would have taken place by way of preparing the members of offer "a pure sacrifice" (14:1). The candidate preparing for baptism is informed of this confession near the end of his/her training (3:14). When one encounters the eucharistic prayers (9f), however, this confession of failings is curiously omitted. So I am puzzled. I strain at the seeming "misplacement" of things. But I am urged on by the discovery that every part of the Way of Life follows an orderly progression. I am also urged on by the discovery that the abstention from food sacrificed to idols was not included in the Way of Life because it would have been chronologically out of place there. Could it be then that there is a reason why the confession of failings does not show up prior to the eucharistic prayers?

My surmise, due to my origination hypothesis, is that this omission of the confession of failings is deliberate and signals what everyone knew—namely that the order of events within the *Didache* follows the order whereby a candidate comes to experience these events. Thus, if my surmise is correct, the eucharist in the *Didache* must represent the "the first eucharist" and the omission of the confession of failings hints at the fact that this public confession was suppressed whenever new candidates were baptized just prior to the eucharist. Many practical and pastoral reasons could be put forward to sustain suppressing a public confession of failings at "the first eucharist." Foremost among them would be the fittingness of joyfully welcoming the new "brothers" and "sisters" who had just been baptized without confronting them with a recital of the failings of permanent members.[30]

For the moment the question is not whether my origination hypothesis is correct or whether I have supplied probable reasons for suppressing the confession of failings at "the first Eucharist." What is important is to notice how my origination hypothesis forces one to probe the text more deeply in order to find out just how far the evidence supplied by the text can be understood to support the explanatory matrix being tested. The origination hypothesis of Schöllgen expects an unorganized movement from topic to topic. Even Niederwimmer expects only the grouping of topics. Audet, for his part, sees the confession of failings as operative prior to every Eucharist, but the absence of blank space on the page prevents him from giving it its rightful place. None of these three expects to find, thus, a hidden logic that guides the narrator from topic to topic from beginning to end.

THE INDEPENDENCE OF THE *DIDACHE* FROM MATTHEW'S GOSPEL

Elsewhere I have offered a detailed examination of the method and the results for determining how one can demonstrate the independence of the

---

[30] Milavec, *Didache*, 237–38.

Didache from the written Gospel of Matthew.[31] For our purposes here, however, let it suffice to consider briefly the case just considered.

Both the *Didache* and Matthew had to deal with backsliders and with misbehaving members. To accomplish this, the *Didache* prescribes confessing personal transgressions before the weekly Eucharist (14:1) and the shunning of members unwilling to amend their lives (15:3). Matthew's Gospel, meanwhile, endorses quite a different procedure. The injured party takes the initiative to resolve a grievance in three well-defined stages: first, privately, then with the help of a few witnesses, and finally with the force of the entire community (Matt 18:15–18). At each stage, the misbehaving member is invited to acknowledge his or her failing and make amends. Only the one who persistently refuses ends up being shunned. In Matthew's community, this procedure is seemingly normative, since Jesus is heard to endorse it in his own words. Had the framers of the *Didache* known of this saying of Jesus (either by reading Matthew's Gospel or experiencing Matthew's community),[32] it would be difficult to understand why

---

[31] My article, "Synoptic Tradition in the Didache Revisited," will be published in the fall 2003 volume of the *Journal of Early Christian Studies,* and it is currently available at www.Didache.info. In part, my study concludes: "When parallel texts are listed or even compared side by side, a plausible case can always be made for dependence upon Matthew's Gospel. More recently, however, more rigorous criteria have been developed in order to establish dependence. Jefford and Tuckett, for example, make the point that verbal agreement, in and of itself, cannot establish literary dependence since, in every case, one has to consider the possibility that the agreement present is due to both the *Didache* and Matthew having access to a common Jesus tradition. Thus, to establish dependence, one has to explore, even in cases of close or exact verbal agreement, to what degree the contexts and meanings overlap. Furthermore, one has to explore to what degree shared issues (fasting, praying, almsgiving, correcting, shunning) are defined and resolved along parallel lines. When these investigations were undertaken, however, they progressively revealed areas of wholesale divergence between Matthew and the *Didache*. In the end, consequently, this present study concludes that Matthew's Gospel and the *Didache* reveal two religious systems that grew up independent of each other. While they occasionally made use of common sources in defining their way of life, each community shaped these sources in accordance with their own distinctive ends. Hence, in the end, even their common heritage directs attention to their diversity."

[32] The mandate to "reprove each other ... as you have it in the good news" (15:3) cannot be used to confirm reliance upon a known Gospel. When the *Didache* itself uses the term *euagellion* ("gospel"), it refers, first and foremost, to the "good news of God" preached by Jesus (as in Mark 1:14; Rom 1:1, 15:16; 2 Cor 2:7; 1 Thess 2:2, 9; 1 Pet 4:17). Thus, in each of the four places wherein the "good news" (*euaggelion*) is mentioned as a source (8:2; 11:3; 15:3, 4), there is nothing

they would not have made use of it. As it is, they had to stretch and strain Mal 1:11 to support the seemingly novel practice of using the Eucharist as a gate for reconciliation: "Everyone having a conflict with his companion, do not let him come together with you [for the Eucharist] until they be reconciled, in order that your sacrifice not be defiled" (14:2). Alternately, instead of citing Mal 1:11 to support this practice, it could be argued that the framers of the *Didache* could have made easy use of Matt 5:23 due to its ready-made juxtapositioning of reconciliation and sacrifice.[33] But they didn't! It becomes very difficult, therefore, to imagine that the framers of the *Didache* were aware of either Matthew's Gospel or of those Matthean traditions that guided the practice of Matthean communities.[34]

---

to suggest that this term refers to a book or "a Gospel." One has to wait until the mid-second century before the term "gospel" takes on the extended meaning of referring to written texts (Helmut Koester, *Ancient Christian Gospels* [Harrisburg, Pa.: Trinity Press International, 1990], 1–48; Werner Kelber, *The Oral and the Written Gospel* [Philadelphia: Fortress, 1983], 144–48). Despite this, "most scholars agree" that the term "good news" found in the *Didache* "refers to some written gospel" (Van de Sandt, *Didache*, 352). When examined closely, however, "nothing in the context of these references indicate the presence of materials that were derived from any known gospel in writing" (50 n. 135). Van de Sandt thus surmises that the term "gospel" within the *Didache* can be "best understood as a reference to oral or written collections of sayings" (50 n. 135). Niederwimmer notes further that these sayings did not pertain to "the Christological kerygma" or "the epiphany, death, and resurrection of Jesus for our sake" (*Didache*, 50) but to a set of practical rules known to members of the Didache communities. For details, see Milavec, *Didache*, 720–23.

[33] One cannot help but notice that Matt 5:23–24 makes an appeal to reconciliation in which the offending party takes the initiative—very much unlike Matt 18:15–18. Furthermore, since it is unclear whether Matthew's community would have celebrated the Eucharist as "a sacrifice," it cannot be supposed that 5:23–24 ever served to define their eucharistic discipline. Within the context of the *Didache*, however, even a chance visitor familiar with 5:23–24 would have called the attention of the community to a saying of Jesus that authorized their eucharistic practice. The absence of 5:23–24 in the *Didache*, consequently, presses one to surmise not only that the framers of the *Didache* were unaware of Matthew's Gospel but that prophets/visitors from Matthew's community never had the occasion to experience the Eucharist within a Didache community.

[34] When it comes to reproving misbehaving members "not in anger but in peace" (*Did.* 15:3), Van de Sandt finds "a marked affinity with Qumran [1QS 5:24–25] concepts" (*Didache*, 353). Thus, when it comes to identifying the "good news" (*Did.* 15:3) source for this practice, he surmises that this source must have been comparable to 1QS and "at variance with our present gospel of Matthew" (352). Van de Sandt expands this argument in the paper included in this volume.

BRIEF CONSIDERATIONS RESPECTING THE DATE AND PROVENANCE OF THE *DIDACHE*

The date and provenance of the *Didache* has been heavily dominated by the question of the sources used in its composition. Adolph von Harnack wrote in his 1884 commentary, "One must say without hesitation that it is the author of the *Didache* who used the *Epistle of Barnabas* and not the reverse."[35] Harnack, accordingly, dated the *Didache* between 135 and 165 C.E. and fixed the place of origin as Egypt since *Barnabas* was thought to have been composed there. It was not until 1945 that E. J. Goodspeed, aided by the Latin versions of *Barnabas* that had no Two-Way section, finally put to rest the assumption that the *Didache* depended upon *Barnabas*.[36]

Once the *Epistle of Barnabas* was no longer considered as the source for the writer of the *Didache*, a fresh impetus was given to the question of which, if any, of the known Gospels were used by the framers of the *Didache*. It is telling that, in 1958, Audet devoted forty-two pages to the *Barnabas*-dependence issue and only twenty pages to the Gospel-dependence issue.[37] Audet concluded that, when examined closely, even the so-called "evangelical addition" of *Did*. 1:3b–5 cannot be explained as coming either from Matthew or from Luke.[38] Audet's enduring accomplishment was to demonstrate that the *Didache* can be best understood when it is interpreted within a Jewish horizon of understanding more or less independent of what one finds in the Gospels. Accordingly, in the end, Audet was persuaded that the manifest Jewish character[39] of the *Didache* pointed to a completion date prior to 70 C.E. in a milieu (Antioch) *that did not yet have a written Gospel*.[40]

---

[35] Adolph von Harnack, *Die Lehre der zwölf Apostel nebst Untersuchungenzuraltesten Geschichte der Kirchenverfassung und des Kirchenrechts* (Leipzig: Hinrichs, 1884), 82.

[36] E. J. Goodspeed published a landmark article in which he was troubled by the Latin versions of *Barnabas* that had no Two-Way section. Goodspeed argued that "early Christian literature usually grew not by partition and reduction, but by combination and expansion," and, from this, it can be deduced that the oldest version of Barnabas must have been prepared without any Two-Way section ("The Didache, Barnabas and the Doctrina," *ATR* 27 [1945]: 228).

[37] Audet, *Didache,* 121–63 with reference to Barnabas independence, 166–86 with reference to Gospel independence.

[38] Ibid., 186.

[39] In effect, it is not just the Jewish character of the *Didache* as such but the early form of its Christology (#5e, #5m), ecclesiology (#9d, #9f), and eschatology (#10m, #10r) that argue in favor of an even earlier date of around 50 C.E.

[40] Audet, *Didache,* 192, 210.

Audet's enduring accomplishment was to demonstrate that the *Didache* can be best understood when it is interpreted within a Jewish horizon of understanding. Following the observations of Jacob Neusner,[41] one can further understand how the halakhic character of the *Didache* emerges within Judaism while the Gospel form did not. It remains very problematic, therefore, to imagine that the framers of the *Didache* would have used or relied upon either a written or oral Gospel. When one combines this with the recognition that the *Didache* communities defined their response to backsliders and misbehaving members (to take just the single example considered above) without any awareness of the Jesus traditions and the practice of Matthew's community, it becomes increasingly certain that Matthew's Gospel and the *Didache* reveal two religious systems that grew up independent of each other. Niederwimmer, a champion of redaction criticism, likewise came to same conclusion: "The *Didache* lives in an entirely different linguistic universe, and that is true not only of its sources but of its redactor as well."[42]

Following upon this, Court's surmise that "the Didache stands in the tradition of St. Matthew's Gospel,"[43] Draper's surmise that "the *Didache* is the community rule of the Matthean community,"[44] and Massaux's surmise that the *Didache* was created "as a catechetical résumé of the first evangelist"[45] cannot stand up to close examination. The Gospel of Matthew and the *Didache*, point after point, evoke two religious systems addressing common problems in divergent ways. Once the venue for Matthew's Gospel is settled upon, therefore, one can know with a high degree of certainty that the *Didache* would not have originated there.[46]

Should *Didache* scholars come to accept this position, the way would be open for an early dating of the *Didache* and for its interpretation as a well-integrated and self-contained religious system that should be allowed

---

[41] Jacob Neusner, *Why No Gospels in Talmudic Judaism?* (Atlanta: Scholars Press, 1988).

[42] Niederwimmer, *Didache*, 48.

[43] Court, "The Didache," 112.

[44] Jonathan A. Draper, "Torah and Troublesome Apostles in the Didache Community," *Novum Testamentum* 33 (1991): 372.

[45] Massaux, "Le problème," 644.

[46] The same thing holds true for the Pauline communities as well. Here again, one discovers that the authentic Pauline letters and the *Didache*, point after point, evoke two religious systems addressing common problems in divergent ways. Jefford argues that the Antioch community had sufficient diversity to include Ignatius (a champion of Paul), Matthew's Gospel, and the *Didache*. As soon as such a mix got down to practical matters such as celebrating a Eucharist, the diversity among them would prove insurmountable.

to speak for itself. One has only to consider how studies devoted to the Letter to the Hebrews, the *Gospel of Thomas,* and the Q Gospel have flourished due to the fact that they have been allowed to stand alone. If the *Didache* were accorded the same treatment, a new era of Didache studies would thus lie open before us.

CONCLUSION

The brief time available does not allow me to elaborate further my origination hypothesis. I will be content, however, if I have offered you enough specific instances such that you can glimpse how the *Didache* might be viewed as a unified production that conceals within its oral logic a hidden key that marvelously accounts for the progression of topics from beginning to end. With what I have provided, you might even be able to make further discoveries for yourself. Being scholars, we always like to have the thrill of discovering things for ourselves rather than simply being told. Then, when reading my thousand-page volume, you will have the prospect of seeing just how far you were able to anticipate and, in many instances, even to outdo my own.[47]

In closing, I would say that the *Didache* has a special relevance within our modern society.[48] Any community that cannot artfully and effectively pass on its cherished way of life as a program for graced existence cannot long endure. Any way of life that cannot be clearly specified, exhibited, and differentiated from the alternative modes operative within the surrounding culture is doomed to growing insignificance and to gradual assimilation. Faced with these harsh realities, the *Didache* unfolds the training program calculated to irreversibly alter the habits of perception and standards of judgment of novices coming out of a pagan lifestyle.[49]

---

[47] My commentary, needless to say, does not just settle with establishing the unity of the *Didache* but goes on to milk every line of the document in order to recover all we can know about the faith, hope, and life of those communities that existentially committed themselves to the Way of Life. Such a reconstruction becomes possible because the unity of the *Didache* has been established as pointing back to living communities fixed in space and time. As long as the *Didache* was viewed as a collage of materials, it necessarily represented multiple points of view held by different persons/groups separated by place and time.

[48] For further reflections on the spirituality of the *Didache* and its relevance for addressing pressing problems within our contemporary society, see Milavec, *Didache,* 842–909.

[49] Michael Polanyi notes that all deep knowing implies a way of being in one's body and a way of being in the world that cannot be transmitted by a mere telling in words. Nor can such knowledge be entirely analyzed, dissected, and made

The content and the modality of this process of human transformation can be gleaned from the verbal clues conveyed within the text itself. Once this is established, then it becomes possible to combine linguistic, historical, and sociological tools to recover the faith, hope, and life of those communities that existentially committed themselves to living the Way of Life. These approaches have taken root during the last decade for investigating the communities that are presupposed by each of the books in the Christian Scriptures. Within recent sessions of the Society of Biblical Literature, comparable approaches have been extended to the *Gospel of Thomas* and the Q Gospel. The time has come for *Didache* scholars to do likewise. This is the way of scholarship. This is the Way of Life.

---

plain such that a detached observer could discern the foundational principles involved and, through progressive steps in clear logic, arrive at the same affirmations as the teller. Polanyi repudiates the ideal of critical, detached knowing as unrealized and unrealizable (both in science as well as in religion), and Polanyi explains that this is so by virtue of the fact that all knowledge is embodied knowledge relying upon tacit skills: "If we know a great deal that we cannot tell, and if even that which we know and can tell is accepted by us as true only in view of its bearing on a reality beyond it...; if indeed we recognize a great discovery, or else a great personality, as most real, owing to the wide range of its yet unknown future manifestations: then the idea of knowledge based on wholly identifiable grounds collapse, and we must conclude that the transmission of knowledge from one generation to the other must be predominantly tacit" (Polanyi, Tacit *Dimension*, 61). In the end, for an adult to learn the ways of a master, he or she has to submit to a prolonged apprenticeship. Polanyi notes that, even in an apprenticeship, learning depends upon a certain sympathy that exists between the novice and master. This sympathy begins in the spontaneous admiration that prompts the novice to establish a master-apprentice relationship in the first place. This sympathy operates throughout the apprenticeship itself, giving the novice the means to enter into and to assimilate the performance skills exhibited by his or her trusted master. For further details, see Aaron Milavec, *To Empower as Jesus Did: Acquiring Spiritual Power through Apprenticeship* (Lewiston, N.Y.: Mellen, 1982), 177–240.

The Gathering of the Church in the Kingdom: The Self-Understanding of the *Didache* Community in the Eucharistic Prayers

Huub van de Sandt
Tilburg University

The prayers for the eucharistic meal in *Did.* 9–10 are older than the *Didache*. They existed prior to the final editing of the work and were incorporated in the document at a later date.[1] The petitions in *Did.* 9:4 and 10:5 run parallel:

4. Just as this fragment lay scattered upon the mountains and became a single [fragment] when it had been gathered,	5. Be mindful, Lord, of your church, to preserve it from all evil [or, from every evil being] and to perfect it in your love. And, once it is sanctified,
so may your church be gathered from the ends of the earth into your kingdom.	gather it from the four winds, into the kingdom which you have prepared for it.
For glory and power are yours, through Jesus Christ, forever	For power and glory are yours forever

---

[1] See, for example, J. Betz, "Die Eucharistie in der Didache," *Archiv für Liturgiewissenschaft* 11 (1969): 10–39; ET: "The Eucharist in the Didache," in J. A. Draper, ed., *The Didache in Modern Research* (AGJU 37) Leiden 1996, 244–75; esp. 245; H. van de Sandt and D. Flusser, *The Didache: Its Jewish Sources and Its Place in Early Judaism and Christianity* (CRINT 3/5), Assen-Minneapolis, 2002, 309–29.

1. THE JEWISH CHARACTER OF THE PRAYER

Both the prayer before the ritual meal (*Did.* 9) and the one concluding the meal (*Did.* 10)[2] have parallels in the Jewish rites. *Didache* 9:2–3 is close to the Jewish table blessing (see *m. Ber.* 6:1),[3] while the supplication in 9:4 resembles the tenth benediction of the *Tefilla* (= Shemoneh Esreh or Amidah).[4] Most scholars nowadays agree that the text in *Did.* 10 evolved from the Jewish Grace after meals (or the Birkat Ha-Mazon), that is, the

---

[2] The clause τὴν ἁγιασθεῖσαν ("the sanctified") in *Did.* 10:5 is translated here as "and, once it is sanctified." The attribute given to the church is often considered to be textually suspect. Since this expression is found in the Jerusalem MS H but is lacking in the Coptic Fragment and in the *Apostolic Constitutions,* it could represent a later gloss. On the other hand, the clause may reflect an authentic reading. The phrase τὴν ἁγιασθεῖσαν in combination with καὶ τελειῶσαι αὐτήν ("and to perfect it") is closely related to the expression in Heb 10:14 where it says that Christ "has perfected [τετελείωκεν] for ever those who are sanctified [τοὺς ἁγιαζομένους]." Moreover, the apposition τὴν ἁγιασθεῖσαν shows agreement with Eph 5:25–26: "Christ loved the church ... that he might sanctify her, having cleansed ['ἵνα αὐτὴν ἁγιάσῃ καθαρίσας] her by the washing of water with the word."

[3] The structure of the separate prayers before the meal (cup-bread) reflects the sequence of these in mainstream Judaism. They are close to the Jewish table blessing in content as well. In the Mishnah, the Jewish blessing over the cup is rendered thus: "(Blessed are you, O Lord, our God, King of the world,) who creates the fruit of the vine" (*m. Ber.* 6:1); and over the bread: "(Blessed are you, O Lord, our God, King of the world,) who brings forth bread from the earth" (*m. Ber.* 6:1).

[4] The tenth benediction of the Palestinian recension of the *Tefilla* reads: "lift up the banner for the gathering of our exiles; praised are you, O Lord, who gathers the dispersed of your people Israel" (for a comparison in parallel columns of the prayers in *Did.* 9–10 and their Jewish sources, see J. W. Riggs, "From Gracious Table to Sacramental Elements: The Tradition-History of Didache 9 and 10," *SecCent* 4 [1984]: 83–101, esp. 92–93; R. D. Middleton, "The Eucharistic Prayers of the Didache," *JTS* 36 [1935]: 259–67, esp. 261–64), and the Babylonian recension of the same supplication is as follows: "lift up the banner to gather all our exiles from the four ends of the earth into our land; praised are you, O Lord, who gathers the dispersed of your people Israel" (See H. L. Strack und P. Billerbeck, *Kommentar zum neuen Testament aus Talmud und Midrasch* 4/1, München 1928, 212; L. Clerici, *Einsammlung der Zerstreuten: Liturgiegeschichtliche Untersuchung zur Vor- und Nachgeschichte der Fürbitte für die Kirche in Didache 9,4 und* 10,5 [Liturgiegeschichtliche Quellen und Forschungen 44], Münster [Westf] 1965, 90; see also the Mussaf prayer for Rosh Hashanah and the benediction before the Shema: "Bring us to peace from the four ends of the earth and lead us straight into our land").

prayer that concludes the Jewish ritual meal.[5] Thus, while the blessings in *Did.* 9 originate from different Jewish sources, those in *Did.* 10 have come from one coherent Jewish liturgical source. Assuming that we get closer to the Jewish setting of Christian prayers as these reflect a single source, one may argue that the text in *Did.* 10 represents the earlier prayer and that *Did.* 9 in its literary form depends on *Did.* 10.[6]

Certain structural patterns, key concepts, and thematic elements of the eucharistic prayer in Did. 10 are similar to the Birkat Ha-Mazon. The first to have closely examined these prayers was Louis Finkelstein, who presented the two texts in parallel columns.[7] Finkelstein's reconstruction is based on manuscripts from the ninth and tenth centuries, however, and his version consequently remains a hypothetical restoration. Furthermore, there is widespread recognition that the precise wording of the Grace was not yet established in the first century.[8] On the other hand, since

---

[5] See, for example, G. Klein, "Die Gebete in der Didache," *ZNW* 9 (1908): 132–46, esp. 140–41; L. Finkelstein, "The Birkat Ha-Mazon," in idem *Pharisaism in the Making: Selected Essays,* New York 1972, 333–84; published previously in *JQR* NS 19 (1928–29): 211–62, passim; Middleton, "Eucharistic Prayers," 263–64; M. Dibelius, "Die Mahl-Gebete der Didache," *ZNW* 37 (1938): 32–41, repr. in H. Kraft and G. Bornkamm, eds., *Botschaft und Geschichte: Gesammelte Aufsätze von Martin Dibelius. 2: Zum Urchristentum und zur hellenistischen Religionsgeschichte,* Tübingen 1956, 117–27, esp. 117, 122–23; J.-P. Audet, *La Didachè: Instructions des Apôtres* (Ebib), Paris 1958, 410; L. Ligier, "The Origins of the Eucharistic Prayer: From the Last Supper to the Eucharist," *Studia Liturgica* 9 (1973): 161–85; published previously as "Les origines de la prière eucharistique: de la cène du Seigneur à l'eucharistie," *Questions Liturgiques* 53 (1972): 181–202; G. Rouwhorst, "Bénédiction, action de grâces, supplication. Les oraisons de la table dans le Judaïsme et les célébrations eucharistiques des Chrétiens syriaques," *Questions Liturgiques* 61 (1980): 211–40; H. Wegman, "Généalogie hypothétique de la prière eucharistique," *Questions Liturgiques* 61 (1980): 263–78; W. Rordorf and A. Tuilier, *La Doctrine des douze Apôtres (Didachè)* (SC 248 bis), Paris ²1998, 178–79 n. 3; K. Niederwimmer, *Die Didache* (Kommentar zu den Apostolischen Vätern 1), Göttingen ²1993 (1989) 194–99; E. Mazza, *The Origins of the Eucharistic Prayer,* Collegeville (Minn) 1995, 16–30.

[6] Riggs, "From Gracious Table," 93. See also Van de Sandt-Flusser, *Didache,* 313.

[7] Finkelstein, "Birkat Ha-Mazon," 215–17.

[8] See J. Heinemann, *Prayer in the Talmud: Forms and Patterns* (SJ 9), Berlin 1977, 37–64, and, concerning the Grace after meals, S. Safrai, "Religion in Everyday Life," in Safrai and M. Stern, eds., *The Jewish People in the First Century: Historical Geography, Political History, Social, Cultural and Religious Life and Institutions* 2 (CRINT 1/2), Assen/Philadelphia 1976, 793–833, esp. 802–3; P. F. Bradshaw, *The Search for the Origins of Christian Worship: Sources and Methods for the Study of Early Liturgy,* London 1992, 207; S. C. Reiff, "The Early History of Jewish Worship,"

Finkelstein's reconstructed text reflects ancient traditions and roughly corresponds to the outline of the three berakhot echoed in the Mishnah (*m. Ber.* 6:8), some form of the later Birkat Ha-Mazon must have been in regular use at the end of the Second Temple period.[9]

However, if *Did.* 10 indeed evolved from the Birkat Ha-Mazon, it is clear that the initial form of the Hebrew Grace after meals underwent a significant development. While the Birkat Ha-Mazon is divided into three strophes, its structure has been adapted to a bipartite use in *Did.* 10.[10] The blessing-thanksgiving-supplication pattern of the Birkat Ha-Mazon becomes a prayer of thanksgiving and supplication. The reorganization of the Grace in the *Didache* reflects the displacement of the entire first pericope (a *berakha* or blessing addressed to God) in the Birkat Ha-Mazon in favour of the second (a *hodaya* or thanksgiving). The *hodaya*, which was found in the Grace at the second place, is located at the beginning in the present structure, and the *berakha*, which was initially the first strophe, has now become part of the *hodaya*. This transposition is not as fantastic as it seems. The Greek verb *eucharistein* ("to be thankful," "to return thanks") may already have been the common designation of "to bless at table" in Hellenistic Judaism (cf. Rom 14:6; 1 Cor 10:30; 1 Tim 4:3-4; and Philo, *De Specialibus Legibus* 2.175), where this alternate form of Grace probably began with this word (*eucharistein*).[11] The thanksgiving in the first pericope of the prayer in the *Didache* has its parallel in the *hodaya*, the thanksgivings in the second pericope of the Jewish Grace.

Another point of difference between the Hebrew Grace and *Did.* 10 concerns the ongoing spiritualization of the prayer in the *Didache*. One may note, for example, the substitution of spiritual food and spiritual drink (10:3) for their physical counterparts and the replacement of the thanks for the "land" for the gratitude that the Lord has his "holy Name ... made

---

in P. F. Bradshaw and L. A. Hoffman, *The Making of Jewish and Christian Worship*, Notre Dame 1991, 109–36; J. A. Draper, "Ritual Process and Ritual Symbol in Didache 7–10," *VC* 54 (2000): 121–58, esp. 139.

[9] The antiquity of the general structure and themes of the Birkat Ha-Mazon is corroborated by the book of *Jubilees* (second century B.C.); it gives an account of Abraham, who, after a "good thank offering"(22:5), pronounces his Grace after meals (22:6–9); see Van de Sandt-Flusser, *Didache*, 316–18.

[10] Cf. Middleton, "Eucharistic Prayers," 263; Th. J. Talley, "From Berakah to Eucharistia: A Reopening Question," *Worship* 50 (1976): 115–37, esp. 125–29; and, also for the following, Van de Sandt-Flusser, *Didache*, 313–25.

[11] J. Laporte, *La Doctrine eucharistique chez Philon d'Alexandrie* (ThH 16), Paris 1972, 82–84; P. Drews, "Untersuchungen zur Didache," *ZNW* 5 (1904): 53–79, esp. 77; and K. Wengst, *Didache (Apostellehre). Barnabasbrief. Zweiter Klemensbrief. Schrift an Diognet* (Schriften des Urchristentums 2), Darmstadt 1984, 57 n. 192.

dwell in our hearts" (10:2). This process of modifying the Grace after meals by spiritualizing the prayers may be assigned to circles in Hellenistic Judaism as well.[12] All this results, as will be shown below, in the conclusion that *Did.* 10 is not a reworking of the Hebrew but of the *Greek* version of the Birkat Ha-Mazon.[13] Instead of taking for granted that the prayer has only one layer of tradition, we have to consider its several stages of development. Structure and expressions in the eucharistic prayers of the *Didache* betray a strong Hellenistic influence. We shall, therefore, assume that the prayer in the *Didache* is a Christianization of the Hebrew prayer after meals used in Greek Judaism.

2. THE PROBLEM: THE CONCEPT OF DISPERSION BEHIND THE PRAYERS

We have seen that, since the prayer in *Did.* 10 was composed from a single source, it may be the more primitive form of the two prayers in *Did.* 9–10. Accordingly, the focus here will be placed primarily on the petition in 10:5. The petition for the gathering of the church "from the four winds" and its being brought home into the "kingdom" reflects the Jewish desire that the people of Israel be gathered and united. According to a reconstruction of Finkelstein, the earliest version of the the third benediction of the Jewish Grace after meals, also called the supplication for Jerusalem, may have read as follows:

> Have mercy, O Lord, our God, on Israel, your people, and on Jerusalem, your city, and on Zion, the resting-place of your glory, and

---

[12] K. G. Sandelin, *Wisdom As Nourisher: A Study of an Old Testament Theme, Its Development within Early Judaism and Its Impact on Early Christianity* (Acta Academia Aboensis, ser. A: Humaniora 64/3), Åbo 1986, 212–18; Dibelius, "Die Mahl-Gebete," passim; Clerici, *Einsammlung der Zerstreuten*, 37. See also Rordorf-Tuilier, *La Doctrine des douze Apôtres*, 179 n. 4.

[13] See above, n. 12. Compare also G. Alon, "Ha-halakha ba-Torat 12 ha-Shelihim," in idem, *Studies in Jewish History* 1, 274–94; 288 n. 67; published previously in *Tarbiz* 11 (1939–40): 127–45; ET: "The Halacha in the Teaching of the Twelve Apostles," in Draper, *The Didache in Modern Research*, 165–94, 185 n. 67; H. Lietzmann, *Messe und Herrenmahl: Eine Studie zur Geschichte der Liturgie* (Arbeiten zur Kirchengeschichte 8), Berlin 1926; ET: *Mass and Lord's Supper. A Study in the History of the Liturgy*, with introduction and further inquiry by R. D. Richardson. Leiden 1979, 233–34; H. Köster, *Synoptische Überlieferung bei den apostolischen Vätern* (TU 65), Berlin 1957, 193; Wengst, *Didache (Apostellehre)*, 48–49, 53 n. 177; R. J. Ledogar, *Acknowledgment: Praise-Verbs in the Early Greek Anaphora*, Rome 1968, 127–28; B. Kollmann, *Ursprung und Gestalten der frühchristlichen Mahlfeier* (GTA 43), Göttingen 1990, 80–89.

on your altar and on your temple. Blessed are you, O Lord, who buildest Jerusalem.[14]

The Greek version of the Birkat ha-Mazon is not known, but it is conceivable that the elements in the third strophe ("Jerusalem, your city"; "Zion"; "your altar"; and "your temple") may have resulted in a prayer for the return to the land of Israel. In any case, the Christian supplication in *Did.* 10:5 recalls the situation of Israel's dispersion. The longing for the triumphant reunion of the church is bound up with the biblical expectation of salvation for the people of Israel.[15] In later Judaism, these ideas continue to flourish,[16] and the future hope of a restored Jerusalem is sustained by prayers.[17] Originally, the dispersion was related to the Babylonian captivity (LXX: διασπορά), a singular event in Jewish history. However, during the Hellenistic age, when the Babylonian captivity had ceased for a long time, the Jewish colonies abroad survived and continued to grow. It is this reality, also frequently expressed in terms like παροικία (meaning "sojourn") or (δια) σκορπισμός (referring to the scattering of Israel), which is envisaged when the eschatological gathering is mentioned.[18]

In this article, we focus on two clusters of questions:

1. In *Did.* 10:5 (and 9:4), the traditional Jewish earthly orientation expressed in the third strophe of the Birkat Ha-Mazon (a compassionate treatment of Israel, the people according to the flesh, of Jerusalem, Zion, and the temple) is conceived in terms of ethical, spiritual, supra-terrestrial, and everlasting goods: the spiritual building of the "church," its deliverance

---

[14] Cf. Finkelstein, "Birkat Ha-Mazon," 233.

[15] See Deut 30:1–5a; Isa 11:12; 27:13; 43:5–7; 49:22; 56:8; Jer 23:8; 31:8, 10; 39:37 (LXX); Ezek 11:17; 20:34; 28:25; 34:11–16; 37:21; 39:27; Mic 2:12–13; 4:12; Pss 106:47; 147:2; Neh 1:8–9; Zech 2:10 (LXX); 8:7–8; 10:6vv; 1 Chr 16:35; 2 Macc 2:7, 18; Tob 13:5; Sir 36:11; 51:12 (f). Cf. also A. Stuiber, "Diaspora," in *RAC* 3 (Stuttgart 1957) 972–82, esp. 974–75.

[16] 2 Macc 1:27; 2:18; *1 En.* 57:1; 90:34; *Pss. Sol.* 8:28; 11:2–6; 17:26, 28, 31, 34–36, 43–44; *2 Bar.* 77–78; *4 Ezra* 13:39; *T. Asher* 7; Philo, *Praem.* 117; *Exsecr.* 165; *b. Meg.* 29a; *b. Pesah.* 117a; etc.; cf. P. Volz, *Die Eschatologie der jüdischen Gemeinde im neutestamentlichen Zeitalter*, Tübingen 1934, 344–50.

[17] Ps 147:2; Sir 36(33):1–16; 51:12a–q (Hebr.); 2 Macc 1:24–29; *Pss. Sol.* 8:27–28; 17:30–31; and the tenth benediction of the *Tefilla* (see above, n. 4); cf. Clerici, *Einsammlung der Zerstreuten*, 65–102; and Niederwimmer, *Didache*, 188 and n. 54.

[18] A. P. J. Arowele, *Diaspora-Concept in the New Testament: Studies on the Idea of Christian Sojourn, Pilgrimage and Dispersion according to the New Testament* (Inaugural-Dissertation), Würzburg 1977, 27–54.

from all evil, its perfection in love, and its ultimate integration into an immaterial reign of God. The earthly, worldly expectation and confidence is replaced by a spiritualized and eschatological hope. The Christian longing for a gathering does not include the Jewish hope for a restoration of Israel and Jerusalem. Is this an attempt to define the Christian community of the *Didache* as distinct from Judaism? Does the *Didache* prayer reflect a separation from the tie that Jews have with the land and Jerusalem? Does it substitute the gathering of the church for the gathering of Israel according to the flesh?

2. The *Didache* prayer recalls the condition of dispersion and the scattering of Israel among the nations of the world. At the same time, however, it is a prayer for the church (ἐκκλησία) and its gathering into the kingdom. What kind of concept of diaspora underlies this prayer? The term *diaspora* was used by Jews to indicate that part of Judaism living outside of Palestine, but what would such a term mean to Christians? Does it say that Christians as such, whether Jewish or Gentile, live in dispersion? Where is this gathering supposed to take place? How to grasp the ultimate significance of the petition in *Did.* 10:5 and 9:4?

Below we will take the following steps. Because the eucharistic prayer clearly recalls a Hellenistic Jewish milieu, our initial concern will be with the concepts of dispersion and gathering in the Hellenistic Jewish writings of Philo of Alexandria, the preeminent representative of Hellenistic Judaism. It will be shown that Philo employs the notions "diaspora" and equivalent terms ("sojourn," "scattering") in a metaphorical way. At variance with their Hebrew Palestinian content, these words do not have a material but a spiritual sense. The same is true for some New Testament writings. This evidence enables us to better understand the motif of return of the dispersed in the Didache prayer (see section 3 below). It does not solve the issue, however, of the disregard of the concrete city of Jerusalem, Zion, and the temple in the *Didache* prayer. On the contrary, one might go so far as to wonder if the figurative understanding of the term "diaspora" does not reflect deviating roles of the physical land of Judea and the concrete city of Jerusalem in contemporary Judaism. Was the purpose of a metaphorical concept of dispersion not to undermine the hope for a future return to the earthly fatherland? And might such a view not have emerged before the Christianization of the Birkat Ha-Mazon, that is, as early as in the Hellenistic stage? It will become clear, however, that the supplication in the *Didache*—without mentioning the physical land of Judea and the tangible city of Jerusalem—reflects a Christian rather than a Jewish longing (see section 4 below). This evidence will finally bring us to the conclusion that the texts of *Did.* 10:5 and 9:4 reflect a Christian community that increasingly distances itself from Judaism.

3. DISPERSION IN A HELLENISTIC-JEWISH AND EARLY CHRISTIAN SETTING

It was established that the eucharistic prayers of the *Didache* have their origin in the Jewish Grace (the Birkat Ha-Mazon) recited by Jews in a Hellenistic milieu. Therefore, one may assume a Hellenistic Jewish provenance for the supplication in *Did*. 10:5. Since the Greek version of the prayer goes back to a Hellenistic Jewish model of the Hebrew supplication for Jerusalem (the Birkat Ha-Yerushalayim),[19] the quest for parallels or similarities in Hellenistic Judaism brings us to Philo.

3.1. PHILO

Although the sources do not provide much information about Philo himself, his writings show him to have been deeply influenced by the Socratic-Platonic view of the dualistic body-soul relationship. He was probably born between 20 and 10 B.C. and belonged to one of the most influential families of Alexandrian Jewry. He had a wide education and was acquainted with many Greek philosophers and writers. At the same time, he was a religious Jew who practised Jewish laws and customs. Because his writings were based on the law of Moses, Philo regarded himself not primarily as an original thinker but as an exegete of Scripture. In his view, Greek philosophy was the intellectual framework of reference within which the books of Moses should be explained.[20]

Philo conceived the reunion out of the dispersion that is prayed for in *Did*. 10:5 as a metaphorical concept, as bridging the distance from the heavenly home. With reference to Lev 25:23 ("for the land is mine; for you are strangers and sojourners with me"), he explains:

> to God they [all creatures] are aliens and sojourners [παροίκων]. For each of us has come into this world as into a foreign city, in which before our birth we had no part, and in this city he does but sojourn [παροικεῖ], until he has exhausted his appointed span of life.[21]

---

[19] The fourth benediction of the Birkat Ha-Mazon is not reflected in either *Jub*. 22:6–9 (see above, n. 9) or in *Did*. 10. It already existed in the Second Temple period but did not become obligatory until after the Bar Kokhba War. See Alon, "Ha-halakha ba-Torat 12 ha-Shelihim," 289–90 (ET: 187); and Finkelstein, "Birkat Ha-Mazon" (1928–29), 221–222.

[20] See, e.g., P. Borgen, *Philo of Alexandria: An Exegete for His Time* (NovTSup 86), Leiden 1997, 1–45. See also E. Schürer, *The History of the Jewish People in the Age of Jesus Christ (175 B.C.–A.D. 135)* 3/2; rev. by G. Vermes, F. Millar, and M. Goodman, Edinburgh 1987, 871–80.

[21] *Cher*. 120; cf. F. H. Colson and G. H. Whitaker, *Philo, with an English Translation* 2 (LCL 227), London-Cambridge MA 1968 (1929), 78–79; see also *Cher*. 121.

In his writings, the idea is found that the life of man is a sojourn and that his original homeland is heaven. He uses terms like πάροικος, παροικία, and παροικεῖν. In its technical use, the term παροικεῖν means "to dwell as a resident alien or stranger" in a place where one is not native or a citizen and does not have civil or native rights.[22] In Philo's texts, πάροικος serves to express the fact that the righteous man is a stranger, a noncitizen, on earth. These qualifications are often used in the LXX, primarily denoting a sojourn in a geographical location. In Philo, however, they show a basic transformation of meaning. The Greek terms no longer refer to any particular geographical location; they now have bearing on the whole of the physical world as it is. There is a clear dualism between this world and the next. Philo portrays the soul as "imprisoned in that dwelling place of endless calamities—the body."[23] The body is the animal side of man. It is the source of all evil and "the grave of the soul, in which it is buried as if in a grave."[24] These statements are entrenched in Philo's overall view of man's fight against the πάθη and the world with his treasures.

Life is a pilgrimage in which the mind of man attempts to get away from the body, which he calls "the foul prison-house."[25] The wise man, who lives in wisdom and virtue, regards his earthly material existence as a temporary domicile. He is a "sojourner":

---

[22] K. L. and M. A. Schmidt, "πάροικος, παροικία, παροικέω" *TWNT* 5:841–53, esp. 851–53. For additional information, see J. H Elliott, *A Home for the Homeless: A Sociological Exegesis of 1 Peter, Its Situation and Strategy*, London 1982 (1st ed. 1981), 24–37.

[23] "Living nature was primarily divided into two opposite parts, the unreasoning and the reasoning, this last again into the mortal and immortal species, the mortal being that of men, the immortal that of unbodied souls which range through the air and sky. These are immune from wickedness because their lot from the first has been one of unmixed happiness, and they have not been imprisoned in that dwelling place of endless calamities—the body" (*Conf.* 176–177); cf. Colson-Whitaker, *Philo* 4 (LCL 261), 1968 (1932), 106–7.

[24] (*QG* 4.75); cf. R. Marcus, *Philo. Supplement 1: Questions and Answers on Genesis* (LCL 380), London-Cambridge MA 1961 (1953), 353. See also R. Williamson, *Jews in the Hellenistic World: Philo* (Cambridge Commentaries on the Writings of the Jewish and Christian World 200 BC to AD 200 1/2), Cambridge 1989, 212–14.

[25] "Depart, therefore, out of the earthly matter that encompasses you: escape, man, from the foul prison-house, your body [δεσμωτήριον, τὸ σῶμα], with all your might and main, and from the pleasures and lusts that act as its jailers" (*Migr.* 9); cf. Colson-Whitaker, *Philo* 4, 136–37. See also, for the following, Williamson, *Philo and the Epistle to the Hebrews*, 483–91; and R. A. Bitter, *Vreemdelingschap bij Philo van Alexandrië. Een onderzoek naar de betekenis van* πάροικος (diss. in Dutch; with a summary in English); Utrecht 1982, 129–69.

This is why all whom Moses calls wise [σοφοί] are represented as sojourners. Their souls are never colonists leaving heaven for a new home. Their way is to visit earthly nature as men who travel abroad to see and learn. So when they have stayed awhile in their bodies, and beheld through them all that sense and mortality has to show, they make their way back to the place from which they set out at the first. To them the heavenly region, where their citizenship lies, is their native land [πατρίδα]; the earthly region in which they became sojourners [ἐν ᾧ παρῴκησαν] is a foreign country [ξένην].[26]

Hellenistic dualism is thus often presented by Philo in the form of a belief that heaven is the true home of the soul. He refers to the soul's heavenly preexistence again and again. On the other hand, man cannot return without difficulty and strain to his celestial origin. Those who achieved perfect virtue are restricted to a privileged few biblical personages like Moses, Abraham, Jacob, and Isaac. In the paragraph following the passage quoted above, Philo makes use of the Greek Bible to substantiate this idea (*De confusione linguarum* 79–82). Reference is made to Gen 23:4; 47:9; and 26:2–3.[27] Those whom Moses calls wise are represented as sojourners since "their souls are never colonists leaving heaven for a new home."

3.2. EARLY CHRISTIAN LITERATURE

It is difficult to determine to what extent Philo's spiritual views and philosophical ideas can be taken as representing his Hellenistic fellow-Jews. However, additional sources, especially the Epistle to the Hebrews and 1 Peter, show a similar strand of Judaism, at least as far as the concept of dispersion is concerned.

---

[26] *Conf.* 77–78; cf. Colson-Whitaker, *Philo* 4, 50–53. See also *Somn.* 1.181: In the course of his allegorical interpretation of the dream of Jacob at Bethel, Philo refers to the statement uttered by God to Jacob in Gen 28:15 ("and I will bring you back to this land") as follows: "Perhaps, too, in these words he hints at the doctrine of the immortality of the soul: for, as was said a little before, it forsook its heavenly abode and came into the body as into a foreign land. But the father who gave it birth says that He will not permanently disregard it in its imprisonment, but will take pity on it and loose its chains, and escort it in freedom and safety to its mother-city, and will not stay his hand until the promises given by words have been made good by actual deeds;" cf. Colson-Whitaker, *Philo* 5 (LCL 275), 1968 (1934), 392–93; further, see *Her.* 267; *Gig.* 61; *Agr.* 65; etc.

[27] In Gen 23:4, Abraham says "I am a stranger and sojourner with you"; in Gen 47:9, Jacob reports, "The days of the years of my life, the days which I sojourn, have been few and evil, they have not reached to the days of my fathers which they sojourned"; in Gen 26:2–3, Isaac is told in an oracle, "Go not down to Egypt, but dwell in the land which I say to you. And sojourn in this land."

Since the Christian community thought of itself as one with a temporary character (Phil 3:20–21; Heb 13:14), it was natural that it tended to appropriate to itself the language of Israel as the sojourning people of God. Addresses to churches in the "dispersion" are found in 1 Pet 1:1 (cf. 2:11), and similar terms appear in the introductions to *1 Clement,* the *Epistle of Polycarp,* and the *Martyrdom of Polycarp.* A fine example of this idea is found in the *Letter to Diognetus,* from which a few verses are quoted here:

> Yet while living in Greek and barbarian cities, according as each obtained his lot, and following the local customs, both in clothing and food and in the rest of life, they (the Christians) show forth the wonderful and confessedly strange character of the constitution of their own citizenship. They dwell in their own fatherlands, but as if sojourners in them [πάροικοι]; they share all things as citizens, and suffer all things as strangers [ξένοι]. Every foreign country is their fatherland, and every fatherland is a foreign country.... They pass their time upon the earth, but they have their citizenship in heaven. (5:4-5, 9)[28]

Just as Philo depicts the Jews as sojourning in foreign countries, so the terminology is used here to depict metaphorically the Christians' state as one of "strangers and pilgrims" upon the earth.

Christian believers are journeying to their true home in heaven as they make their way through the present transitory life. This is also the conviction of the author of the Letter to the Hebrews. In Heb 11:13–16, the patriarchs are said to have confessed that they were "strangers [ξένοι] and sojourners [παρεπίδημοι] on the earth." The terms "stranger" and "sojourner" denote the stranger who stays for a short time in a place, the transient alien without rights of citizenship.[29] The author of Hebrews at the same time establishes, however, that these patriarchs, while living in Canaan, their country of adoption, did not attempt to return to their country of origin. Although they had the opportunity to go back, they did not do so. A literal explanation of their confession to be "strangers and sojourners on the earth" was, therefore, not appropriate. To him, it is clear that these two terms are symbolically used, that is, that "they desire a better country, that is a heavenly one." Heaven is the homeland of God's people (cf. Heb 12:22–24).

The alien typology that 1 Peter employs puts him in the same Hellenistic Jewish traditional stream, which we have seen to be strongly represented in Philo and Hebrews. In 1 Peter, the recipients of the letter

---

[28] English translation by K. Lake in *The Apostolic Fathers in Two Volumes* (LCL 25), vol. 2, London 1970 (1913), 358–61.

[29] See, e.g., Elliott, *Home for the Homeless,* 21–58.

are addressed as "chosen sojourners of the dispersion in Pontus..." (ἐκλεκτοῖς παρεπιδήμοις διασπορᾶς Πόντου ... κτλ.; 1 Pet 1:1). Terms like διασπορά and παροικία or πάροικος are appropriated as easily as the use of παρεπίδημος. The writer of 1 Peter implores his Christian addressees as "aliens and sojourners [παροίκους καὶ παρεπιδήμους] to abstain from passions of the flesh" (2:11), that is, to maintain their status as spiritual pilgrims to their heavenly home.[30] The believers are urged to behave in such way as to attain the goal to which they have been called. This is also the drift of 1:17, where their strangeness is emphasized with the same term, παροικία (sojourning in a foreign land), so as to indicate an ethical behaviour that does not ruin their Christian status. Since these terms appear in contexts which do not consider any geographical specifics (except for 1:1), one may suppose that the "dispersion" community of 1 Peter seems to have had a predominantly Gentile background (1 Pet 4:3; cf. 1:14, 18). There is no need to find a Jewish address behind the use of διασπορά and related terms. Peter is addressing all Christians—Jewish and Gentile—as chosen exiles in dispersion.[31] Their true homeland is not to be found anywhere on earth but in heaven.

The above observations partially answer the questions in cluster 2. *Didache* 10:5 and 9:4 assume the church to be dispersed but mention neither the location of the kingdom nor the spot where the church was to be gathered. Like Philo, the Christians of the *Didache* community probably understood the gathering of the church from the ends of the earth in a metaphorical sense. Christians were said to live in *diaspora* because they dwelled on earth and God would bring them together into his kingdom.

---

[30] "Die Metaphern vom Fremdling, der nur vorübergehend an einem für ihn fremden Ort lebt (παρεπίδημος: V 1; 2,11), und vom Fremden ohne Bürgerrecht in einer Stadt (πάροικος: 2,11) sowie von der Diaspora verstehen christliche Existenz, wie sich immer deutlicher zeigen wird, als Nicht-Angepasst-Sein an den verbreiteten Lebensstil, als Verweigerung von Identität und Zustimmung, als eine die greifbaren Lebensbedingungen transzendierende Hoffnung, die das Leben unter diesen Bedingungen reguliert. »Heimat« haben die Christen also anderswo"; cf. N. Brox, *Der erste Petrusbrief* (EKKNT 21), Zürich und Neukirchen-Vluyn 1979, 57. For the Christian adoption of πάροικος and related terms, see K. L. and M. A. Schmidt, "πάροικος, παροικία, παροικέω," 851–53. See also K. L. Schmidt, *TWNT* 2:101–4, on διασπορά in the New Testament and W. Grundmann in ibid., 64–65, on παρεπίδημος.

[31] This seems apparent from Peter's parallel in 2:10 to Rom 9:25: "Once you were no people but now you are God's people." In Jas 1:1, the address αἱ δώδεκα φυλαὶ ἐν τῇ διασπορᾷ is found. At variance with 1 Pet 1:1, this expression might quite realistically refer to Christians, whether Jews or Gentiles, who do in fact live in dispersion, without an "accompanying spiritual sense"; cf. Schmidt, "διασπορά," 103 n. 14.

On the other hand, the outlook in the *Didache* is significantly different from the position of Philo. According to Philo, the soul belongs to another world and is imprisoned in the body, whereas the prayer of the *Didache* does not seem to know a cosmological dualism or any heavenly preexistence of the soul. In *Did.* 10:5, the praying congregation opens its heart to God so that he might purge it, perfect it, and make it holy. The ethical phrases lend a special meaning to the community vis-à-vis the world. The belief had practical implications in everyday life. Conversion to Christianity appears to have significantly altered the *Didache* believers' social interaction with non-Christians. *Didache* 9:4 goes a step further as it expresses the gathering of the diaspora of the church through the metaphor of the bread. The very act of eating one bread (συναχθὲν ἐγένετο ἕν) at the Eucharist is regarded as anticipating the future eschatological gathering, the day on which God will collect (οὕτω συναχθήτω) his church in his reign.[32] The church's self-understanding has become part of liturgical practice.[33]

---

[32] The church is compared here to a "piece of bread that was scattered" and then gathered together. As a loaf is made into a whole through the gathering of widely scattered corn, so this payer asks that the scattered church be likewise brought together from the ends of the earth into God's reign. It is likely that the image of the bread used for the reunion of the church was a novel Christian idea. It is similar to the terminology in 1 Cor 10:16–17, where the cup of wine and the bread symbolize the unity of the church: "Because there is one loaf, we, who are many, are one body, for we all partake of the one loaf." The passage in 1 Cor 10:16–17 is particularly relevant to our subject since the rite of the cup and the rite of the bread are mentioned in reverse order to the usual structure in the accounts of the Last Supper in the New Testament (Matt 26:26–29; Mark 14:22–25; 1 Cor 11:23–26). The same (reversed) cup-bread sequence is found in *Did.* 9:2–3 and Luke 22:15–19. Paul reproduces in 1 Cor 10:16 the liturgy of the eucharistic supper celebrated by the Christian community of Corinth: "The cup of blessing [τὸ ποτήριον τῆν εὐλογίας] which we bless, is it not a participation in the blood of Christ? The bread which we break, is it not a participation in the body of Christ?" In v. 17, he goes on to point to the unity implied in the bread of the Christian rite because there is only one body of Christ: "Because there is one bread, we who are many are one body, for we all partake of the one bread." The first-person plural of the various verbs in verses 16–17 (εὐλογοῦμεν, κλῶμεν, ἐσμεν, μετέχομεν) tells us about the form of the eucharistic celebrations in Corinth. It suggests that Paul assumes that the Corinthians would recognize their celebration in his description of the meal. Furthermore, because the efficacy of the ceremony with regard to unity is formulated in rhetorical questions (οὐχὶ ... οὐχὶ), the rite of the cup and of the bread must be ritual facts, which the Corinthians experienced in the way Paul describes them. In this letter, the two celebrations are different, the one (11:23–25) dealing with apostolic tradition about Jesus and confronting the Corinthians with a

One might expect that the concrete historical belief in a return to Jerusalem would have become less urgent and pressing in this metaphorical way of speaking. This assumption brings us back to our initial questions with respect to Jerusalem (cluster 1). Because the *Didache* community conceived of the diaspora in figurative terminology, the prayers in *Did*. 10:5 and 9:4 need not necessarily reflect a deliberate dejudaization innovated by Christians. They may witness to an archaic tendency that was already firmly rooted in Hellenistic Judaism. If this was the case, however, the abandonment of the hope that the people of God would return to Jerusalem may have occurred before the Christianization of the Birkat Ha-Mazon. Entirely different views of the earthly Jerusalem would have become apparent between the Palestinian and Hellenistic Jews at an early stage.

Since the Greek version of the Birkat Ha-Mazon has been lost to us, we are not in a position to establish whether terms like "Jerusalem," "Zion," and "temple" were already lacking in the third *berakha* of the Hellenistic synagogue. Perhaps it is possible to apply some other tests to the question at issue. First, it is worthwhile to investigate if the spiritualization emerging in Philo goes hand in hand with an increasing alienation from the earthly Jerusalem in his writings. Second, it is particularly instructive to find out what the status of Jerusalem was to Hellenistic Jews in the first century A.D.

4. JERUSALEM AS A TEST CASE

At first sight, Philo appears to be interested in the spiritual conquest of virtue and in universalizing Jewish laws rather than identifying himself

---

model to follow, while the other (10:16–17) considers the actual liturgy of the local community (see Van de Sandt-Flusser, *Didache*, 307–8). The evidence may thus indicate that there was already a pre-Pauline liturgical tradition where the bread of the Eucharist symbolized the unity of the participants. A similar idea is found in the letter of Ignatius, the bishop of Antioch, to the Ephesians. In the closing statement to the body of the letter (20:2), the major theme is repeated, namely, the need to come together in unity under bishop and presbytery (W. R. Schoedel, *Ignatius of Antioch: A Commentary on the Letters of Ignatius of Antioch* [Hermeneia], Philadelphia 1985, 95–96.) The emphasis on the *one* bread (ἕνα ἄρτον κλῶντες) suggests that Ignatius, too, must have known the tradition.

33 According to John, the prophecy of Caiaphas explained that Jesus not only died for the (Jewish) people but also to gather together (συναγάγῃ εἰς ἕν) "the children of God who are scattered abroad [διεσκορπισμένα]." There is no need, however, to suppose that the *Didache* was influenced by John here since the phrase in *Did*. 9:4 and John 11:52 may depend on a common liturgical tradition; see also John 10:16.

with and paying attention to the politics of his Palestinian homeland. It is wrong, however, to suppose that Philo's approach to Judaism is philosophical and spiritual only and that national eschatology is completely lacking in his thought. He and other Diaspora Jews were interested in Judea and Jerusalem. The situation among the early Christians was quite different. We will see that, at variance with the Jewry of Alexandria and Philo, some early Christian writings toned down the importance of the earthly and physical city of Jerusalem in favour of the celestial one.

4.1. THE SIGNIFICANCE OF JERUSALEM IN DIASPORA JEWRY

Philo clearly showed an interest in practical nationalism once he was chosen to head the delegation, sent by the Jewish community of Alexandria, to the emperor Gaius Caligula in A.D. 39–40. He was also eager to advance the participation of the Jews in Hellenistic cultural institutions and to help them attain full citizen rights in Alexandria. Furthermore, in his view, the survival of the Jewish people in the homeland was fundamental to Jewish identity. Although he thought of the temple of Jerusalem primarily as allegorical, he believed it to be a prominent symbol of Judaism as well.[34] He writes about the pilgrimages to Jerusalem, undertaken by Jews from the Diaspora, and portrays how Jews from all over the world congregated and enjoyed fellowship in Jerusalem:

> Countless multitudes from countless cities come, some over land, others over sea, from east and west and north and south at every feast. They take the temple for their port as a general haven and safe refuge from the bustle and great turmoil of life.[35]

Philo may have made the pilgrimage to Jerusalem and have worshiped in the temple, although his familiarity with contemporary Palestinian Judaism is debated.[36]

---

[34] J. J. Collins, *Between Athens and Jerusalem: Jewish Identity in the Hellenistic Diaspora,* New York 1983, 111–17.

[35] *Spec.* 1.69; cf. F. H. Colson, *Philo, with an English Translation* 7 (LCL 320), London-Cambridge MA 1968 (1937), 138–39. See Borgen, *Philo of Alexandria,* 20–21. Cf. also S. Safrai, "Relations between the Diaspora and the Land of Israel," in S. Safrai and M. Stern, eds., *The Jewish People* 1 (CRINT 1/1), edited in cooperation with D. Flusser and W. C. van Unnik, Assen-Philadelphia 1974, 185.

[36] Collins, *Between Athens and Jerusalem,* 116 and n. 50; Schürer, *History of the Jewish People,* 3/2, 818; P. Borgen, "Philo of Alexandria" in M. E. Stone, ed., *Jewish Writings of the Second Temple Period: Apocrypha, Pseudepigrapha, Qumran Sectarian Writings, Philo, Josephus* (CRINT 2/2), Assen-Philadelphia 1984, 257–59.

Philo's practical nationalism reflects the general outlook of Diaspora Judaism as a whole that always remained in touch with Palestine. Of course, the view that sacrifice is of no avail if a man acts unjustly toward his neighbour may have been more widespread in the Diaspora than in Jewish Palestine.[37] The influence of the environment may have prevented some Jews in the Greek environment from observing all specifically Jewish laws and customs so as to pave the way for tolerance from their Hellenistic surroundings. Nevertheless, the eyes of all pious Jews—in the land and in the Diaspora—were directed to Jerusalem. Those abroad sent gifts to the temple in order to contribute to the sacrificial cult. If they were able, they went on pilgrimage on the three great feasts.[38] Jerusalem was the city of salvation in the eschatological age where God would take up his residence again and inaugurate his royal rule. The hope that the Diaspora would return to the lofty city was kept alive.

For all Jews, in Palestine and in the Dispersion, Jerusalem is the "holy city" (ἱερόπολις)[39] or the "mother-city" (μητρόπολις).[40] Mount Zion is

---

[37] See also D. R. Schwartz, "Temple or City: What Did Hellenistic Jews See in Jerusalem?" in M. Poorthuis and Ch. Safrai, eds., *The Centrality of Jerusalem: Historical Perspectives*, Kampen 1996, 114–27, esp. 117–24.

[38] Safrai, "Relations," 191–201.

[39] "As for the holy city [ἱεροπόλεως], I must say what benefits me to say. While she, as I have said, is my native city she is also the mother city [μητρόπολις] not of one country Judaea but of most of the others in virtue of the colonies sent out at divers times to the neighbouring lands Egypt, Phoenicia, the part of Syria called the Hollow and the rest as well and the lands lying far apart, Pamphylia, Cilicia, most of Asia up to Bithynia and the corners of Pontus, similarly also into Europe, Thessaly, Boeotia, Macedonia, Aetolia, Attica, Argos, Corinth and most of the best parts of Peloponnese" (*Legat.* 281; cf. F. H. Colson, *Philo 10: The Embassy to Gaius* [LCL 379], London-Cambridge MA 1971 [1962], 142–43). See also *Legat.* 225, 288, 299, 346.

[40] Not merely for Jews in Palestine but for Jews everywhere who "hold the Holy City [ἱερόπολιν] where stands the sacred Temple of the most high God to be their mother city [μητρόπολιν]"; Philo, *Flacc.* 46; cf. F. H. Colson, *Philo, with an English Translation* 9 (LCL 363), London-Cambridge MA 1967 (1941), 326–29. Compare also *Legat.* 203, 278, 281, 294, 305, 334. See W. C. van Unnik, *Das Selbstverständnis der Jüdischen Diaspora in der hellenistisch-römischen Zeit*, bearbeitet von P. W. van der Horst (AGJU 17), Leiden 1993, 135–36; A. Kasher, *The Jews in Hellenistic and Roman Egypt: The Struggle for Equal Rights* (TSAJ 7), Tübingen 1985, 236–37. For the concept of Jerusalem as "our mother," see Isa 49:14–21; 50:1; 51:18; 54:1; 60:4; etc; see also below. For the early passages in which the church is represented as a mother, see J. C. Plumpe, *Mater Ecclesia: An Inquiry into the Concept of the Church As Mother in Early Christianity* (The Catholic University of America Studies in Christian Antiquity 5), Washington D.C. 1943.

called the "midst of the navel of the earth" (*Jub.* 8:19; cf. also Josephus, *Bellum judaicum* 3.52).[41] In apocalyptic apocrypha, Zion-Jerusalem is called the mother of all Israelites[42] who has brought up her children (Bar 4:8–10).[43] The Jews, though scattered throughout the ancient world, maintained the bond with the motherland and the holy city. The dispersion was seen as a painful experience, the bitter destiny of the people of God.[44] They had to live with the hard fate of the Diaspora and envisaged the restoration to be reserved for the messianic age. Diaspora is a substantiation of eschatological hope for the future return to the earthly fatherland.

Philo also seemed to expect that some day God would gather the exiles from the ends of the earth into the homeland. His *De Praemiis et Poenis* 165–172 presents an elaborate portrayal of the eschatological fulfilment of the hope of the Jews. It starts thus:

> When they have gained this unexpected liberty, those who but now were scattered [σποράδες] in Greece and the outside world over islands and continents will arise and post from every side with one impulse to the one appointed place, guided in their pilgrimage by a vision divine and superhuman unseen by others but manifest to them as they pass from exile to their home. (*Praem.* 165)

The passage continues by emphasizing that the nation would be gathered as a people, peace would be established, and Israel's enemies would be

---

[41] For the passage in *Jub.* 8:19, see Ph. S. Alexander, "Jerusalem As the Omphalos of the World: On the History of a Geographical Concept," in L. I. Levine, ed., *Jerusalem: Its Sanctity and Centrality to Judaism, Christianity, and Islam*, New York 1999, 104–19.

[42] "Sion mater nostra omnium" in *4 Ezra* 10:7, 38–44; cf. also *2 Bar.* 3:1–3; and see *5 Ezra* where, in 2:2, 4, 5–6, Jerusalem is called the mother of Israel but, in 2:15, 17, 31, is referred to as the mother of the church and of the Christians; see G. Stanton, "5 Ezra and Matthean Christianity in the Second Century," *JTS* NS 28 (1977): 67–83, esp. 71–73.

[43] In the New Testament, Jesus addresses Jerusalem as a mother when he states, "O Jerusalem, Jerusalem, killing the prophets and stoning those who are sent to you! How often would I have gathered your children [τὰ τέκνα σου] together..." (Matt 23:37; cf. Luke 13:34). Weeping over her, Jesus predicts, "For the days shall come upon you, when your enemies... will dash you to the ground, you and your children [τὰ τέκνα σου] within you" (Luke 19:43–44).

[44] See, e.g., R. Feldmeier, *Die Christen als Fremde: Die Metapher der Fremde in der antiken Welt, im Urchristentum und im 1. Petrusbrief* (WUNT 64), Tübingen 1992, 63–69.

destroyed.[45] This hope would never be abandoned but would continue to be cherished.

4.2. THE SIGNIFICANCE OF JERUSALEM IN SOME EARLY CHRISTIAN WRITINGS

The earliest indication that Christians regarded themselves as aliens and pilgrims on earth is found in the letters of Paul. Paul believes that Christians belong to the Jerusalem above, or the heavenly community (Gal 4:26; Phil 3:20). They are not at home on earth but pertain to that heavenly domain where the glorified Lord dwells (cf. 2 Cor 5:1-5, 6-9; 1 Thess 1:10; 4:17). In the polemical passage of Gal 4:25-26, Paul is clearly attacking his opponents who claim that the present Jerusalem is their mother, probably suggesting that their views emphasizing the observance of the law were supported by Jerusalem. Paul counters this position by appealing to a higher instance in contradistinction from the earthly Jerusalem: "Now Hagar is Mount Sinai in Arabia; she corresponds to the present Jerusalem, for she is in slavery with her children. But the Jerusalem above is free, and she is our mother."

Paul uses the phrase of the heavenly Jerusalem in his argumentation without any explanation, as if his readers are familiar with it. One may thus assume that the image of the "Jerusalem above" was widely accepted by the early Christians. It takes up the expectation in Jewish apocalyptic tradition of the preexistent city that is built by God in heaven with glory and magnificence and comes down to the earth in the end.[46] In rabbinic literature, the designation "the Jerusalem above" or "the Jerusalem of the age to come" as distinct from "the Jerusalem of this age" is found.[47] In these examples, the latter is an image of the original in heaven. Out of love for the city on earth, God has erected the city in heaven, and he swears not to enter the celestial one until that below is restored.[48]

---

[45] *Praem.* 165-172; cf. Colson, *Philo* 8 (LCL 341), London-Cambridge MA 1968 (1939), 417-23. For comments on *Praem.* 163-172, cf. Borgen, *Philo of Alexandria*, 276-80; see also Van Unnik, *Das Selbstverständnis der Jüdischen Diaspora*, 133-34; Collins, *Between Athens and Jerusalem*, 115.

[46] Cf. *4 Ezra* 7:26; 10:27, 54; 13:36; *1 En.* 90:28-29; Rev 21; cf. also Volz, *Eschatologie der jüdischen Gemeinde*, 372-75 about the variations in the ideas of the heavenly Jerusalem. See also P. Lee, *The New Jerusalem in the Book of Revelation: A Study of Revelation 21-22 in the Light of Its Background in Jewish Tradition* (WUNT 2/129), Tübingen 2001, 72, 129-39.

[47] Cf. Strack-Billerbeck, *Kommentar zum Neuen Testament* 3 (1926) 573 and also 3:795-96; 4:883-85, 919-31.

[48] See G. Dalman, *Die Worte Jesu: Mit Berücksichtigung des nachkanonischen jüdischen Schrifttums und der aramäischen Sprache* 1, Leipzig ²1930, 106. See also H. Bietenhard, *Die himmlische Welt im Urchristentum und Spätjudentum* (WUNT 2), Tübingen 1951, 123-25.

Apparently, then, the celestial city shares the hardships of the earthly Jerusalem's fate.

For Paul, however, the earthly Jerusalem stands in sharp contrast to the celestial one. The heavenly Jerusalem is preexistent and remains in heaven. By setting the two in opposition, he demonstrates that salvation is not to be transferred to an indeterminate future but has come already. Those who are to dwell in it must move upward.[49] If the Christians have their real commonwealth in heaven, it follows that they are aliens on earth.

First Peter and the Epistle to the Hebrews also reveal that the present city of Jerusalem, to which the Christians should have no desire to return, has been replaced as the centre of hope. The first letter of Peter does not show any indication of a positive concern for Judaism nor any interest in Israel. The letter to the Hebrews makes it clear that the new and better covenant provides access to the heavenly Jerusalem, the city of the living God. In 13:13–14, Christians are exhorted to "go out to him" (= Jesus), "outside the camp" since the blood of Jesus was poured on an altar "outside the gate." Like Abraham, who went out to "a place that he was to receive as an inheritance" (11:8), they too had to go out to witness the impermanence of this world in search of a city that had foundations (11:10). Because Jesus died outside the earthly city of Jerusalem, Christians had to leave the city that was not "a continuing city" (13:14). They had to experience an insulted and unsettled life on their journey to the eternal city of the heavenly Jerusalem.[50] By remaining with Jesus outside the camp of Judaism, Christians show that the present city, to which they should have no desire to return, has been replaced as the centre of hope.

5. CONCLUSION

The Christian longing for a gathering of the dispersed church into the kingdom in the eucharistic prayers of *Did.* 9–10 does not include the Jewish hope for a restoration of Israel and Jerusalem. A similar separation—and in some cases even estrangement—from the historic Jewish setting is found in several other early Christian writings. In the *Didache* prayer, the alien status of the Christian in the world probably arises from the demands of faith irrespective of any particular historical event or situation. The longing

---

[49] H. D. Betz, *Galatians: A Commentary on Paul's Letter to the Churches in Galatia* (Hermeneia), Philadelphia ²1984, 246.

[50] "Das Heilsziel liegt nicht im Diesseits, sondern im Jenseits. Insofern gibt V 14 der dualistischen Weltsicht des Hebr klassischen Ausdruck. Christen sind »Wanderer zwischen beiden Welten«"; cf. E. Grässer, *An die Hebräer*, 3 Teilband: Hebr 10,19–13,25 (EKKNT 17/3), Zürich und Neukirchen-Vluyn 1997, 386–87 and n. 28.

to be gathered from the four winds into the kingdom is a description of the actual situation of the church, which is set apart from the world by its Christian heterogeneous character.

The terminology also indicates the Christian character of the supplication. In Jewish texts, even the LXX, no instances are found where the *dispersed* people of God are designated ἐκκλησία ("church"). The idea of the assembling of the believers "from the four winds" (*Did.* 10:5) or "from the ends of the earth" (9:4) is reflected in the Gospels as well. In Matthew, it is said that when the Son of Man comes, "he will send out his angels with a loud trumpet call, and they will gather his elect from the four winds, from one end of heaven to the other" (24:31; cf. Mark 13:27). The "loud trumpet call" in Matthew may imply the sign for the raising of the deceased righteous to meet the Lord.[51] In John 11:52, the Son of Man not only gathers the members of the Jewish nation but also the Gentile believers, the scattered children of God, to bring them together and make them one (cf. 10:15-16). Furthermore, while the texts in Matthew and Mark seem to presuppose a gathering place on earth, it is important to note that, according to the Gospel of John, Jesus is supposed to have said "and I, when I am lifted up from the earth, will draw all men to myself" (12:32; see also 1 Thess 4:15-17; 2 Thess 2:1). *Didache* 10:5 contains a congenial tradition as it links the gathering of the church to the end time, when the church will enter God's kingdom.

The *Didache* probably originated in a Jewish community that made Jesus the core of its understanding. The community had close affinities with Jewish antecedents and still felt a high regard for Israel. The texts of *Did.* 10:5 and 9:4, however, reflect an alienation from Judaism. These verses represent a discontinuity in the people-of-God concept, since the gathering of the church into God's kingdom no longer has any connection with the gathering of Israel. The prayer for the political restoration of Israel in the third benediction of the Birkat Ha-Mazon has turned into a prayer for the gathering of the church. Palestine and Jerusalem are no longer linked to the Christian eschatological hope.

The ecclesial existence takes on the character of dispersion not because its communities are scattered in the world but as a result of the fact that the believers must behave as if they are transient aliens sojourning on earth in the hope of an inheritance. The inheritance, a word belonging to the "land" terms in the Hebrew Bible, is spiritualized to a high degree without mention of the concrete land, Zion, or Jerusalem. The kingdom is made supraterrestrial, stripped of all earthly limitations and qualifications. The prayers of *Did.* 9:4 and 10:5 may have been formulated in a community which had moved away from close contact with Judaism.

---

[51] Clerici, *Einsammlung der Zerstreuten,* 80.

God's Provision for the Well-Being of Living Creatures in Genesis 9

Simon J. De Vries
Methodist Theological School in Ohio

The account in this chapter is not narrative in the usual sense of the word. It has no plot, no character development, and no story-line. Nor is it, apart from the aphorism in verse 6 and the recital in verses 12–16, anything like lyrical poetry. The one is a wisdom saying in rhythmical form and the other shows the style of a theological liturgy. The Priestly writer (P), though not creating beautiful verses in the high style of the psalmists and prophets, characteristically expresses himself in series of rhythmical utterances having less the structure of synonymous parallelism than that of the heaping up of item upon item in order to create a whole. The general effect upon the reader may be to occasion monotony, yet in great theological texts such as the creation story in Gen 1:1–2:4a and the account of a new creation in Gen 9:1–17, it conveys a sense of solemnity and gravity. It may be said that it displays in both these passages an ascerbic and disciplined minimalism, rather than fulsome expansiveness or aimless repetition. The careful reader realizes that each word, each phrase, and each clause must be treasured and carefully evaluated.[1]

TEXT AND STRUCTURE

1. A blessing on Noah and his sons 1–7
    a. Narrative introduction 1a
    b. Encouragement to abundant proliferation 1b
    c. Nonhuman flesh appointed as food for mankind 2–3
        (1) All animals placed in subjugation 2
        (2) Nonplant food made equal to plant food 3

---

[1] This question is treated extensively in Sean E. McEvenue, *The Narrative Style of the Priestly Writer* (AnBib 90, Rome: Biblical Institute Press, 1971).

      d. Restrictions relating to the shedding of blood 4–6
          (1) Prohibition against eating blood with living flesh 4
          (2) Prohibition against the shedding of human blood 5
      e. Aphorism about shedding human blood 6
      f. Encouragement to abundant proliferation 7[2]
  2. God sets up a covenant to preserve all flesh 8–16
      a. Narrative introduction 8
      b. Decree of protection 9–11
          (1) The parties 9–10
              (a) God over against Noah and his descendants 9
              (b) God over against the animal world 10[3]
          (2) Benefits 11
      c. Appointment of a binding sign 12–16
          (1) Strophe I: Divine designation of the sign 12
          (2) Strophe II: The rainbow in the clouds 13–15
              (a) A sign of the bond between Creator and creation 13
              (b) The sight: Out of clouds the rainbow appears 14
              (c) A reminder of his covenant with man and animals 15
          (3) Strophe III: A reminder of a perpetual covenant 16
  3. Concluding summary 17

The translator and the exegete should accept the responsibility of thoroughly dissecting the Hebrew text of Gen 9:1–17. The overall structure of this passage is governed by four statements of God's act of speaking (9:1, 8, 12 and 17), which define a beginning and an ending with two internal breaks, to create three separate sections. Two details show, however, that the three sections are not equal. The first detail is that the verse 12 creates an *inclusio* with verse 17 regarding the sign of the covenant. The second is that verses 12–17, thus defined, is closely attached to verses 8–11, where God promises never to bring another flood. Thus verses 8–11 and verses 12–17 are closely attached to each other. Verses 1–7 concerns God's blessing of abundant proliferation, together with the conditions and restrictions defining it. The term, "covenant" (*berît*) is not found here, yet it stands clearly defined over against verses 8–17 by the counterbalancing *weʾattem*, "as for you," in verse 7, juxtaposed with *waʾanî*, "now I on my part," in verse 9.

One further formal detail deserving attention is the presence of links back to the P creation account in chapters 1–2 and to the beginning of the

---

[2] Since *ûrebû* is already the second verb in the first stich, it seems probable that it is a haplograph supplanting an original *ûredû*, found at this position in the verse being quoted, Gen 1:26.

[3] LXX omits this clause, followed by the RSV.

P flood story in chapter 6. The encouragement to be abundantly prolific in verses 1 and 7, the arrangement of living beings into three or four orders in verses 2 and 10, and the mention of God's previous provision of human food in verse 4 are direct references to the creation story, the effect of which is to require that details of this account be interpeted in the light of what is stated there. Also, the mention in verses 11 and 15 of devastation through the flood echoes God's decision to bring the flood in 6:13 as well as the reason for it, which was that the earth was corrupt and that "all flesh" had corrupted its/their "way" (*derek*), that is, their order and manner of life. Thus the passage we are studying has been composed both as a conclusion to the divine act of destroying corrupt life and as a continuation or renewal of the original divine act of creating life. The blessing, the covenant, and the sign mentioned in chapter 9 are designed to put an end to all devastation, past, present, and future, while providing a beginning to a new life that God has designed.

THE ANIMAL CREATURES

It is apparent that P conceives of animal life and human life as inseparable. True, the subordination of animals to man has already been made evident in mankind's creation as a second phase of the fourth-day act of creation (Gen 1:24–25, 26ff.) as well as in the statement in 9:2 that the various types or orders of animals had been delivered into the hand of man and placed under the fear and dread of him. This is in fact the first part of the blessing that was bestowed on Noah and his posterity (9:1ff.). An essential part of the subordination of the animals to man was, furthermore, that man might now benefit from the flesh of animals as food, alongside the plants that had previously been approved according to 1:29. Access to plant food had not, in matter of fact, been man's exclusive privilege, for it had been assigned as well to every order of animal life as well (1:30). In any case, nothing is said about the animals being given human flesh to eat; in fact, if an animal eats a human being, the shedding of blood must be punished in the same way, and to the same measure, as if it had been done by another human being (9:5).

In spite of this subordination, the two orders of being, human and animal, are treated as alike in their guilt, in their punishment through the flood, in their preservation by the ark, and in the life and fecundity that they are to share in the new creation envisaged in this chapter. Even though the encouragement to abundant fruitfulness is spoken only to the human survivors of the deluge (but cf. Gen 1:22), and in spite of the fact that the animals preserved in the ark are now put under the fear and dread of man, part of the new covenant is that not only man, but the animals as well, shall never again be "cut off" in another flood. According to P, not mankind alone, but "all flesh," are both needed and valued within God's new world.

It is worthwhile to pay close attention to the references to animals within the Priestly narrative of the flood. "Flesh" (*baśar*) is something specific in 9:4, where it means "meat"—an important ingredient in whatever is covered by the word, "food," something in addition to the previously authorized green plants. "All flesh" (*kol baśar*) occurs in Gen 6:12, 13, 17; 7:15, 16, 20; 9:11, 15–17 (also "from among [i.e., 'some of'] all flesh" in 6:19; 7:15–16; 8:17); this expansion is modified by the phrase "in which is the spirit of life" in 6:17 and 7:15. Another modifier, "every living thing of all flesh," occurs at 6:19 and 8:17. The distinction intended in Gen 8:1 between "all that was alive and every beast" is not clear; nor is that of the phrase "every living thing of all flesh" both in 8:1 and 8:17; nor is that of the phrase "every living creature" in 9:10 and that of "all life on earth" in 9:2.

In distinction from *kol baśar*, *kol ḥaḥayyâ* and *kol nepeš ḥaḥayyâ* refer exclusively to animals. In 9:5 the phrase "at the hand of every animal [*miyyad kol-ḥayyâ*] and at the hand of man [*miyyad ha'adam*]" makes this distinction certain. The expressions, "and between every living animal that may be with you unto perpetual generations" (*ûben kol nepeš ḥayyâ 'ašer 'ittekem ledorôt 'ôlam*) in 9:12 and "and between every living animal out of all flesh" (*ûben kol-nepeš ḥayyâ bekol-baśar*) in 9:15–16 are inclusive expressions pertaining to all varieties of animal life in distinction from human life. In any event, "all flesh" represents the wider category to which "every living being" belongs.

The same term may however be given a more precise definition when it is applied to the distinct orders of animal being. Thus in Gen 1:20 God, on the third day, causes the seas to bring forth *šereṣ nepeš ḥayyâ*, "a swarm of living animals." This is explicated in 1:21, where it is said that he also creates from the sea (1) great monsters, (2) *kol-nepeš haḥayyâ haromešet*, and (3) winged birds. According to 1:24, God, on the fourth day, commands the earth to bring forth another order of *nepeš ḥayyâ*, one that includes the three kinds, cattle (*behemâ*), creeping things (*remeś*), and wild animals of the earth (*ḥayetô 'ereṣ*), but it is remarkable that in the report of compliance that follows in verse 25, these three are presented in a different order, *ḥayat ha'areṣ*, *habbehemâ* and *kol-remeś ha'adamâ*. This listing of three orders has not acquired the status of a stereotype and is less schematic than the Deuteronomistic formulation found in Deut 4:16–18, which lists four orders: the beasts on the earth, the birds in the air, that which creeps (?) on the ground, and the fish in the water under the earth. The apocalyptic passage Ezek 38:20 has the same four orders, though in a different sequence: fish of the sea, birds of the air, beasts of the field, and all *haremeś haromeś 'al-ha'adamâ*.

WHAT IS *REMEŚ* AND *ROMEŚ*?

The foregoing discussion places details of the account in Gen 9 within a preliminary framework of understanding, but questions remain concerning two crucial identifications, that of the group with the name *remeś* and that of an overarching category known as *kol- baśar*. The first is of crucial exegetical importance for an understanding of this passage because it pertains to the animal food that mankind is permitted to eat. Are Noah and his family permitted to eat only lizards and beetles and other creeping sorts of things? Most of us would be inclinded to think: Not much of a privilege!

It may be pointed out that P in Gen 9:2 agrees with Deut 4:16–19 and Ezek 38:20 in mentioning four rather than three orders — though this may not be original. The four are: (1) the group known as *kol-ḥayat ha'areṣ*, (2) the group known as *kol-ʿôp haššamayim*, (3) the group verbally designated as *kol 'ašer tirmoś ha'adamâ*, and (4) the group called *kol-degê hayyam* (v. 2). Usually the word *behemâ* is in first place, though "every living being" is sometimes substituted for it, as here, and may be intended as its synonym, or at least its equivalent. The birds and the fish are readily identified with the proper habitats, the sky and the sea, which they claim as their own, with neither man nor beast to supplant them. It is the third group, referred to in a participial phrase, that remains out of focus.

The noun *remeś* and the participle *romeś* have been translated "creeping thing," "moving thing," "that which slithers," "worms," "maggots," and the like, but these are vague, generalized, and generally misleading. They are mostly guesses based on rabbinical tradition and do little or nothing to clarify the archaic Hebrew term. For definitions, dictionaries and lexicons have resorted to the context, but this is often doubtful or even contradictory. There is an Akkadian cognate, but it is as ill-defined as the Hebrew. The Hebrew word occurs in the *Damascus Code* (CD XII 12), but merely as a copy of the biblical phrase upon which it depends.

The Hebrew text of Sir 10:11 has four terms (*rmh wtwlʿ knym wrmś*) that have been reduced to three in the LXX and the RSV based upon it, "For when a man is dead, he will inherit creeping things, wild beasts, and worms." It is apparently Greek *erpeta*, "snakes, worms," that translates *rmś*, but apparently in the wrong order. The LXX translator probably gave up trying to render all of these words, leaving us in the dark as to which Hebrew word *erpeta* is translating.[4] Thus this passage is of little help to the lexicographer, and all that can be deduced with confidence is that *rmś* as such is in Sirach's Hebrew text and has come to mean something defiling,

---

[4] Skehan and Di Lella in *Anchor Bible,* 225, suggest that, in this diatribe against vain rulers, the language is deliberately vague.

stinking, or draining from a corpse. The word appears in Middle Hebrew (*Nidd.* 3:2, *Sanh.* 8:2), probably in the meaning, "creeping thing," "worm," "snake," but the vocalization seems to require that it be pronounced as *šeqeṣ*, "that which defiles."

In an effort to avoid futility and confusion, along with the fallacy of defining something by itself, we should observe the following data:

1. From the P creation account in Gen 1–2: It designates one of three orders, usually but not always with this mysterious word as the third in sequence. The order may live and swarm in the sea but usually occupies the earth or ground.[5]
2. From Gen 6:20: The P order of animals entering the ark is: "some" (*min*) of the birds, "some" of the beasts (*habbehēmâ*), "some" of all the *remeś hāʾadāmâ*.[6]
3. From Gen 7:21: The "all flesh" that die in the flood according to P is further defined as *haromeśet ʿal haʾareṣ*, which is further described as consisting of five orders: birds, cattle (*behēmâ*), wild animals (*ḥayâ*), "that which swarms [*šereṣ*][7] on the earth," and mankind.
4. From Gen 7:23: God wipes out "all that exists [*yeqûm*][8] on the face of the ground." This entity is comprised of two inclusive groups of two each: (1) "those from man to beast" (*behēmâ*) and (2) "those from *remeś* to the birds of the sky."
5. From Gen 8:17: "Every animal" (*haḥayâ*) emerging from the ark is said to belong to the wider category "all flesh," which in turn consists of three orders: birds, beasts (*behēmâ*), and "every sort of *haremeś*"; the last is further defined and limited by the participial phrase *haromeś ʿal haʾareṣ*.[9]
6. From Gen 8:18–19: Here the *remeś/romeś* come first, but the report of Noah's compliance with the divine command seems to be garbled and the LXX may represent a secondary restoration.
7. From Gen 9:2: There are four orders, "every animal of the earth," "every bird of the sky," "everything that *rmś* [the verb] the ground," and "every fish of the sea," that are subjected to man. All except the third—a participial phrase—are in nominal

---

[5] The two terms, *ʾereṣ* and *ʾadāmâ* are virtual synonyms in spite of the fact that the latter is the most distinctive and therefore the most probable setting for the *remeś*.
[6] Cf. J at 7:9.
[7] Cf. Gen 1:20.
[8] Cf. Deut 11:6.
[9] According to Gen 1:21, the last mentioned may also live in the sea.

form. We should raise the question whether the fourth order may constitute an after thought in this text because "the fish" are generally not included in P's tabulations. If P's syntactical shift to the verbal clause is to be interpreted as more than a stylistic flourish, there must be a special reason for this variation. What this reason may be is suggested by the fact that the following verse 3 commences with a parallel participial phrase, *kol-remeś ʾašer hûʾ-ḥay,* "every *remeś* that lives." Unless verse 3 comes from a separate literary source,[10] it is to be assumed that its function is to define something important about the contents of the verbal phrase in verse 2.

8. The Psalms and prophetic literature have references to this order in the following passages: Ps 69:35 [Eng 34], in which the order of the *romeś* are said to live in the sea, adding there to God's praise; Ps 104:20, which speaks of some of the same who live in the forest doing their thing—whatever that is—at night; Ps 104:25, which speaks of the *remeś* inhabiting the sea in great numbers; Ps 148:10, which simply mentions them in parallelism with beasts, cattle, and birds (*ḥaḥayyâ wekol-behemâ, remeś weṣippôr kanap*), without suggesting what they are or what they do; 1 Kgs 5:13 [Eng 4:33], in which Solomon is said to have encyclopaedic knowledge of beasts, birds, *haremeś,* and the fish; Hos 2:20 [Eng 18], which speaks of an eschatological covenant with the wild beasts, the birds, and the *remeś haʾădāmâ;* Hab 1:14, which states that Yahweh makes men like fish of the sea who are without a ruler like *the remeś;* Ezek 8:10, which describes abominable images of this particular order of animals; Ezek 38:20, exhibiting the familiar four orders but in another sequence, while defining it by itself in the expression, *kol haremeś haromeś ʿal haʾădāmâ.*[11]

9. In the cult-legislative literature this changes. Leviticus 11:46–47 reads *zōʾt tôrat habbehemâ wehaʿôp wekol nepeš ḥaḥayyâ haromeśet bammayim,* "This is the law of beast and bird and every living being that *romeśet* in the waters." The clause that is added to this does nothing to clarify it: *ûlekol-nepeš haššôreṣet ʿal haʾāreṣ,* "and every living being that swarms upon the earth." The parallelism seems to be largely stylistic in view of the artificiality of the phrase, "any swarming thing

---

[10] As suggested by R. Smend, Holzinger, and McEvenue, among others.
[11] Cf. Gen 8:17.

that swarms," occurring in verse 44; yet it is strange to hear of this order of animals doing their thing in the waters, while the defiling creatures that "swarm" do this on earth.
10. Leviticus 20:25 definitively states that "everything that *romeś* the ground is an abomination that makes a person unclean." With Lev 11:46–17, it may have been influential in turning the order of the *romeś* into something that defiles in the literature of postbiblical Judaism.

Three important conclusions arising from this analysis are: (1) the living beings belonging to this order may exist on the land or on the sea; (2) their order is distinct from the *behemâ* and the *ḥayya*, though often confused with them; and (3) except in very late passages, they are certainly not something odious or defiling in themselves. Else, how could *remeś* serve as food (= meat) for mankind in God's new era of blessedness?

But we still do not know who or what they are and precisely what they do. They are not a species or even a biological class or order. Perhaps Ps 104:25 may give us the clue we need: "Yonder is the sea, great and wide, where there is *remeś* beyond counting, living things [*ḥayyôt*] both small and great." We cannot dismiss this as mere metaphorical language. It is the language of classical Hebrew and Near Eastern wisdom that we are hearing. We realize that the *remeś* belongs mainly on the earth or ground; we know also that it is found in the sea and even in a forest (v. 20). It can consist of large or small creatures, but out in nature, not in a stable or a barnyard.

Thus the individual beings belonging to *remeś* may "swarm" in the sea or prowl the jungle. The main thing is that they are too many for anyone to count and are beyond human control or manipulation. They seem to vary so much among themselves that they bring wonder and amazement to those who try to understand them and describe them. This is why P speaks of them with apparent inconsistency. They are all of the things described; they may do any of things assigned to them.

From the observation that the third order appearing in the list in Gen 9:2 is not given a name like the other three but is designated by a relative clause, *kol ʾašer tirmoś haʾadamâ*, I draw the conclusion that P recognizes that there are animal beings that do not fit readily within any of the other categories mentioned, "beast of the earth," "bird of the air," or "fish of the sea"; he therefore speaks of what they do rather than of what they are. Still, God includes them among the creatures given into the power of man.

A reasonable explanation for the vagueness and variegation with which this order is depicted might be that the root *rmś* is primarily verbal, normally appearing in inflected or participial forms even though the simple noun is also employed. It is understandably the verbal/participial constructions that tell where (on the earth/ground or in the sea) and when (even at night) they do their special thing[12]; among passages having the nominal form,[13] only Gen 1:25; 6:20; Hos 2:20; and Ezek 38:20 tell where they are to be found. An additional reason is that the entity *remeś* appears to be a category larger and more extensive than any other order and therefore cannot be subsumed under or coordinated with a specific group of living beings.

This perhaps explains why it usually appears as third in sequence when a tabulation is being made, following the mention of more cohesive and recognizable groups—those well known, those frequently seen, those who can be managed to human advantage through the skills of animal husbandry. *Remeś* is added apparently as a catch-all term for all orders and may include some or all, but it refers especially to those that lurk in obscure places and out of sight.

One passage expressing this perspective rather clearly is Gen 7:21, where we read, "And all flesh—*haromeś* upon the earth—died, both bird and beast, both animal life [*ûbaḥayyâ*] and that which swarms upon the earth, as well as man." *Kol baśar* is the main subject but is qualified immediately by *haromeś ʿal haʾareṣ*, a term that qualifies and limits this term as used since the flood had killed only the land creatures. Nevertheless, it will be seen that the second term coordinates with the first. *Kol baśar*—at least that which exists on the earth—is tantamount to, if not equivalent with, *haromeś*! This compound expression is in turn broken down into the smaller groups, the first two of which appear as pairs: (1) birds and (domestic) cattle, (2) wild animals and creatures that swarm, (3) mankind.

Certain verses in this passage seem to confuse this distinction, but it is easy to understand why, for P's description remains vague and complex. It is best simply to ask, What does the *remeś* or *romeś* do? Whatever the various species do is not what they do, yet they do what all species do: live, breathe, and move about.

Since we need an English equivalent, no matter how imperfect, if we wish to translate this biblical passage, we may have to resort to an equivalent that we cannot prove, such as "moving thing," but certainly we must avoid prejudicial terms such as "creeping thing." The term, "moving animal," though it may be an oxymoron, may be more appropriate because Gen 9:2–3 clearly does intend to make a sharp distinction between the plants that stay unmoved in their places and are therefore easy to gather

---

[12] Gen 1:21, 26, 28, 30; 7:8; 8:17, 19, 21; Lev 11:44, 46; 20:25; Deut 4:18; 9:2, Deut 4:18; Ezek 38:20; Pss 69:35; 104:20

[13] Gen 1:24, 25, 26; 6:7, 20; 7:14, 23; 8:17, 19; 9:3; 1 Kgs 5:13; Hos 2:20; Ezek 8:10; 38:29; Hab 1:14; Pss 104:25; 148:10

for food and now these animals that move about on the ground or in the sea, and must be caught.

GOD PUNISHES AND BLESSES "ALL FLESH"

It seems strange to read in Gen 9:9 that God makes a covenant with Noah and his descendants and then in verse 10 that he includes animals, both those that are with Noah in the ark and—presumably—those who are not.[14] Verse 15 repeats that the covenant is extended to "every living creature of all flesh." The content of the covenant is a promise never again to send a flood to destroy all living beings. It is not actually a covenant like the one in Gen 17:2–17 but an agreement or arrangement,[15] like that of Gen 6:18,[16] to save Noah's family and representative individuals of all creaturely orders from the coming flood by bringing them all into the ark.[17] This has to stand as an exemplar of the most perfect kind of divine grace bestowed upon the animals—that for which the beneficiaries would do nothing whatever in order to deserve or reciprocate for—what God was doing on their behalf. Noah and his family did labor to build the ark, gather the animals, and perform the chores of feeding and watering—especially to do so in the face of what would have been a jeering, persecuting crowd of onlookers; they would certainly demand signicant participation in working toward their own salvation, thus making themselves available and accessible for the working of divine grace. What needs to be said is that yes, certainly, the animals needed a covenant with God too! God had appointed mankind to have dominion over the wild creatures (Gen 1:28), but clearly this excluded exploitation of the animals, demanding rather their diligent care. God valued them highly enough to provide the means

---

[14] Because the LXX omits the final phrase in v. 10, *lekol ḥayyat ha'areṣ*, the RSV places it in a footnote but does not translate it. If it is retained, the meaning would be that God saves animals both from the ark and from the dry land. Though this might disturb the logic of claiming that all animals still living had been in the ark, the author may intend to say that the covenant is to extend not only to those that had actually been in the ark but to all those who eventually inhabited the earth.

[15] This does not deny that the full weight of divine self-giving stands behind the two promises. It is full of solemnity and authority. Nevertheless, the old theologians went far astray in speaking of a "Noachian covenant" as an agreement on God's part to accept mankind's good works as a satifaction to him.

[16] "But I will establish my covenant with you; and you shall come into the ark . . . ."

[17] Martin Luther's Genesis commentary makes great sport at speculating about where so many animals had to be kept and how much labor was to be expended in shoveling out all the manure that accumulated over many days.

of rescuing the animals from the flood and in preserving them alive unto perpetuity!

In this light it should not surprise us that, according to the Priestly writer of Genesis, God deliberately included the animals in his covenant of restoration guaranteed by the sign of the rainbow. There are Old Testament passages that give special recognition to the essential role that animals may play in human well-being. Deuteronomy 11:15 mentions God's provision of grain for the cattle in order that mankind might have plenty. Psalm 104:21 states that the young lions seek their food from God. Psalm 145:15–16 says that the Lord upholds, raises up, gives food to all—apparently not just all human beings—opening his hand to satisfy the desire of every living being (*maśbîaʿ kol-ḥay raṣon*). Psalm 147:9 mentions that "he gives to the beasts their food, and to the young ravens that cry."

Sometimes the animals participate in the ritual of contrition with their human masters. So do the beasts, herds and flocks who wore the Ninevites' sackcloth (Jonah 3:7–9) to induce Yahweh to change his mind about destroying their city, and in the end he expresses his intent to save "many cattle" along with innumerable innocent humans (4:11). There are times, too, when an animal, such as the ass of Balaam, speaks out in good Hebrew to protest the impiety as well as the cruelty of his master (cf. Num 22:28–30). In addition, there are occasions in which erring animals require being haled before the court of justice, as regulated by Lev 20:15–16:

> If a man lies with a beast, he shall be put to death and you shall kill the beast. If a woman approaches any beast and lies with it, you shall kill the woman and the beast; they shall be put to death, their blood is on them.

Or again, according to Exod 21:28, 29, 32:

> When an ox gores a man or a woman to death, the ox shall be stoned and its flesh shall not be eaten.... If the ox gores a slave, male or female, the owner shall give to their master thirty shekels of silver, and the ox shall be stoned.

In accordance with the principle of mutual responsibility governing both animals and humans, Gen 9:5 specifies, "For your blood I will surely require a reckoning; of every beast I shall require it and of man." In the new order that God is creating, P speaks of animals as though they were ethical and responsible agents. If they transgress the standards laid down in God's creation, they must be punished for it—punished not as one punishes a stubborn mule or a wayward horse in order to make them obey, but punished for a moral wrong. This is to be a rule in God's covenant with the "all flesh" who survive the flood.

This brings us to the reason why, according to P, there had to be a flood. As says Gen 6:12, this was because "all flesh" had "corrupted their way upon the earth." The first question to raise here is, Who is or are "all flesh"? In Gen 6:19; 7:15–16; 8:17; and 9:15 it refers explicitly to animals, and to animals alone, but in Gen 6:12–13, 17; 9:11, 15–17 it probably refers both to human beings and to animals, while in Gen 7:21 it cannot exclude man, who is mentioned last in a sequence governed by this expression. The explanation for this interesting variation is that it is determined by the contexts' demands, which in one passage may be limited to animals alone because it is concerned with them alone, or in another passage it may include both animals and human beings because they are dealt with according to a common principle. An important question is whether this expression ever refers exclusively to human beings, because that is what most interpreters have assumed about Gen 6:12–13, which is usually taken to refer to all humanity, all nations. But this is an unwarranted assumption drawn from the introductory material in the J account beginning in verses 5–7, which does refer exclusively to the delinquency of mankind, and of it alone.

The P flood account is introduced in verse 11 with a summary statement, "And the earth was corrupt in God's sight, so that the earth was filled with violence"; this is immediately followed by the narrative statement of a declaratory judgment, "And God saw the earth, and behold, it was corrupt, for all flesh had corrupted their way upon the earth" (v. 12). The account has next a narrative introduction with God's explanation to Noah that he had determined to make an end to "all flesh" because the earth was filled with violence through "all flesh" and that he was determined to destroy all who were included in this category along with the earth that they had corrupted (v. 13). The earth had been made corrupt because "all flesh" had corrupted its way upon earth (*darkô ʿal haʾareṣ*).

Mention of a "way" gives us a clue that the problem is ethical and behavioral rather than theological and spiritual, as in the J account.[18] Accordingly, there is no good reason for excluding a delinquency on the part of the animals from P's complaint, and in view of what has been said about the personification of animals in this account, there should be no hesitation about including animals along with man in this, the very first, use of "all flesh" within the P flood account.[19]

---

[18] In vv. 5–6 Yahweh observes that it is the great wickedness of man that must bring the flood because "every imagination of the thoughts of his heart was only evil continually." This description makes perfectly clear that man alone is the cause and that the created animals must suffer solely on his account.

[19] In view of the fact that every other instance of this expression in the P account includes the animals, with or without man, it would be difficult to understand why only here it should mean man alone in this introductory verse.

What in particular the corruption is that has occurred among men and animals is neither explained nor described by P. The "violence" that results from this corruption is likewise left unclarified. There are numerous instances of corruption and violence within the Old Testament to which we might turn for illustrations, but we do not need them because it is safe to assume that P is thinking of these as the opposites of the harmony, wholeness, and peace that God had created in Paradise. Keeping in mind that it is "their way" (i.e., pattern of behavior) that has become corrupt and violent, we may assume that it primarily includes the all the shedding of blood, abuse of animals, and human injustice that causes the flood. Only a deluge would be sufficient to stifle the violence and to cleanse the corruption so that a new creation might begin.

This is the point at which this discussion may benefit from an illustrative comparison with parallel material from another ancient Near Eastern culture, in this instance, the Epic of Atrahasis, with its fragments of a flood story.[20] Here are some poignant lines from this remarkable document:[21]

> The land became wide, the people became numerous,
> The land bellowed like wild oxen,
> The god was disturbed by their uproar.
> Enlil heard their clamor
> And said to the great gods,
> "Oppressive has become the clamor of mankind,
> By their uproar they prevent sleep."
> ....
>
> "In the morning let him cause ... to pour down,
> Let it extend though the night [ ]
> ....
>
> Enki [opened] his mouth,
> Saying to En[lil]:
> "Why hast thou sworn [ ]
> I will stretch out my hand at the [ ]
> The flood which thou commandest [ ]
> ....
>
> [Atrahasis] opened his mouth,
> [Saying to his lord:]
> [ ] make known unto me its content
> [ ]that I may seek its. . . ."
> [Ea] opened his mouth.
> Saying to his servant:

---

[20] More elaborate is the flood account in the better-known Epic of Gilgamesh
[21] James B. Pritchard, ed., *Ancient Near Eastern Texts Relating to the Old Testament,* 2d ed., 1955, 104–6

"Thou sayest 'let me seek....'
The task which I am about to tell thee
Guard thee well:
'Wall, hearken to me,
Reed hut, guard well all my words!
Destroy the house, build a ship,
Renounce (worldly) goods,
Keep the soul alive!
The ship that thou shalt build.'"
....

"[ ] I will loosen.
[ ] he will seize all the people together,
[ ] before the flood appears.
[ ] as many as there are,
I will cause overthrow, affliction ...
[ ] build a large ship.
[ ] of good ... shall be its structure.
That [ship] shall be an ark, and its name
Shall be 'Preserver of Life.'
[ ] ceil (it) with a mighty cover.
[Into the ship which thou shalt make,
[Thou shalt take] the beasts of the field,
The fowl of the heavens."
....

[ ] At the stated time of which I will inform t[hee]
Enter (the ship) and close the door of the ship.
Aboard her [bring] thy grain, thy possessions, thy goods,
Thy (wife), thy family, thy relations, and the craftsmen.
Beasts of the field, creatures of the field, as many as eat herbs,
I will send to thee and they shall guard thy door.

The people's rowdiness and clamor is identified as the cause of the flood in this remarkable parallel, and that does not fit the biblical account from the ideological point of view. It is, however, the raucous behavior of mankind as a formal equivalent to the "corruption" and "violence" that causes the flood according to P. Again, the problem is not depicted as a deeply spiritual matter but as a matter of behavior. The things of the heart may remain hidden, and so long as they are, they are unlikely to bring a flood. But if wild disturbance and disruption occurs in the world and in society, nothing less than a flood can remedy the situation. This rioting and misbehavior is bad enough when only man is at fault, but when even the beasts burst their bonds, all hell breaks loose![22]

---

[22] On this theme, we may think of the calculated horror created in films such as *Jurassic Park* and *Godzilla*.

Thus a covenant must be made both with Noah and his descendants, and with the animals, comprising "all flesh" together. The rainbow is for them all. I leave room for additional exposition of Gen 9. Suffice it to say that every individual item referred to in chapter 9 of Genesis must be explained in terms of a new possibility of salvation and a new creation, or creation renewed. Definitely, this includes the special rules about the shedding of blood. If even the wild animals are to be held indictable for the shedding of human blood, how much more human beings who shed each other's blood!

But let it not be left unsaid that this passage is protective also of the rights and needs of the animal world, and in equal measure with those of mankind. They are put in fear and dread of man—obvious enough! Their flesh may be utilized as food, but humanely and respectfully.[23] P says that, but few seem to listen any more. The sad truth of our day is that nature is being harrowed and raped by mankind; animals that escape being shot with rifles are often deprived of the habitat necessary for living as God intended them to live—under a wise and protective management on the part of those under whose hand they must now exist.

No, there will never be another deluge to destroy the world. God has promised that. When the world is destroyed, it will be because the land has been eroded away, the trees have been cut down, the waters fished out, and the animals who remain alive are consigned to zoos!

The animals that remain on the earth, in the sea, and in the air would welcome being dealt with in strict accord with the covenant of Gen 9, but in the main mankind daily disregards it. Has the earth been again corrupted by man? Has a violence far worse than in Noah's time taken over the earth?

I think the God of Noah still desires his *remeś* to prowl the forest, cavort in the lakes and seas, fly through the air. He still desires luxuriant plant growth, full of nourishment for animals and for mankind, beautiful enough to lift men's spirits and give joy and comfort both to the beasts and to mankind.

---

[23] And why not? Is it better to leave their carcasses rotting in the field? Humans may as well benefit from them as to consign them to the vultures and the maggots!

DOES YHWH *NAḤAM?*
A QUESTION OF OPENNESS

Donald C. Raney II
Mansfield, Texas

John Calvin once wrote that "God is not sorrowful or sad; but remains forever like himself in his celestial and happy repose."[1] While his sentiments certainly reflect those of traditional Christian orthodox belief, are they in line with the biblical portrait of God? In recent decades a growing number of scholars have begun questioning the biblical basis for many of the pillars of traditional orthodoxy. Although many of the conclusions of these scholars have been a part of scholarly debate for a long time, they have found a name and a popular audience only during the past fifteen years. The name is "open theism," and the entry of these ideas into the public arena has sparked considerable controversy and debate, particularly among evangelicals. The majority of these debates have focused on the questions that the open theists raise concerning God's relation to and knowledge of future events. Yet the real issue concerns the larger fundamental question of what kind of God the God of the Bible is. Is God the immutable, impassable, and wholly transcendent being of traditional orthodoxy? Or is God the intensely emotional being who has entered into genuinely personal and mutually affective relationship with humanity, as the open theists maintain? This paper seeks to contribute to this discussion by examining the teaching of the Hebrew Bible concerning the repentance of God. Such a concept clearly challenges the classical idea of God as omniscient and impassable deity. Such a god would be far removed from the need for regret or a change of mind. The study will focus on the uses of the Hebrew verb נחם, which is most frequently used in this connection. It will begin with a brief exploration of the meaning and uses of the root, followed by a survey of representative verses that address the issue.

---

[1] John Calvin, *Commentaries on the First Book of Moses Called Genesis* (trans. J. King; Grand Rapids: Eerdmans, 1948), 1:249.

MEANINGS AND USES OF נחם IN THE HEBREW BIBLE

There is some disagreement among scholars as to the general meaning of the root נחם. Several suggest that the original meaning of this term seems to have been "to draw a deep breath," apparently as a sign of relief or sorrow, and thus conclude that the primary sense of this verb is "be sorry."[2] Others hold that a simple change of mind or attitude without any necessary connection with sorrow or regret is the basic meaning.[3] A survey of the treatment of the root in the standard lexicons seems to confirm that נחם indeed involves both a change of purpose as well as an expression of deep emotions.

The Old Testament contains five nonverbal uses of this root. First, there are seven distinct proper names in the Hebrew Bible derived from נחם, including those of Nehemiah and the prophet Nahum.[4] None of these, however, provides significant information concerning the meaning of the root. Second, נחמה, which occurs only in Ps 119:50 and Job 6:10, is translated "comfort" and "describes the life-giving effect of God's word in the midst of affliction."[5] Third, תנחומים carries the idea of "consolation" in each of its five uses and is said to bring joy to the soul in times of anxiety.[6] Fourth, נחום which speaks specifically of God comforting those whom he punishes, could be translated "compassion" since the contexts in which it appears describe God's feelings for the one needing comfort.[7] The final nonverbal derivative of this root, נחם, occurs only in Hos 13:14, which speaks of God withholding his compassion during judgment. These nonverbal forms of נחם, while revealing only limited information about the meaning of the term, clearly indicate not only an emotional quality within the root but also an intimate and caring relationship between the parties involved.

---

[2] R. B. Girdlestone, *Synonyms of the Old Testament* (Grand Rapids: Eerdmans, 1948), 87; G. F. Moore, *Judaism in the First Centuries of the Christian Era* (Cambridge: Harvard University Press, 1927), 1:510–11; H. Van Dyke Parunak, "A Semantic Survey of NHM," *Biblica* 56 (1975): 513.

[3] Norman Snaith, "The Language of the Old Testament," in *Interpreter's Bible* (ed. G. A. Buttrick; New York: Abingdon-Cokesbury, 1925), 1:225; James Mays, *Amos,* , (ed. P. Ackroyd and J. Barr; OTL; Philadelphia: Westminster, 1969), 129–30.

[4] F. Brown, S. R. Driver, and C. Briggs, *Hebrew and English Lexicon* (Peabody, Mass.: Hendrickson, 1979), 637.

[5] Parunak, "Semantic Survey of NHM," 515.

[6] See Ps 94:19. This term also describes the gentle words from God that Eliphaz brings to Job in Job 15:11.

[7] This term is used in Isa 57:18; Zech; 1:13; and Hos 11:8, each of which clearly speaks of God's compassion for his people.

The root appears fifty-three times in the Piel and Pual stems and is uniformly translated "comfort" or "console."[8] This translation fits well into the various contexts in which these stems appear. These passages speak of comfort or consolation in the face of death, danger, misfortune, or divine anger.[9] Both God and other humans are variously presented as the provider of the comfort in these contexts.[10] A number of these passages place נחם in a parallel relationship with the root נוד, which literally means "to nod" but by extension can mean "to pity."[11] The parallel use of these terms seems to indicate that the comfort involved contains a deeply emotional quality. In fact, as one scholar has pointed out such, "sympathetic pain, or 'compassion,' lies at the heart of the biblical concept of comfort."[12]

Of primary interest for the current study, however, are the occurrences of נחם in the Niphal and Hithpael. Of the fifty-five occurrences of נחם in these stems, God is the subject thirty-five times. Although the majority of the uses of these stems are in contexts that describe the repentance of God, difficulty exists in interpreting their meaning due largely to the varied meanings offered by the standard lexicons. The four meanings that are most often given are: (1) "moved to pity" or "have compassion," (2) "rue" or "repent," (3) "be comforted," and (4) "ease oneself."[13] Thus these verbal forms not only maintain the emotional quality of the root but also suggest that this emotional response may lead to a change of intent or attitude. One scholar has examined the semantic uses of נחם in these stems and has found six meanings that clearly demonstrate this dual meaning. H. Van Dyke Paranuk's definitions are: (1) "suffer emotional pain," (2) "be comforted, comfort oneself," (3) "execute wrath," (4) "retract punishment," (5) "retract blessing," and (6) "retract (a life of) sin."[14] Finally, Hans Wolff

---

[8] See Brown, Driver, Briggs, *Hebrew and English Lexicon*, 636–37; William Holladay, *A Concise Hebrew and Aramaic Lexicon of the Old Testament* (Grand Rapids: Eerdmans, 1971), 234; Julius Fuerst, *A Hebrew and Chaldee Lexicon to the Old Testament* (trans. S. Davidson; London: William & Norgate, 1867), 922.

[9] For examples of these, see Gen 37:35; Ps 23:4; Job 2:11; and Isa 12:1, respectively.

[10] See Ruth 2:13; 1 Chron 7:22; and Isa 52:9. In Ps 23:4 it is God's "rod and staff" that provide comfort to the psalmist.

[11] William Gesenius, *A Hebrew and Chaldee Lexicon to the Old Testament* (trans. E. Robinson; Boston: Crocker & Brewster, 1854), 655. This parallelism occurs in Isa 51:19; Nah 3:7; Ps 69:21; Job 2:11; 42:11; and Jer 16:5.

[12] Parunak, "Semantic Survey of NHM," 517.

[13] Brown, Driver, Briggs, *Hebrew and English Lexicon*, 637; Fuerst, *Hebrew and Chaldee Lexicon*, 921–22; Holladay, *Concise Hebrew and Aramaic Lexicon*, 234.

[14] Parunak, "Semantic Survey of NHM," 519–25. Obviously, the last of these meanings does not occur when God is the subject since God does not sin.

recognized these various elements when he defined נחם as "a change of mind prompted by the emotions, a turning away from an earlier decision on the part of someone deeply moved."[15]

THE NONREPENTANCE OF GOD

The idea that God does not repent is found in eight Old Testament passages.[16] Of these, five describe God's refusal to change his mind concerning the judgment of his people in 587 B.C.E., and one, Ps 110:4, speaks of his nonrepentance in relation to the eternal priesthood and order of Melchizedek. The remaining two verses, Num 23:19 and 1 Sam 15:29, appear to place the idea of divine nonrepentance in a standard statement of principle, namely, "God is not a man that he should change his mind." Because of this these two passages have often been used to combat the idea of God's repentance. A closer examination of each, however, shows that they do not state that nonrepentance is a characteristic or attribute of God but reveal God's unwillingness to change his mind concerning two specific decisions.

Numbers 23:19 is set within the larger context of the Balaam narrative found in Num 22–24. Balaam, having been hired by the king of Moab to curse the Israelites, instead pronounced a series of four oracles of blessing upon them. The current text is found within the second of these oracles. In his defiance of the king, he defends his action by stating that he would not curse what YHWH had blessed. Verse 19 then reads, "God is not a man, that he should fail, or the son of man that he would change his mind. Has he said, and will he not do it? Or spoken and will he not fulfill it?" This statement seems to state clearly that God never needs to change his mind, yet two issues need to be considered. First, the implication of Balak's instructions to Balaam is that he should entice God into changing his mind concerning Israel. Having heard of the Israelites' successes, the king certainly would have assumed that YHWH had blessed them and was able and intent on maintaining that blessing. Thus at a minimum YHWH would have to choose to allow a curse to have effect.

Second, the rhetorical questions at the end of verse 19 address God's truthfulness and determination specifically in comparison to humans. The repeated statement that "God is not a man" emphasizes this important

---

[15] Hans Walter Wolff, *Joel and Amos* (trans. Waldemar Janzen, S. Dean McBride Jr., and Charles Muenchow; Hermeneia; ed. S. Dean McBride; Philadelphia: Fortress, 1977), 298.

[16] Num 23:19; 1 Sam 15:29; Ps 110:4; Jer 4:28; 20:16; Ezek 24:14; Hos 13:14; and Zech 8:14.

difference between Creator and creature. The first of these statements, "God is not a man, that he should fail," is reinforced by the first rhetorical question, "Has he said and will he not do it?" Similarly, the second statement, "or the son of man that he should change his mind," is strengthened by the second question, "or spoken and will he not fulfill it?" Thus unlike humans and contrary to Balak's wishes, YHWH was not capricious in distributing blessings and curses, and would not remove the blessing on his chosen people.

First Samuel 15 is primarily concerned with the events surrounding God's final rejection of Saul as king of Israel in response to Saul's actions concerning the Amalekites. After Saul defied God's instructions, God informed Samuel that he regretted making Saul king and would give the kingdom to another. The second half of verse 11 states that Samuel cried out to God all night, apparently in an attempt to convince God to change his mind. When Samuel later confronted Saul with an awareness of his sin and its consequences, Saul denied responsibility. Samuel, however, knew the truth and informed Saul of the irrevocability of God's decision.

Due to the apparent contradiction between the statement of God's non-repentance in verse 29 and the statements affirming God's repentance in verses 11 and 35, many scholars question the unity of this chapter. Some have suggested that verse 29 may have been penned by a redactor to whom the suggestion of a divine change of mind was unacceptable.[17] This view seems to be based on the conclusion that verse 29 refers to God's refusal to change his mind regarding his rejection of Saul. While verses 11 and 35 clearly indicate God's repentance concerning his decision to make Saul king, the immediate context of verse 29, however, indicates that God's nonrepentance refers to his choice of David as the new king.[18] Verse 28 states that God has given the kingdom to another, and thus it seems that verse 29 affirms that it is this decision which is irrevocable. Thus, as in the Numbers passage discussed above, verse 29 does not state that God never repents but merely that he will not change his mind concerning his choice of David to be king. When one considers the significance of these two divine choices for the people of Israel, it is easy to understand why the

---

[17] William McKane, *I and II Samuel* (ed. J. Marsh and A. Richardson; Torch Bible Commentaries; London: SCM, 1963), 103; Fabrizio Foresti, *The Rejection of Saul in the Perspective of the Deuteronomistic School* (Rome: Edizioni del Teresianum, 1984), 28–29.

[18] For this conclusion, see Terence Fretheim, "Divine Foreknowledge, Divine Constancy, and the Rejection of Saul's Kingship," *Catholic Biblical Quarterly* 47 (1985): 595–602.

biblical writers would seek to remove the possibility of a divine change of mind concerning them.

THE REPENTANCE OF GOD

When one examines those verses which affirm that God does repent, one finds that there are several different factors which motivate God's change of mind, each of which involves a response to human actions. God is pictured as repenting in response to human disobedience, human repentance, and intercessory prayer. Another small group of verses, however, seem to describe God's repentance as a divine attribute. Each of these literary contexts provides important insight into the biblical conception of God.

GOD'S REPENTANCE AS A RESPONSE TO HUMAN DISOBEDIENCE

The story of Noah in Gen 6–9 is easily one of the most familiar stories of the Bible. Yet for all its popularity, certain passages within these chapters remain the source of great difficulty for modern scholars. This is particularly true of 6:1–8. Verses 1–4 describe what appear to be divine-human intermarriages and serve to tie the genealogy of chapter 5 to the account of the flood. The spread of sin that was introduced in chapter 3 seems to reach a climax in the events described in 6:1–4. Verse 5 clearly depicts this by emphasizing that *every* human thought and plan was continuously evil. This statement provides a clear moral motivation behind the sending of the flood. This is important because such a moral basis does not appear in the other ancient myths concerning the flood. Second, 5b shows that God's decision to destroy creation came only after the wholesale corruption of a generation had taken place. Finally, by revealing God's sorrow over the situation, verse 6 shows that God is not vengeful in his administration of justice but grieves because he must punish.

This final point is demonstrated most clearly by the fact that in verse 6 עצב, "deeply saddened," is used to parallel נחם. Gordon Wenham points out that the root עצב is most often used to "express the most intense form of human emotion, a mixture of rage and bitter anguish."[19] It is also significant that עצב is further supplemented by "in his heart" since this is the only time that this combination of terms occurs in the Hebrew Bible. Franz Delitzsch saw this combination as describing a "heart-piercing sorrow" within God.[20] The rampant evil that controlled the hearts of humanity,

---

[19] Gordon Wenham, *Genesis 1–15* (Word Biblical Commentary; Waco, Tex.: Word, 1987), 1:144.

[20] Franz Delitzsch, *A New Commentary on Genesis* (trans. Sophia Taylor; Edinburgh: T&T Clark, 1888), 1:233.

Does YHWH Naḥam? A Question of Openness

according to versw 5, is thus contrasted in verse 6 with the deep grief and disappointment that resulted in the heart of God, and it is this grief that led to God's decision to destroy all of creation.

GOD'S REPENTANCE AS A RESPONSE TO HUMAN REPENTANCE

Jonah 3:1–4 record Jonah's journey to Nineveh and his brief proclamation of the city's impending destruction. In response to this revelation, the people declare an immediate fast and the king calls for the people to pray and repent in verses 5–8. While it is unclear whether the king recognized the judgment as coming from YHWH or one of the gods in the Ninevite pantheon, he did correctly link the announcement of destruction to the behavior of the people and called for change. This response on the part of non-Israelites is remarkable in light of the fact that Jonah's message mentioned neither the possibility nor conditions for repentance.

In calling for the people to repent of their evil ways, the king recognized that no god could be forced to act in a particular way. His decree reflects this uncertainty through the use of the phrase מִי־יוֹדֵעַ יָשׁוּב וְנִחַם in verse 9. The first two terms in this expression represent the Hebrew idiom "Who knows?" and carry the idea of "perhaps." These four terms appear in the same order in Joel 2:14, where they are also used in connection with a call for fasting and praying. The phrase יָשׁוּב וְנִחַם, which also appears in Joel 2:14, is curious since each term may be translated "repent." It seems that in this case נחם should be translated "be compassionate," while the idea of repentance is carried by שׁוּב. It is thus even more remarkable that this pagan king not only recognized the possibility that YHWH would repent but that that repentance would be due to YHWH's compassion. Jonah 3:9 then further defines this by expressing the hope that God would turn from his anger. The singular hope of the king in Jon 3:9 is therefore expressed in three different ways: that God might repent of his decision to destroy the city, have compassion on a praying people, and turn from his anger over their sin. Verse 10 then reports that God did repent concerning the destruction of the city. It is important to note that God's change of mind was not due to the prayers and fasting of the people. Verse 10 makes it clear that God was moved to repentance by the turning of the people from their wicked behavior. God has therefore shown that true human repentance will be met with divine repentance.

GOD'S REPENTANCE AS A RESPONSE TO INTERCESSORY PRAYER

Forty days after their leader climbed Mount Sinai, the Israelites persuaded Aaron to build a golden calf. Exodus 32:7–10 records that God informed Moses of the people's idolatry and announced his intention to destroy them. God's anger is clearly evident as he seemed to disown the people by telling Moses that they were "*your* people, whom *you* brought up from the land of Egypt." Yet in verse 10 God seems to provide Moses with a hint that God may be persuaded to repent by telling Moses to "leave me alone that I may punish them." Yet while this may be a test for Moses, this should not be misunderstood as diminishing the seriousness of the people's sin or of God's threat. The people were guilty of a grave sin, and God was fully justified in deciding to destroy them, but God here expressed a desire to repent of that decision only if Moses was faithful in his responsibility as God's prophet to pray for the people.

Moses' response in verses 11–13 shows that his main concern was not only with the people but also with God's reputation. First, he reversed God's statement in verse 7 and clearly stated that the Israelites were *God's* people and that it was *God* who was responsible for bringing them out of bondage. Second, he pointed out that the destruction of Israel would provide other nations with the grounds by which to slander the name of YHWH. Third, by using the imperative form of נחם in a parallel relationship to the phrase "turn from your anger," Moses pointed to God's compassionate nature and called on that compassion to temper his anger.[21] Fourth, Moses invoked the promise that God had made to the patriarchs and thereby urged God to remain faithful to his word. Moses' prayer had the desired effect, as verse 14 reports that God did repent of his decision to destroy the people. The intensity of Moses's intercession along with God's compassion led him to temper without waiving his judgment. Many scholars have unfortunately underestimated Moses's role in these verses by overemphasis on God's sovereignty. Yet the text makes it clear that it was a combination of God's power and Moses's prayer that was responsible for the continued welfare of the people.

God's Repentance As a Divine Attribute

Both Joel 2:13 and Jon 4:2 include the repentance of God in a list of divine attributes. Nearly identical lists, lacking only the reference to divine repentance, appear in Exod 34:6; Neh 9:17; Pss 86:15; 103:8; and 145:8, while partial lists may be found throughout the Old Testament. Because of similarities in vocabulary and structure, these statements seem to reflect a common cultic formula. If this is true, one is left to wonder whether Jonah and Joel preserved the full original saying while the others offer abbreviated versions or whether the prophetic texts represent early midrashic exegesis in which each author adapted the original meaning of

---

[21] The only other occurrence of the imperative of נחם in the Old Testament is in Ps 90:13, which is also attributed to Moses and where it clearly has the idea of "be compassionate toward."

an authoritative text in order to address contemporary issues.[22] Whichever of these may be the case, this confession provides a wealth of insight into the divine character.

The oracle against Judah in Joel 2:1–17 may be easily divided into two sections. Verses 1–11 contain a detailed description of the invasion and destruction of Judah that would accompany the coming of the "day of the Lord." The graphic tone of these verses clearly emphasizes the certainty and finality of the coming destruction. Yet even as Joel envisions the final phase of the invasion he recognizes that the possibility still existed that God would change his mind if the people would repent. In order best to convey this message, Joel used a well-known confessional formula within the worship of the community as motivation for repentance. Thomas Dozeman states that this "confession of Yahweh's gracious character is a hinge in the prophet's speech between the finality of the divine judgment that was reflected in the description of the Day of Yahweh in Joel 2:1–11 and hope in Joel 2:14."[23]

The first term used to describe God is רחום, which is most often translated "merciful" but comes from a root that means "have compassion" and therefore may be translated "compassionate." Of the forty-seven Old Testament uses of this term, thirty-five refer to God. Since the term also is associated with the Hebrew word for "womb," it has been suggested that it also carries the idea of "motherly compassion as well as fatherly mercy."[24] God is then described as חנן, which means "gracious." While the verb form occurs in a variety of contexts, the adjective is used only with God as the subject. When applied to God, this term denotes an active interest in the well being of the godly.

God is next described as being ארך אפים, which is nearly always translated "slow to anger." This phrase is highly anthropomorphic in that the word translated "anger" may also be translated "nose." The picture is of God slowly drawing a deep breath as he calms his wrath. Yet while praising God for his great patience, this phrase does remind the reader that anger is an emotion that God possesses but chooses to restrain. Finally, God is described as possessing great חסד. This word is certainly one of the most significant words in the Hebrew Bible. While there is some debate concerning the precise meaning of the term, it is frequently used directly

---

[22] It is generally accepted that Exod 34:6 represents the original form of this liturgical confession. See Allen, 80. See also Thomas Dozeman, "Inner-Biblical Interpretation of Yahweh's Gracious and Compassionate Character," *Journal of Biblical Literature* 108 (1989): 209.

[23] Dozeman, "Inner-Biblical Interpretation" 212.

[24] Thomas Raitt, "Why Does God Forgive?" *Horizons in Biblical Theology* 13 (1991): 50.

or indirectly in connection with God's covenant with Israel as an expression of God's faithfulness and loyalty to that covenant. Katherine Sakenfeld suggests that by placing this term alongside those discussed above, this attribute formula suggests that God is "so great in faithfulness that he is willing even to forgive breach of relationship."[25]

Each of these four attributes clearly possesses strong emotional characteristics and appears to present a different aspect of God's love. It therefore seems reasonable that, as Joel included נחם in his list of divine attributes, he had in mind the emotional quality of this term.

The people could know that their repentance would lead to a removal of the threat because of YHWH's grace, mercy, and constant faithfulness to his covenant. For Joel, the fact that God changes his mind concerning judgment in response to human repentance was as sure as the fact that God is compassionate, gracious, and great in steadfast lovingkindness.

CONCLUSION

So, what does it mean to say that God repents? Peter Toon offered an excellent summary when he wrote that "God as perfect Deity does not change in his essential nature; but because he is in relationship with people who do change, he himself changes his relation and attitude from wrath to mercy and from blessing to judgment, as the occasion requires."[26] By entering into a personal relationship with humanity, God chose to condition his actions on the actions of his covenant people. This does not mean that God's will is subjected to that of man, for God is constantly at work to fulfill his ultimate and changeless purposes. Yet in order to maintain humanity's freedom to choose to obey, God's individual acts toward those purposes are not predetermined.

This study, therefore, affirms two complementary aspects in the biblical portrait of God that have great significance for modern believers. First, the unchangeable nature of God assures individuals that they are not in the hands of an unstable and capricious force. God's essential holiness, infinite love, and limitless ability to meet human needs cannot increase and never decreases. His faithfulness to his people and to his ultimate purposes also knows no change. Second, the mutability of God's mind assures individuals that they are not in the hands of an unfeeling iron-clad fate. God has entered into a relationship with his creation in which his love compels him

---

[25] Katharine Sakenfeld, *The Meaning of Hesed in the Hebrew Bible* (Missoula, Mont.: Scholars Press, 1978), 119.

[26] Peter Toon, "Repentance," in *New International Dictionary of the Bible* (ed. J. D. Douglas; Grand Rapids: Zondervan, 1987).

to be responsive to human individuals. His responses are not controlled by capricious expressions of his emotions but are always in line with his unchanging being and purposes. Although God must punish those who chose to disobey, mankind may then rest in the knowledge that they are in a relationship with a compassionate God who is ready and willing to change his mind in order to demonstrate his perfect love to anyone who would turn to him. It would thus appear that the God of the Bible certainly appears to be much closer to the truly relational God of open theism than the distant impersonal deity of classical orthodoxy.

(Re)presentations of Violence in Philo

Torrey Seland
Volda University College, Norway

INTRODUCTION

The issue of violence and the Bible has come into focus for several reasons in recent years. In reading the Bible, however, it is also important to see how other writers and—as in our case—interpreters of the biblical texts at the beginning of our time considered violence. One of these persons who should be invited to speak is Philo of Alexandria. Living from roughly 10 B.C.E. to 50 C.E. made him a contemporary of both Jesus and Paul. Being an author of an extensive number of commentaries on biblical books and issues makes him an even more interesting personage of his time. A presentation of readings from his texts should not be carried out, however, without providing some considerations about Philo and the nature of the topic studied. Hence some comments on my presuppositions in this regard.

SOME MODELS AND PERSPECTIVES

When investigating the prevalence of representations of violence[1] in the works of Philo, there are two sets of presuppositions to clarify: first, what are we looking for; secondly, who was Philo, and what was his social location in the world of his time? Then the major question can have a closer presentation: How did Philo deal with the issue of violence?

---

[1] The issues focused in both this Society of Biblical Literature session and the former last year are "questions of intra-religious violence, that is Jews against Jews and/or Christians against Christians" (from the invitation letter to participate). Hence I will not deal with the role of violence in, e.g., situations of war, but deal with various forms of inter- and intragroup conflicts as presented by Philo.

WHAT IS VIOLENCE?

The issue of violence is deeply embedded in the social structures of the time and culture concerned, and any investigations of such a theme should make explicit the applied concept, that is, how one defines the phenomenon of "violence." Recent studies emphasize that presentations of violence are closely related to standpoint and social location. Hence presentations of "violence" may be differently evaluated according to the position of the reporters as, for example, a perpetrator, a victim, or a witness. Discussions of (re)presentations of violence without such awareness of standpoint may bring out some viewpoints but will be hard to assess as to the value of the inherent evaluations of the topic studied.

In a much-cited book, D. Riches defined "violence" as "an act of physical hurt deemed legitimate by the performer and illegitimate by (some) witnesses."[2] In a more recent collection of articles following up the stimulus set by the book of Riches, this definition is upheld, not at least because of its "abstractness which allows for cross-cultural comparability, and in its addressing the essential ambivalence <of violence> as instrumental and expressive action."[3] B. J. Malina too has recently defined "violence" in a similar way: "Violence transgresses the limits of acceptable coercion; it is aimed at harming another illegitimately."[4] Several aspects of determining the nature of violence are focused in these definitions: first, the relation of violence to force and coercion; secondly, its relation to current laws and social norms; and lastly, the relevance of possible diverging viewpoints stated by a perpetrator, victim, or witness.

First of all, one should differentiate between *coercion, violence,* and *force.* Not all use of coercion is violence. Every society has some kinds of rules set by the system to regulate the use of coercion, whether performed by the regime or private individuals. In the following the term *coercion* is used to denote "acts intended to harm others or their value possessions."[5] Such a definition includes a vast array of acts from the slight and the subtle to the extensive and overt. But common to all coercive acts is that they are intended to harm in one way or another. What constitutes harm,

---

[2] D. Riches, "The Phenomenon of Violence," in *The Anthropology of Violence,* (ed. David Riches; Oxford: Oxford University Press, 1986), 8.

[3] Ingo W. Schröder and Bettina E. Schmidt, "Introduction: Violent Imaginaries and Violent Practices," in *Anthropology of Violence and Conflict,* (ed. Ingo W. Schröder and Bettina E. Schmidt; London: Routledge, 2001), 4.

[4] See Bruce J. Malina, *The Social Gospel of Jesus: The Kingdom of God in Mediterranean Perspective* (Minneapolis: Fortress, 2001), 42.

[5] Peter C. Sederberg, *Terrorist Myths: Illusion, Rhetoric and Reality* (Englewood Cliffs, N.J.: Prentice Hall, 1989), 11.

however, may be further defined in light of the particular societies studied; that is, it is culturally dependent.⁶

Coercion is further closely related to violence and force, but these latter terms represent two different kinds of coercion: "Acts of coercion that violate the limits within a particular community may be termed 'violence,' whereas acceptable coercion may be called 'force.'"⁷ Hence some coercion may be acceptable in light of a particular society's code of law, but the acceptable degree of coercion may be different from community to community. The important element here is that outbreaks of violence (as unacceptable coercion) do not signify the breakdown of law and order or of politics, but politics, considered as all deliberate efforts to control mutual interaction, determines which forms of coercion are considered to be violent.

Secondly, the various forms of violence may have strong expressive functions of meaning; establishment violence is one of these, terrorism another. The ready use of violence to maintain or defend the status quo is a form of behavior here to be called "establishment violence" or "vigilantism."⁸ In investigations of history of law the term "self-redress" is often used for the kind of actions here termed establishment violence. Furthermore, "self-redress" or "self-help" is often used to denote the oldest and most primary form of punishment brought upon persons who were thought to deviate from the accepted norms of their societies.⁹ By the establishment of greater formation of communities and the development of a more "advanced" form of jurisdiction, "self-redress" was not immediately abolished or denied, but it underwent some regulation. In the further

---

⁶ Ibid., 14–15.

⁷ Ibid., 13.

⁸ Cf. ibid., 60ff. H. J. Rosenbaum and P. C. Sederberg, "Vigilantism: An Analysis of Establishment Violence," in *Vigilante Politics* (ed. H. J. Rosenbaum and P. C. Sederberg; Philadelphia, 1976), 3–29. "Terrorism" will not be much focused here. Sederberg understands it as "a coercive tactic used by the contending sides of a political struggle that deliberately violates ... two rules of war. Noncombatants are the targets of terrorism, and the means chosen to destroy these targets are relatively indiscriminate" (*Terrorist Myths*, 31).

⁹ Cf. B. Cohen, "Self-Help in Jewish and Roman Law," *Revue Internationale Des Droits de l'Antiquité* 3 (1955): 107: "A system of self-redress, in the form of private vengeance preceded everywhere the establishment of a regular judicature." On this issue in the ancient Greek and Roman world, see further K. Latte, "Beiträge zum griechischen Strafrecht," in *Zur griechischen Rechtsgeschichte*, (edited E. Berneker; Wege der Forschung 45; Darmstadt, 1968), 262–314; and R. Köstler, "Die homerische Rechts- und Staatsordnung," in Berneker, *Zur Griechischen Rechtsgeschichte*, 172–95.

development of law and jurisdiction some remnants of the institution of self-redress were retained as a right of self-defense in certain circumstances. But these last-mentioned forms of what might also be called "regulated or legalized self-help" must be distinguished from the form of "self-redress" proscribed in the political system of the societies concerned, that is, vigilantism.

Defined in this way, self-redress is not something to be found only in old "primitive" societies before the establishment of regular judicature. In communities where the regular way of prosecuting nonconformers is hindered by some higher authorities, as for example in occupied nations or in pariah groups, or where conservative elements of the population consider the regime to be too tolerant or ineffective, the only way to fulfill the demands of their own law may be "to take the law into their own hands." Rosenbaum and Sederberg differentiate between three forms of vigilantism according to the kind of targets: crime-control vigilantism, social-group vigilantism, and regime-control vigilantism.[10] Recent times have seen several cases of establishment violence or vigilantism where conservative elements of the population considered their values threatened by "modernizing" attitudes, and social-anthropological research has also focused on the occurrence of killing by self-redress in societies relatively close to the present time.[11]

The Jews of both the Diaspora and in the occupied land of Israel can be considered as having lived in situations concerned with social frontiers. And as establishment violence has been characterized as typical for what may be called a frontier mentality, this model commends itself for a study of conflicts among the first century Jews.

Accordingly, the issue of "violence" involves several aspects to be considered; it concerns actions of coercion considered illegitimate by some (perpetrators, victims or witnesses), it always has functions of meaning, and it may be variously categorized in relation to its expressive role.

WHO WAS PHILO?

Philo belonged to a rich and influential family in Alexandria. His brother Alexander Lysimachus was "alabarch," perhaps an office concerned with administration of the paying of taxes and customs.[12] Josephus says that Alexander "surpassed all his fellow citizens both in ancestry and

---

[10] Cf. Rosenbaum and Sederberg, "Vigilantism," 3–29.

[11] H. Jon. Rosenbaum and Peter C. Sederberg, *Vigilante Politics* (Pennsylvania, 1976).

[12] Cf. the comments in Josephus (LCL) to *Ant.* 18.159.

in wealth" (*Ant.* 20.100). Philo thus undoubtedly belonged to the elite segment of the Jewish Alexandrian community.¹³

In *Ant.* 18.259 Josephus comments on an Alexandrian delegation—headed by Philo—that was sent to Rome to intercede for the Jews at emperor Gaius Caligula. Josephus here presents Philo as "a man held in the highest honor [ἀνὴρ τὰ πάντα ἔνδοξος], brother of Alexander the alabarch, and no novice in philosophy" (φιλοσοφίας οὐκ ἄπειρος). It is also obvious from Philo's own writings that he had official positions in the city, and his story of the delegation to Rome is told in his *De Legatione*.

Philo must also have been influential as a writer.¹⁴ Not only did he write exegetical commentaries on the Penteteuch (i.e., the Law of Moses), the Jewish constitution, but he also wrote philosophical treatises and apologetic works and dealt with contemporary political issues.¹⁵ If I should venture to make a comparison with our own world and time, I might conjecture that had he lived today he would probably have been a learned professor or rabbi—or both—with his own television program and web site, commenting on both political and religious issues of his time and world (cf. *Ad Flaccum* and *Legatio*). I do not consider him a solitary scholar, sitting in his office writing theoretical expositions of the old scriptures, but read him as one deeply engaged philosophically, politically, and religiously in the life and circumstances of his Jewish community. In fact, he was much of an agitator of his view of Judaism both among his fellow-Jews and neighboring non-Jews.¹⁶ Hence his works focused on both intermural and intramural aspects of Jewish life in Alexandria.

---

¹³ See also my summary in Torrey Seland, *Establishment Violence in Philo and Luke: A Study of Nonconformity to the Torah and Jewish Vigilante Reactions* (Biblical Interpretation Series 15; Leiden: Brill, 1995), 82–93; and now also Peder Borgen, *Philo of Alexandria, An Exegete for His Time* (Supplements to Novum Testamentum 86; Leiden: Brill, 1997), 14–26.

¹⁴ About forty of his works are still extant, but indications in his own works as well as remarks by some of the so-called church fathers suggest that his works must have consisted of at least twenty more titles.

¹⁵ For a more comprehensive presentation of Philo's works, see Borgen, *Philo of Alexandria*.

¹⁶ Cf. here also Peder Borgen ("Philo of Alexandria A Critical and Synthetical Survey of Research since World War II," *ANRW* 21.1:98–154), who states that "Philo's intention is to conquer the surrounding culture ideologically by claiming that whatever good there is has its source in Scripture and thus belonged to the Jewish nation and its heritage. In this way Philo represents the dynamic and offensive movement of the Jews who infiltrated the environment of the alexandrian citizens around the gymnasium" (151).

With regard to the social location of the members of the Jewish community he belonged to in Alexandria, they were probably situated along various stages of the social ladder with regard to wealth, but they did not in general belong to the elite groups holding positions in the political and religious institutions outside their own *politeuma* structures. I have suggested that the Jewish communities in the Diaspora in some respects could be characterized as representing a community type to be designated "pariah community."[17] They represented minority groups, though in such cities as Alexandria they might have constituted a considerable part of the population. The presence of Jews in several parts of the Roman world antedated that empire by centuries; hence during our period they had long been a part of the economic and social system of the Diaspora. Nevertheless, in the letter of Claudius to the Alexandrians (41 C.E.) he stated that the Jews were living in a city "not their own."[18] Thus, they were not then considered indigenous to their host country by the Roman authorities. Philo relates that in Alexandria there were five quarters, named after the first letters of the alphabet: "Two of these are called Jewish because most of the Jews inhabit them" (*Flacc.* 55). We know also that most Jews in Rome lived in a special sector of that city (cf. *Legatio* 155). However, they did not comprise ghettos, for they resided in various other parts of the city too. In some cities many Jews gathered together, perhaps according to professional activities, as was usual in such preindustrial cities.

According to Philo, they considered Jerusalem as their μητρόπολις,[19] even though they might have belonged to families that had lived in the Diaspora for several generations. It is also to be kept in mind that for many the Diaspora situation was a provisional arrangement: one day all the Jews of the Diaspora should return to Israel, their own land (see *Praem.* 164f, and Deut 30:1–5). On the other hand, many Diaspora Jews might have considered their Diaspora residence their "fatherland" too. Hence, while some social aspects demonstrate the pariah character of their existence, other points show that this was not necessarily the only dominant character of their own conceptions of their Diaspora life.

Furthermore, and very important for our topic, the Jews had a sociopolitical organization that was acknowledged by the Roman authorities. They had an institution with its own constitution and administration, and through this they could perform certain in-group functions and also some

---

[17] Seland, *Establishment Violence in Philo and Luke*, 89–93.

[18] For the text of this letter, see H. I. Bell, *Jews and Christians in Egypt* (Westport, 1924), 29.

[19] For the significance of this term, see Y. Amir, *Die hellenistische Gestalt des Judentums bei Philon von Alexandria* (Neukirchen-Vluyn, 1983), 52ff.

of a juridical character. These were limited, however, as the Jews lacked the right to impose capital punishment, even though the Torah prescribed such measures in several cases.[20] In an agonistic culture as the first-century Mediterranean world, the character of their Jewish community as a minority community and the limitations on their own jurisdiction are all aspects that are important for understanding the (re)presentations of "violence" in the works of Philo.

(RE)PRESENTATIONS OF VIOLENCE IN PHILO'S WORKS

(Re)presentations of acts of "violence" are thus dependent on several points of view. In the following I will primarily use the works of Philo belonging to the so-called *Expositio* and his historical works, investigating what they might tell us about Philo's views on "violence."[21] However, in reading his works, it soon becomes very evident here too that "violence" cannot be studied as an abstract phenomenon. It is always socially located, socially conditioned, and socially understood. Hence in the following I will try to differentiate between Philo as a victim/witness of anti-Jewish "violence" and Philo as a witness of intra-Jewish "violence."

PHILO AS A WITNESS/VICTIM OF ANTI-JEWISH "VIOLENCE"

Several of the works of Philo have an obvious apologetic agenda; among these *Hypothetica, In Flaccum,* and *De Legatione ad Gaium* are the most noticeable. In the two last mentioned, Philo deals with contemporary

---

[20] That the Jews did not have the rights of capital punishment is scarcely to be doubted. See J. Juster, *Les Juifs dans l'Empire Romain: Leurs condition juridique économique et sociale* (Paris, 1914), 2:156ff. Juster adds, however (157): "Cependant, les Juifs avaient adopté la pratique du lynchage dans les cas ou un des leurs commettait quelque attentat grave contre la religion juive." Cf. E. R. Goodenough, *The Jurisprudence of the Jewish Courts in Egypt* (1929; repr., Amsterdam [New Haven], 1969), 25: "That Jews ever had the formal and official right in Alexandria, especially under Roman rule, to execute sentence of death is most unlikely." Goodenough's own solution is, however, that this "by no means prevents the conclusion that the Jewish courts could sentence to death subject to the approval of the Roman ruler, just as was done in the case of Jesus." Cf. pp. 253ff. This theory is hardly tenable and in any case impossible to prove. See my discussion in Seland, *Establishment Violence in Philo and Luke,* 17–42. See also R. Taubenschlag, *The Law of Greco-Roman Egypt in Light of the Papyri 332 BC–640 AD* (Warszaw, 1955), 372: "In the Roman period the highest jurisdiction in all the land, civil and criminal ... belonged to the prefect. He was also invested with ius gladii."

[21] For the sake of convenience I use the term "violence" in quotation marks as the general term, but the reader should remember my definition presented above.

political events crucial for the existence and well-being of the Jewish community in Alexandria at his time. Pivotal among the events dealt with are the pogrom in Alexandria in 38 C.E.

The pogrom was a result of several political events and circumstances both on the imperial level in Rome and locally in Alexandria concerning the local Jewish rights. We cannot here discuss the historical questions concerning the chronology of the particular events,[22] nor the way Philo describes these issues in light of his symbolic and theological universe,[23] but present some comments on the "violence" in the riots against the Jews as described by Philo.

The riots of 38 C.E. were due to several factors. Among these, one of the most crucial was the political weakness of the then governor Flaccus. Due to the death of his patron, the emperor Tiberius, he was politically ineffective for some time. The time before the reestablishment of the local governor's ability of authority was taken advantage of by some of his enemies and exploited in verbal and physical attacks against the Jews. When Gaius Caligula became emperor, the conditions in Alexandria grew even worse. The attacks, when first initiated, soon evolved into severe riots: the Jewish synagogues were attacked and desecrated or burned down (*Legat.* 133–134), and the governor was made to issue a proclamation that the Jews were "foreigners and aliens" (*Flacc.* 54) in Alexandria. This was followed by an expulsion of the Jews from the various parts of the city into one section alone, which thus soon was converted into a ghetto, "the first known ghetto in the world."[24] As the anti-Jewish riots developed, the cruelty increased: houses were pillaged, many fled out of the city to the beaches (*Legat.* 124), and many were publicly exposed and dishonored in several ways. Some were physically attacked, mob-lynched, scourged, dragged through the market; some were burned, others crucified (*Legat.* 130–131; *Flacc.* 65ff.). Finally, it seems to have resulted in an attack by Flaccus on the pivotal institution of the Jews, their senate or "gerousia," their council of elders. The members were scourged, some of them to death in a way that was utterly felt as a humiliation to the Jews (*Flacc.* 75–85). Philo himself describes this as "the height of harshness"; the elders were not scourged in the usual way due to their status, but in the same ways as the native Egyptians; that

---

[22] See here E. M. Smallwood, *The Jews under Roman Rule: From Pompey to Diocletian* (Studies in Judaism in Late Antiquity 20; Leiden, 1981), 235–42; and now especially Pieter Willem van der Horst, *Philo's Flaccus: The First Pogrom: Introduction, Translation, and Commentary* (Philo of Alexandria Commentary Series 2; Leiden: Brill, 2003).

[23] On these aspects, see, e.g., Borgen, *Philo of Alexandria*, 176–93.

[24] Smallwood, *Jews under Roman Rule*, 240.

is, "they were treated like Egyptians of the meanest rank and guilty of the greatest iniquities" (*Flacc.* 80).

Philo is eloquent in his descriptions of the actions taken against the Jews, as well as when he later describes the consequences that befell Flaccus the governor. After Claudius had become the emperor in Rome, Flaccus was arrested, deprived of his property, sentenced to banishment and exiled to one of the Aegean islands, and finally killed by the Romans. Smallwood is right in stating that Philo's interest "in Flaccus' fate is moral, not judicial."[25] He is convinced that Flaccus's agony was caused "by his treatment of the Jews, whom in his craving for agrandisement he had resolved to exterminate utterly" (*Flacc.* 116). Philo ends his book on Flaccus by stating that "it was the will of justice [δίκη] that the butcheries which she brought on his single body should be as numerous as the number of the Jews whom he unlawfully put to death" (*Flacc.* 189) and that Flaccus "thereby became an undubitable proof that the help which God can give was not withdrawn from the nation of the Jews" (*Flacc.* 191).

How does Philo consider the "violence" exhibited in this pogrom? In this case Philo was an observer and, as a part of the Jewish community in Alexandria, also a victim. As might have been expected, he does not deal so much with the enforcement of coercion displayed in the riots, as with the legal and moral disgracement involved. This is evident throughout his narrative but most manifest in his descriptions of the dishonor conferred on the Jews and especially on the council of elders. These features are quite understandable in light of the culture at that time and place. Alexandria, as well as the larger Mediterranean area, was part of an agonistic culture in which values such as honor and shame played unescapably roles. As in any agonistic culture, coercion and even violence in various forms were pervasive. This is also to be seen in his descriptions of both the pogrom and the fate of Flaccus: the Jews suffered excessive and unjust violence; Flaccus got what he—according to Philo—deserved, an extremely bloody death.

In light of the model presented here, the kind of coercion perpetrated against the Jews in the pogrom should be termed *establishment violence*. Due to the social progression of the Jews felt and feared by their native neighbors, especially by the local citizens, the Jews were attacked in order to reduce their influence and possibilities of social advancement. Back to basics! And as far as the pogrom also was rather indiscriminate as to the victims, the establishment violence could be further defined as a kind of social group control vigilantism, or even vigilante terrorism.[26]

---

[25] Ibid., 241–42.
[26] See further on this Sederberg, *Terrorist Myths,* 60–62.

PHILO AS A WITNESS OF INTRA-JEWISH VIOLENCE

If we then turn to what we may find in the works of Philo about "violence" in an intramural Jewish context, it might be interesting to ask how he treats the many narratives in the Hebrew Bible about excessive coercion, even violence, against fellow-Jews. How does he treat the "violence" recorded in the Scriptures? Does he give voice to any criticism of the degree of coercion exhibited? Or does he perhaps occasionally rather strengthen the coercive or violent features of events recorded? Furthermore, as he applies the legal matters of the law of Moses to contemporary issues, how does he actualize these laws? We shall present a few test cases of how he deals with episodes recorded in the books of Moses; then we will try to demonstrate how he in some cases even intensifies some of the legislation of Moses in his contemporizing expositions.

SOME CASES OF "VIOLENCE" IN THE HEBREW BIBLE. Being aware of the danger of running into anachronistic readings of the works of Philo, one might nevertheless take a point of departure in some texts that modern readers often find rather repulsive in their use of coercion, violence, and force. We focus briefly on Philo's representations of the sacrifice of Isaac (Gen 22), the rape of Dinah (Gen 34), the slaughter of the Levites (Exod 32), and the Phinehas episode of Num 25.

Philo has a major exposition of *the sacrifice of Isaac* (Gen 22) in *Abr.* 167–208, but he comments explicitly on the inherent "violence" of the story neither here nor in his other scattered references to this episode (*Somn.* 1.195; *Fug.* 132; *Congr.* 43; etc.). He knows, however, that there were some "quarrelsome critics who misconstrue everything and ... do not think Abraham's action great or wonderful, as we suppose it to be" (*Abr.* 178). They level against Philo that many others have offered their children in order to be redeemed from some danger. Hence they do not see why the willingness to offer Isaac should be considered special. It is not clear who these critics were, whether Jews or Gentiles.[27] M. Niehoff argues that Philo was more sympathetic to the idea of child sacrifice than both Josephus and the rabbis.[28] Be that as it may, it is obvious from Philo's exposition of Gen 22 that the "violence" as such did not bother him here; at least he does not focus on this aspect.

---

[27] Niehoff finds them to be Jewish opponents (Maren Niehoff, *Philo on Jewish Identity and Culture* [Texts and Studies in Ancient Judaism 86; Tübingen: Mohr Siebeck, 2001], 173), while Feldman thinks they were "non-Jews who condemned the Jews for misanthropy" (Louis H. Feldman, "Philo's Version of the 'Aqedah,'" in *The Studia Philonica Annual. Studies in Hellenistic Judaism XIV 2002* [ed. David T. Runia and Gregory E. Sterling; Brown Judaic Studies 335; Providence, R.I.: Brown University Press, 2002], 66–86).

[28] Niehoff, *Philo on Jewish Identity and Culture,* 174.

Philo has also just a few comments on the *rape of Dinah* and the subsequent revenge of her brothers (Gen 34) in *Migr.* 223 and *Mut.* 194. He here uses the story in a highly allegorical exposition. Contrary to Gen 34:30, where Jacob is reproaching his unmerciful sons, Philo is positive toward their action. As the editors of the Loeb edition state in their footnote to *Migr.* 223, Philo "takes great liberties with the story," ignoring the seduction and the circumcision of the male persons in Shechem, but is led to be appraisive of Jacob's sons. No further comments on the excessiveness of the coercion involved are voiced by Philo.

In Exod 32 we have the story of the Israelites in the desert worshiping *the golden calf*. After Moses came down from the mountain, he in his anger called upon those who wanted to be on the Lord's side, and the Levites rallied to him. They were then told to "put your sword on your side, each of you! Go back and forth from gate to gate throughout the camp, and each of you kill your brother, your friend, and your neighbor." The sons of Levi did as Moses commanded, and about three thousand of the people fell on that day. For this, the Levites were later rewarded with the priesthood.[29]

Philo returns several times to this episode (see esp. *Mos.* 2.159ff.; 270ff.; *Spec.* 1.79; 3.124–125; 3.155; *Ebr.* 67–68; *Sacr.* 130; *Fug.* 90). He uses very emphatic terms, applauding the action taken by the Levites: "They were held to have done a truly religious deed, driven by godly zeal" (*Spec.* 1.79); they carried out a "righteous slaughter" (3.124), performing the "most illustrious act of heroism that has ever been achieved" (3.126). But most of all they are praised because they disregarded any family ties and championed the honor of God alone: they "acknowledged no love nor kinship but God's love" (3.126–127; *Mos.* 2.273). The willingness to serve God is considered by Philo to be the primary tie of affinity, and the love of one's neighbors or relatives is subordinated to this commitment.[30] We find the same emphasis of Philo also in his version of Gen 22 in *Abr.* 67 and in other descriptions of how to relate to apostates. In *Spec.* 3.155b he states that "Those whom we call our kinsfolk or within the circle of kinsmen our friends are turned into aliens by their misconduct when they go astray; for agreement to practice justice and every virtue makes a closer kinship than that of blood, and he who abandons this enters his name in the list not only of strangers and foreigners but of mortal enemies" (cf. *Spec.* 1.317–318).

---

[29] For the further exposition of Exod 32, see B. S. Childs, *Exodus: A Commentary* (Old Testament Library; London, 1977), 553–81.
[30] See further on this Seland, *Establishment Violence in Philo and Luke,* 155–58.

We find similar emphases in his use of the *Phinehas episode* from Num 25.[31] The Phinehas episode is mentioned in eight passages from Philo's works: five in his allegorical works and three in his *Expositio*.[32]

In the Torah (Num 25) the sin of the people is depicted as both adultery and idolatry, the former issue reported of Zimri though no offering by him is explicitly stated. The issue of sexual sin made it easy for Philo to use the episode in his expositions on the fight to be fought against pleasure, and this is the explicit context of his use of the Phinehas episode in *Leg.* 3.242; *Post.* 183; *Mut.* 108; and *Mos.* 1.301ff. (cf. 1.263ff.). It is also more or less inherent in the other passages of *Ebr.* 73 and *Conf.* 57. This emphasis colors Philo's exposition of such elements in the story as the name Phinehas, his spear, the womb of the woman, and Phinehas's reward. The expositions of the Phinehas episode in these passages thus contain rather extensive allegorizations, but Philo nevertheless keeps firmly in mind the picture of Phinehas in Num 25 in his comments.

Among the most interesting features of his expositions here are his descriptions of Phinehas as driven by ζῆλος, a ζῆλος even characterized as a "zeal for God" (*Post.* 183) or "zeal of God" (ὁ ζηλώσας τὸν ὑπερ θεοῦ ζῆλον, *Leg.* 3.242). Not to be ignored is the comment Philo adds in *Ebr.* 74 showing that the historical situation is not denied in the allegorical passages:

> Surely such a one must pass for a murderer in the judgement of the multitude [παρὰ πολλοῖς], and be condemned by custom the woman-like, but in the judgement of God the all-ruling Father he will be held worthy of laud and praise beyond reckoning and of prizes that cannot be taken from him—two great and sister prizes, peace and priesthood.

Philo's use of the Phinehas episode in the *Expositio* is given in his works *Mos.* 1.301–304; *Spec.* 1.56–57; and *Virt.* 34ff. By some additions to the story as recorded in Num 25, Philo emphasizes the role of Zimri.

In both Philo's *Spec.* 1.54–57 and *Mos.* 1.303–304, as well as in some rabbinic texts, Phinehas's action is given in highly positive terms; he was acting as a mediator between God and men. This positive application of the Phinehas episode is corroborated by the fact that the feature of the

---

[31] Ibid., 132–36; Louis H. Feldman, "The Portrayal of Phinehas by Philo, Pseudo-Philo and Josephus," *Jewish Quarterly Review* 92 (2002): 315–45.

[32] In the allegorical writings, *Leg.* 3.242; *Post.* 182; *Ebr.* 73; *Conf.* 57; *Mut.* 108; in the *Expositio, Mos.* 1.301; *Spec.* 1.56–57; *Virt.* 34ff. (Phinehas is not explicitly mentioned in the last). In the *allegorical writings* Philo uses the Phinehas episode in various contexts, but that of the fight against pleasure is the most prominent, and he gives allegorical explanations for several aspects of Phinehas and his action.

criticism of Phinehas found in Phinehas traditions in Pseudo-Philo *Biblical Antiquities* 47:1 and in some later rabbinic traditions is absent in the works of Philo. His use of the episode is positive and endorsing.

I admit the danger of anachronistic readings of these texts when using them as evidence for Philo's views on "violence." They nevertheless demonstrate how he in his social world of Alexandria, and in the context of his symbolic universe, used these cases from the Torah. And to understand him, we have to familiarize ourselves with his contexts too. To Philo these texts represented cases from the law of God and as such represented part of the constitution of Israel, a people "living under the best of constitutions" (*Conf.* 141). He finds this law to be in accordance to nature and righteous and good. These aspects are also inherent in his presentation of the importance of *ius talionis* (*Spec.* 3.181ff.);[33] the punishments prescribed has to resemble the crimes condemned (3.182):

> Our law exhorts us to equality when it ordains that the penalties inflicted on offenders should correspond to their actions, that their property should suffer if the wrongdoing affected their neighbour's property, and their bodies if the offence was a bodily injury, the penalty being determined according to the limb, part or sense affected , while if his malice extended to taking another's life his own life should be the forfeit.

The *ius talionis* is thus strongly upheld, though Philo is also aware of that the particular circumstances of a crime has to be taken into consideration when meeting out the punishments to be inflicted (3.183).

The love of God (see above) and the willingness to serve God is to be the primary tie and focus of affinity. It has been stated that Philo never quotes the Old Testament injunction of loving one's neighbor as oneself (Lev 19:18b, 34), nor does he seem to allude to it in any of his works. His all-embracing emphasis is rather on the love toward God: that is, the θεοφιλής aspect is emphasized.[34] This is not correct. Philo uses Lev 19:34 in *Spec.* 1.51–53 and *Virt.* 102–104.[35] The obligation to love one's neighbors or relatives is, however, restricted by Philo in several texts. As demonstrated above, Abraham is praised for his disregard of family ties both in connection with his departure form his father's house (*Abr.* 67) and in his willingness to sacrifice Isaac (*Abr.* 167–199), and the Levites are similarly praised (*Spec.* 3.124–125; *Mos.* 2.170–173; etc.). Instead of affirming

---

[33] Cf. here Exod 21:24; Lev 24:19–21; Deut 19:21.

[34] A. Nissen, *Gott und der Nächste im antiken Judentum* (Wissenschaftliche Untersuchungen zum Neuen Testament 15; Tübingen, 1974), 304–5.

[35] Peder Borgen, "The Golden Rule, with Emphasis on Its Usage in the Gospels," in *Paul Preaches Circumcision and Pleases Men* (Trondheim: Tapir, 1983), 99–114.

here such ties of friendship or family, Philo declares that there should be one tie of affinity, the willingness to serve God, and that every word and deed should promote the cause of piety and "the honor of God, which is the dissoluble bond of all affection which makes us one." The same willingness to disregard family ties is also emphasized in his exposition of Deut 13 on how to cope with false prophets (*Spec.* 1.315–318).

CASES OF ESTABLISHMENT VIOLENCE?

In another work I have dealt with some texts in *De Specialibus Legibus* in which I find Philo arguing for actions to be taken by way of "establishment violence" against Jewish transgressors of the law.[36] I shall here comment further on two of these texts in light of our particular topic, namely, *Spec.* 1.54–57 and 1.315–318. For a fuller treatment of these texts, I must refer to the work just mentioned.

Both texts are part of Philo's exposition of the two first commandments of the Decalogue (1.12–345); the first deals with those who "betray the honor due to the one God"; the second deals with false prophets and family members seducing into worshipping other gods.

SPEC. 1.54–57. Philo states this case thus: "But if any members of the nation betray the honor due to the One, they should suffer the most severe penalties." And concerning the actions to be taken against such transgressors, he says: "And it is well that all who have a zeal for virtue should be permitted to exact the penalties offhand and without no delay, without bringing the offender before jury or council or any kind of magistrate at all." Then he legitimates this procedure further with a brief reference to the Phinehas episode from Num 25 ("There is recorded in the Laws the example of...").

The crime described is introduced by the pregnant expression "betray the honor due to the One" (καθυφίενται τὴν τοῦ ἑνὸς τιμήν).[37] This should be read as a strong expression denoting shaming their God by apostasizing. The direct object for the verb καθυφίενται in 1.54 is given as τοῦ ἑνὸς τιμήν: "the honor due to the One." To understand the importance of this aspect in the present text, it must be read in light of Philo's emphasis on the oneness of God and the honor due to him. To Philo, the honoring of God is closely related to observance of the law and to the worship of the one true God. The gravest mistake a man can make is to fail to honor the One, the only living God (*Legat.* 347), the Creator of all things (*Legat.* 293).

---

[36] See here Seland, *Establishment Violence in Philo and Luke,* esp. 103–181.

[37] Καθυφίενται, pres. med. of καθυφίεμι is here used transitively like active. It is to be found only here and in *Spec.* 3.61 among the works of Philo. Liddell and Scott lexicalize it as having the meaning of "to give up, surrender treacherously."

That God is the only truly existent God is stated in Philonic expressions that function almost as formulas (see *Spec.* 1.313, 331; *Virt.* 34, 40, 102, 114; *Praem.* 123).

The description of the measures to be taken against the culprits is first stated very briefly: "they should suffer the utmost penalties" (ταῖς ἀνωτάτω τιμωρίαις ὀφείλουσι κολάζεσθαι). The expression is very short, but it is most probable that the punishment it signifies is capital punishment. This interpretation can be supported by several observations: first, by the expression ταῖς ἀνωτάτω τιμωρίαις as used in other Philonic texts, then by the description of the practice and legitimation that follow in 1.55–57, and lastly from the description of the capital punishment to be inflicted on the transgressors of the five first commandments, as stated in *Spec.* 2:242ff.[38]

Our interpretation of the expression ταῖς ἀνωτάτω τιμωρίαις ὀφείλουσι κολάζεσθαι as an injunction to kill the transgressor on the spot is strengthened by Philo's outright denial of any need to consult the courts or any officials concerned with regular trials. Instead, the agents are to consider themselves as executing the functions usually carried out in court procedures (*Spec.* 1.55):

> And it is well that all who have a zeal for virtue should be permitted to exact the penalties offhand and with no delay, without bringing the offender before jury or councilor any kind of magistrate at all, and give full scope to the feelings which possess them that hatred of evil and love of God which urges them to inflict punishment without mercy on the impious. They should think that the occasion has made them councillors, jurymen, high sheriffs, members of assembly, accusers, witnesses, laws, people, everything in fact, so that without fear or hindrance they may champion religion in full security.

Thus, the punishment suggested by Philo for betraying the honor due to the One God is death. Its execution, furthermore, should not be given over to those responsible for regular court procedures but carried out on the spot. When such gross transgressions were discovered "in flagrante," the situation itself would make the witnesses liable to perform all the functions usually carried out by regular court procedures and functionaries. Hence Philo here does not present the punishment to be inflicted as a measure of disciplinary punishment, but—in light of the categories of our model and from the viewpoint of official law—as measures of "vigilantism." How these actions were to be carried out is not, however, explicitly stated by Philo. Stoning might have been thought of as the most regular

---

[38] See further on this Seland, *Establishment Violence in Philo and Luke*, 122–25.

means (cf. *m. Sanh.* 9:6), but whatever means available at the crucial moment might have been acceptable.

The persons to take action against the transgressors are described in *Spec.* 1.55 thus: "And it is well that all who have a zeal for virtue [ἅπασι τοῖς ζῆλον ἔχουσιν ἀρετῆς] should be permitted to exact the penalties offhand and with no delay" (cf. 1.316; 2.252–254). Then, having stated that they should not bring the offender before any jury, and so forth, Philo characterizes the situation thus: they should "give full scope to the feelings which possess them, that hatred of evil and love of God which urge them to inflict punishment without mercy on the impious" (ἀλλὰ τῷ παραστάντι μισοπονήρῳ πάθει καὶ φιλοθέῳ καταχρῆσθαι πρὸς τὰς τῶν ἀσεβῶν ἀπαραιτήτους κολάζεις). Important issues here are the "affective emphasis" of the agents denoted and the question whether some particular groups are meant by these descriptions.

The characterization in the present passage, furthermore, receives a additional specification in 1.56–57, where the Phinehas episode is used as a legitimating example. Phinehas is the great figure associated with ζῆλος in the history of Israel.[39] In several passages Philo too, associates him with the performance of ζῆλος (cf. *Leg.* 3.242; *Conf.* 57; *Post.* 183; *Mut.* 108).

The "affective emphasis" of this ζῆλος, so typical in descriptions of "the Zealots" in Palestine[40] is indicated by several features as present here too. The expression νομίσαντας κτλ. of 1.55 represents an aspect in some other comparable texts of Philo. In *Spec.* 1.316 (see below) it is said that those who would rush to take vengeance on the unholy seducer would do so κρίνοντες εὐαγὲς τὸ κατ' αὐτοῦ φονᾶν ("deem it a religious duty to seek his death"). A similar statement is given in *Spec.* 3.96, which deals with the measures to be taken against μάγοι and φαρμακευταί: "And therefore it is right that even the most reasonable and mild-tempered should seek the blood of these, that they should lose hardly a moment in becoming their executioners, and should *hold it a religious duty* to keep their punishment in their own hands and not commit it to others" (καὶ νομίσαντας εὐαγὲ τὴν τιμωρίαν ἐπιτρέπειν ἀλλ' ἑαυτοῖς). Similar sayings are also to be found in Philo's retelling of the Levites' action in the desert (*Spec.* 3.26–27) and of Moses' killing the Egyptian (*Mos.* 1.44). Accordingly, there are cases where it is right to kill on the spot a violator of the Torah, and such an action should be deemed holy, as "a religious duty" (*Spec.* 3.128). These aspects surely point to features of "affective emphasis" among the agents thus

---

[39] Cf. Martin Hengel, *The Zealots: Investigations into the Jewish Freedom Movement in the Period from Herod I until 70 A.D.* (trans. David Smith; Edinburgh: T&T Clark, 1989), and Seland, *Establishment Violence in Philo and Luke*, 42–72, 126–36.

[40] Hengel, *Zealots*, 62.

described. Furthermore, in 1.55 this aspect is described thus: They should "give full scope to the feelings which possess them, that hatred of evil and love of God which urges them to inflict punishment without mercy on the impious" (ἀλλὰ τῷ παραστάντι μισοπονήρῳ πάθει καιφιλοθέῳ καταχρῆσθαι πρὸς τὰς τῶν ἀσεβῶν ἀπαραιτήτους κολάσεις). Here this comes as an explanation of their zeal and is in accordance with *Spec.* 4.14, where Philo says that "everyone who is inspired with zeal for virtue [ζῆλος ἀρετῆς], is severe of temper and absolutely implacable against manstealers." The "affective emphasis" of this ζῆλος was thus well known to Philo. The same emotional aspect is followed up by the injunction to exact the penalties "offhand and with no delay"[41] and "without fear or hindrance" (*Spec.* 3.96) and by the statement that the punishment is to be inflicted "without mercy" on the impious.[42] Hence we have here not only a text where Philo admonishes zealous persons to take action but one where he also explicitly points to their feelings of anger and suggests a rapid and violent action on the spot.

The question whether some particular groups are meant by such descriptions is more difficult to decide. But texts as 1 Maccabees and *m. Sanh.* 9:6 seem to attest that violent zealous measures against some nonconformers to the Torah was considered to have been carried out. As I comprehend these texts, Philo—though living in a different time and place—gave injunctions to similar vigilante behavior. The descriptions of the "zealots" in *Spec.* 1.56–57 are rather close to those of *m. Sanh.* 9:6. Both deal with transgressions of the Torah; both concern measures not needing regular court procedures; and both characterize the agents as "zealous." According to J.-A. Morin, it is "tout à fait remarquable où l'exégète alexandrin ... décrit des ζηλωταί qui ressemblent étrangement à ceux de la Mishna."[43] It may be remarkable, but it is hardly to be denied.

---

[41] See the expression ἐκ χειρός ("offhand") as an expression denoting killing on the spot. In *Spec.* 3.91 and 4.10 Philo uses αὐτοχειρία ("with his own hand"). But this could as well be translated "on the spot" or "offhand." Cf. also *Ebr.* 66; *Mos.* 1.303, 308; *Spec.* 3.96.

[42] The expression here translated "without mercy," the Greek ἀπαραιτήτους, meaning "inexorable," "inevitable," "not to be turned away with prayer," signifies the absence of mercy in several descriptions of punishment for specific severe crimes. See *Legat.* 305; *Ebr.* 3.135 on the case of priests entering the holy of holies, *Legat.* 212 on Gentiles entering the temple, *Spec.* 3.76 on sexual intercourse with a betrothed girl, and 4.19 on manstealers. Cf. further on those imitating Phinehas at Sittim (Num 25): *Mos.* 1.303; on the anger of Gaius Caligula: *Legat.* 192 and 244; and lastly of the wrath of God: *Gig.* 47; *Immut.* 48.68; *Ebr.* 116.

[43] J. A. Morin, "Les deux derniers des douze: Simon le zélote et Judas Isakariôth," *Revue Biblique* 80 (1975): 340–41. The Mishnaic text that Morin has in mind is *m. Sanh.* 9:6. Cf. ibid., 340.

SPEC. 1.315–318. According to our reading of this text, Philo here, by his exposition of Deut 13:1ff., advocates zealotic self-redress or establishment violence to be carried out against some seducers to apostasy, taken in flagrante. The crime is described very closely to Deut 13:1ff.[44]

The most relevant section concerning the way to cope with such seducing prophets, friends, or family members is 1.316b:

> We must punish him as a public and general enemy, taking little thought for the ties which bind us to him: and we must send round a report of his proposals to all lovers of piety, who will rush with a speed which brooks no delay to take vengeance on the unholy man, and deem it a religious duty to seek his death.

In Deut 13, the regulations on what is to be done with the seducers to idolatry is given both after the description of the false prophet (Deut 13:6) and after the warning against family members (13:10). Philo, however, presents his understanding of the measures first after his description of the seductive family members. In addition, he makes some other important deviations in describing the measures to be taken.

In 317 Philo motivates the recommended action by an elaboration of his understanding of the really significant kinship (οἰκειότης) to be kept and retained even at the loss of relationship based on blood. But preceding this he presents his understanding of the LXX expression ἀναγγέλλων ἀναγγελεῖς (Deut 13:10). Philo's interpretation of this issue seems to indicate he is not thinking about punishment to be taken by the authorities, especially not by Roman authorities, but rather about measures taken by self-help on the spot.

Philo's description of the punishment to be inflicted upon the seducer is important for understanding his view of the disruptive consequences of such seductive activities. The seducer must be punished ὡς δήμιον καὶ

---

[44] The texts of Philo runs thus: "Further, if anyone cloaking himself under the name and guise of a prophet and claiming to be possessed by inspiration [σχῆμα προφητείας ὑποδύς, ἐνθουσιᾶν καὶ κατέχεσθαι δοκῶν] lead us on to the worship of the gods recognized in the different cities, we ought not to listen to him and be deceived by the name of prophet. For such a one is no prophet, but an impostor [γόης γὰρ ἀλλ' οὐ προφήτης ἐστιν ὁ τοιοῦτος], since his oracles are falsehoods invented by himself. And if a brother or son or daughter or wife or a housemate or a friend, however true, or anyone else who seems to be kindly disposed, urge us to a like course, bidding us fraternize with the multitude [συνασμενίζειν τοῖς πολλοῖς], resort to their temples, and join in their libations and sacrifices, we must punish him as a public and general enemy, taking little thought for the ties which bind us to him."

κοινὸν ἐχθρόν, "as a public and general enemy." He is to be treated as an enemy of the Jewish community as he has incited his own folk to leave their ancestral traditions of honoring the one and only God. Therefore, one must not consider the incidental family ties (οἰκειότητος) that may exist as a hindrance to his punishment but take his life as soon as possible. This is most clearly borne out by what follows in the text of Philo.

Philo has no explicit injunctions as to *how* the seducer is to be killed. It is not explicitly stated in the text of the Torah how the false prophet is to be killed (Deut 13:6), but only that he is to be done away with (καὶ ἀφανιεῖς τὸν πονηρὸν ἐξ ὑμῶν αὐτῶν). The text of Deut 13:11, however, clearly prescribes the punishment of stoning for the other seducers (cf. the expression καὶ λιθοβολήσουσιν αὐτὸν ἐν λίθοις, καὶ ἀποθανεῖται; cf. also Deut 17:2ff., where stoning is presented as the punishment for idolatry).

The relevant part of *Spec.* 1.315–318, dealing with the agents, can be translated thus (1.316c):

> we must punish him as a public and general enemy, taking little thought for the ties which bind us to him: and we must send round a report of his proposals to all lovers of piety [πᾶσι τοῖς εὐσεβείας ἐρασταῖς], who will rush with a speed which brooks no delay to take vengeance on the unholy man, and deem it a religious duty to seek his death.

The text used as basis here is Deut 13:6ff., especially verse 10, the latter that in its Septuagintal form reads: ἀναγγέλλων ἀναγγελεῖς περι αὐτοῦ, αἱ χεῖρές σου ἔσονται ἐπ' αὐτὸν ἐν πρώτοις ἀποκτεῖναι αὐτόν, καὶ αἱ χεῖρες παντὸς τοῦ λαοῦ ἐπ' ἐσχάτῳ, καὶ λιθοβολήσουσιν αὐτὸν ἐν λίθοις, καὶ ἀποθανεῖται. Philo does not mention the stoning, and his exposition of how the punishment is to be carried out seems to be more dependent upon his understanding of the Greek LXX expression ἀναγγέλλων ἀναγγελεῖς. Philo's interpretation of this expression seems to indicate that he is not thinking about punishment taken by the authorities, especially not by the Roman authorities, but rather about measures taken on the spot.

The most natural interpretation of the Masoretic Text and the translation of the LXX is to take the Old Testament expression as an injunction to report the seducer to the authorities (cf. Deut 17:2ff.). But in Philo the relevant expression ἀναγγέλλων ἀναγγελεῖς has been changed to διαγγελτέον πᾶσι τοῖς εὐσεβείας ἐρασταῖς, who are then supposed to take immediate action. There is no good reason to interpret this as a description of the authorities. The expression εὐσεβείας ἐρασταῖς is found only here and in *Virt.* 218, the latter being a description of Abraham striving for virtue. It may be more helpful to compare the expression concerned here with *Spec.* 1.54, where the true adherents of the Mosaic constitution are described as belonging to the τάξιν εὐσεβείας καὶ ὁσιότητος and even with those described there as having "zeal for virtue." Its significance may be illuminated by reference to the action taken by Phinehas against the Midianites, an action Philo describes as being a battle for εὐσεβείας καὶ ὁσιότητος (*Mos.* 1.307) and, further, the Levites' actions taken against their kinsmen after the episode with the golden calf in the desert (*Spec.* 1.79; 3.127; *Mos.* 2.173, 274). This last proposal of mine is strengthened by the fact that the expression κρίνοντες εὐαγές (1.316c) or similar formulations are especially associated by Philo with the action of taking reprisals against apostates or idolaters. In *Spec.* 1.79 it is said that the Levites who were thus "carrying to the end their championship of piety [ὑπὲρ εὐσεβείας ἀγῶνας] were held to have done a truly religious deed" (εὐαγὲς ἔδοξαν ἔργον εἰργάσθαι; cf. also *Spec.* 1.96 and *Mos.* 1.44).

Philo, then, does not have the authorities in mind as subjects for the measures to be taken against the seducers, but his injunction is to be understood as an admonition to all lovers of piety to kill the seducer, keeping the execution in their own hands. Hence the measures to be taken should not be considered as official disciplinary measures carried out by the legal authorities, but as measures of violence of the kind here categorized as establishment violence. Philo himself legitimates this thus (*Spec.* 1.317–318):

> For we should have one tie of affinity [οἰκειότης], one accepted sign of goodwill, namely the willingness to serve God and that our every word and deed promotes the cause of piety. But as for these kinships [συγγένειαι], as we call them, which have come down from our ancestors and are based on blood-relationship, or those derived from intermarriage or other similar causes, let them all be cast aside if they do not seek earnestly the same goal, namely the honor of God, which is the indissoluble bond of all the affection which makes us one.
>
> For those who are so minded will receive in exchange kinships of greater dignity and sanctity. This promise of mine is confirmed by the law, where it says that they who do "what is pleasing" to nature and what is "good" are sons of God. For it says, "Ye are sons to your Lord God," clearly meaning that He will think it fit to protect and provide for you as would a father. And how much this watchful care will exceed that of men is measured, believe me, by the surpassing excellence of Him who bestows it.

THEORETICAL OR PRACTICAL ADMONITIONS?

Are there then no mitigating aspects in Philo's texts on the use of coercion, violence, and force? Is he always a stern, zealotlike, Torah-observing Jew who knows no compromises in his actualizing comments and expositions of the law? Or is he only dealing with theoretical expositions? If not, how can Philo, the apologete, be harmonized with these stern expositions of the Torah? These problems may partly be due to the fact that Philo is never in these texts dealing with the phenomena of "violence" as such. On the other hand, a closer reading of his texts may reveal some compromising attitudes. We admit they are not many but shall point briefly to three aspects: the role of allegory in some of his expositions, the issue of *philanthropia*, and his awareness of the still-pending eschatological realization of the perfect.

Philo's writings testify to the existence of several groups, or rather tendencies, within the Alexandrian communities concerning the interpretations of the Hebrew scriptures. Most important here are the so-called literalists and the allegorizers. These again may be further divided into faithful literalists or allegorizers and unfaithful literalists or allegorizers. And there are some that use both approaches.[45] According to *Migr.* 89–93, Philo upheld both a literal and an allegorical reading of the Torah. To him they belong together as body and soul. He may, however, nevertheless occasionally prefer an allegorical interpretation (*Det.* 95; 167), especially in order to avoid anthropomorphic understandings of God. Sometimes he may offer both literal and allegorical interpretations without making reservations or preferences concerning the one or the other (e.g., in his *De Abrahamo*).

In *Spec.* 4.173–180 he offers both kinds of interpretations, but it looks like he himself here prefers the allegorical. The text deals with the punishment to be inflicted upon a woman who in a heated situation of conflict caught hold of the genitals of a male opponent (Deut 25:11–12). According to a literal reading of the Torah, her hand is to be cut off. Philo, however, seems to find this to be too far-going and introduces an allegorical interpretation offered by some who "think that most of the contents of the law-book are outwards symbols of hidden truths" (4.178), and he even adds another allegorical exposition of himself (4.180). Philo does not explicitly present this because of the cruelty of the literal reading but as one he has "heard from highly gifted men" (4.178).

Furthermore, in his treatise *On the Virtues* (*De Virtutibus*), sections 50–174, he deals with the human aspect of the Mosaic law, with the φιλανθρωπία. Here Philo is highly apologetic and tries to argue against accusations of the Jewish law as being misanthropic.[46] He points to the

---

[45] See further on these issues some recent articles: e.g., David M. Hay, "Philo's References to Other Allegorists," *Studia Philonica* 6 (1979–80); idem, "Defining Allegory in Philo's Exegetical World," in *Society of Biblical Literature Seminar Papers, 1994* (ed. Eugene H. Lovering Atlanta: Scholars Press, 1994), 55–68.

[46] Cf. on this section Peder Borgen, "Philantropia in Philo's Writings: Some Observations," in *Biblical and Humane: Festschrift for John Priest* (ed. Linda Bennett

willingness of the law to accept proselytes, drawing upon Lev 19:34 (*Virt.* 102–104), and he adds the laws concerning the treatment of enemies in wartime (*Virt.* 109–115) as examples and proof of their φιλανθρωπία. But in a passage to which I have found no true parallel in his works, he admits that the conditions envisaged by Moses the lawgiver are still a part of the eschatological fulfillment to come (*Virt.* 119–120):

> This is what our most holy prophet through all his regulations especially desires to create, unanimity, neighbourliness, fellowship, reciprocity of feeling, whereby houses and cities and nations and countries and the whole human race may advance to supreme happiness. Hitherto, indeed, these things live only in our prayers, but they will, I am convinced, become facts beyond all dispute, if God, even as he gives us the yearly fruits, grants that the virtues should bear abundantly.

But I have to admit, these features are very rare in Philo's expositions. Philo is an expositor of the law of God; he does not focus here on the issue of "violence" as such but on the role of the law in establishing and confirming the people as the people of God and the promotion of the honor of God.

Finally, this last question remains: Did Philo really support such zealotic and "violent" attitudes and actions as discussed above? Is it really plausible that the "historical Philo" supported "establishment violence"? These are much-discussed questions.[47] Any answer should at least consider the following aspects: As we nowhere have a report in Philo's works of actual cases of Jewish intramural establishment violence being carried out, we have no such evidence to argue from. And we do not have any other sources witnessing that Philo engaged in some ways in such actions. What we have, however, are his discussions of such capital cases as the texts presented above (see also *Spec.* 2.252–254).

But then one should also pay attention to some other aspects. Philo apparently knew about zealous persons being present in Alexandria. In *Spec.* 2.253 he presupposes the presence of "thousands ... full of zeal for the laws, strictest guardians of the ancestral institutions, merciless to those who do anything to subvert them." In spite of the obvious rhetorical exaggerations in the expression ("thousands"), Philo obviously expected the interference of such persons as a real possibility (cf. here also 1.55; 1.316b; 4.7–10). Furthermore, according to *Spec.* 2.252–254 and its parallel *Spec.*

Elder, David L. Barr, and Elizabeth Struthers Malbon; Atlanta: Scholars Press, 1996), 173–88; Borgen, *Philo of Alexandria*, 243–60.

[47] See my review of the history of such questions in Seland, *Establishment Violence in Philo and Luke*, 17–42.

2.27–28, Philo knew about two different punishments for the crime of perjury: the lash or death. More importantly, however, Philo explicitly states that he favors the more strict: death (*Spec.* 2.252; cf. 2.27). In *Spec.* 2.28 he characterizes those favoring death as "the better-kind whose piety is extra-fervent." This characterization should then be read as an implicit self-characterization.

Philo can thus be read as giving expositions of the Torah, supporting actions on the spot against violators of the law taken "in flagrante." Arguments against such interpretations are not credibly supported by assertions as "it is difficult to believe that a philosopher and ethical teacher, as Philo was, would have justified any practice of mob killing or mob violence."[48] Neither should the actions argued for by Philo be classified by negative expressions such as "mob killing" or "mob violence," nor should sweeping propositions of what "a philosopher" could propagate be used.[49] G. Alon has suggested, furthermore, that *Spec.* 1.54 attests that Philo here reveals his knowledge of an ancient halakah that was suppressed in later rabbinic traditions, a halakah "which was acted upon in Eretz-Israel and in the Diaspora in Philo's days."[50] He further tries to substantiate his case by pointing to *m. Sanh.* 9:6.[51]

Hence we can conclude: though we have no sources from Philo available that explicitly record actual cases of establishment violence, we have nevertheless his expositions of cases of gross nonconformity to the Torah in which he argues for coercive actions to be taken on the spot. He legitimates his expositions by drawing upon traditions of the great hero Phinehas, and he admonishes the agents to carry out the countermeasures quite independently of any decision of court. In so far as this was contrary to the jurisdiction granted to the Jews in Alexandria, his expositions dealt with here may very well be taken both then and now as evidence for an endorsing attitude to what should be termed "establishment violence." Philo is thus a witness of a trajectory of zealotic "violence" that was in force not only in Palestine but also in the Diaspora. This tradition of "violent" zeal became crucial for both Jews and Christians and their interrelationships in the first century C.E.[52]

---

[48] N. Bentwich, "Philo As Jurist," *Jewish Quarterly Review* 21 (1931): 154.

[49] Cf. the statements by Rosenbaum and Sederberg, "Vigilantism," 25, that "vigilante organisations seem to be composed of members from all segments of society."

[50] G. Alon, "On Philo's Halakha," in idem, *The Jews, Judaism and the Classical World* (Jerusalem, 1977), 89–132.

[51] See also *Jub.* 30:7; 30:14–15; and *b. Sanh.* 8b, 80b. and *m. Sanh.* 4:4.

[52] See, e.g., Torrey Seland, "Once More—The Hellenists, Hebrews and Stephen: Conflict and Conflict Management in Acts 6–7," in *Recruitment, Conquest, and*

SUMMARY

We summarize the main arguments of our discussion on (re)presentations of "violence" in the works of Philo thus:

- Philo was a member of the elite sectors of the Jewish community in Alexandria, writing voluminous works in which he commented on biblical books and contemporary problems and issues.

- the Jewish community in Alexandria had an institution of their own called "politeuma," but they nevertheless were not granted the right of carrying out death penalties, even though such punishments were described and prescribed in their own law, the Torah of Moses.

- in his expositions, Philo very seldom explicitly argued against the laws laid down in the Torah on capital punishments; however, he occasionally strengthened the measures of the Torah (*Spec.* 1.54–57; 1.315–318) and might sometimes even argue for death penalty in cases where no such measures were given in the Torah (e.g., *Spec.* 2.252 on perjury).

- Philo adhered to, and thus confirmed, the rule of *ius talionis* of the Torah, arguing that the penalties inflicted should correspond to the actions; "an eye for an eye'.

- pivotal value in upholding the law and its standards were the honor due to the one God; even ties of kinship were subordinated to this commitment. Several examples from the Torah were used by Philo in arguing this point, the Levites being a major example.

- in several cases Philo could adduce the value of zeal for God as a legitimating aspect for taking actions on the spot against transgressors of the Torah, especially when they were taken "in flagrante." Phinehas was the primary role model in this regard.

- if the term "violence" is replaced by coercion, "violence" can be defined as "illegitimate coercion," and "legitimate coercion" as "force." In light of the Roman laws, the actions of the pogrom in 38 C.E. should be termed social group control vigilantism (establishment violence). In light of the Roman laws Jewish actions on the spot against their own culprits might be labeled establishment violence too, that is, illegitimate coercion in defense of status quo of the Jewish law. In light of the Torah, however, such actions were to be considered legitimate coercion (though carried out in an illegitimate way), hence "force."

Conflict: Strategies in Judaism, Early Christianity, and the Greco-Roman World (ed. Peder Borgen, Vernon K. Robbins, and David B. Gowler; Emory Studies in Early Christianity; Atlanta: Scholars Press, 1998), 169–207; L. W. Hurtado, "Pre-70 CE Jewish Opposition to Christ-Devotion," *Journal of Theological Studies* 50 (1999): 35–58; Torrey Seland, "Saul of Tarsus and Early Zealotism: Reading Gal 1.13–14 in Light of Philo's Writings," *Biblica* 83 (2002): 449–71.

Tradition in Transition, or Antioch versus Sepphoris: Rethinking the Matthean Community's Location

Aaron M. Gale
West Virginia University

PRELIMINARY OBSERVATIONS: MATTHEW'S COMMUNITY AS A CITY CHURCH

It is likely that Christianity grew within urban environments.[1] Therefore a plausible place to locate the Matthean community is in a major city. A brief survey of scholarship reveals that this is a reasonable premise. For example, Jack Dean Kingsbury states, "Indeed, there is good reason to believe that the Matthean community was a 'city church' that was materially well off."[2] Evidence for this position also comes from the text. For instance, Matthew favors the word πόλις ("city"), in contrast to Mark's usage of the term κώμη ("village").[3] Matthew utilizes the former term twenty-six times, but κώμη only four times. Matthew 11:1 states, "And when Jesus had finished instructing his twelve disciples, he went on from there to teach and preach in their cities." Mark, however, uses

---

[1] A good example of this theory is found in the work of Wayne A. Meeks. See *The First Urban Christians: The Social World of the Apostle Paul* (New Haven: Yale University Press, 1983), 10–11 and passim. Although Meeks concentrates mostly on Paul, he does note that the cities played a role in the development of Christianity beyond the apostle's work. On page 10 he states, "This preoccupation with the cities was not peculiar to Paul. Before Paul's conversion the believers in Messiah Jesus had already carried their new sectarian message into the Jewish communities of the Greco-Roman cities."

[2] Jack Dean Kingsbury, "The Verb Akolouthein ('to Follow') as an Index of Matthew's View of His Community," *Journal of Biblical Literature* 97 (1978): 66.

[3] Jack Dean Kingsbury, *Matthew As Story* (Philadelphia: Fortress, 1986), 125. The following statistics come from here as well.

πόλις only eight times, instead opting to use κώμη seven times. Often Matthew omits Mark's mention of the "village" altogether or changes the term to "city." For instance, Mark 8:23 reads, "And he took the blind man by the hand, and led him out of the village." This line is not found at all in the Matthean Gospel.

Even where that Mark's Gospel does use πόλις, it is often coupled with κώμη. Mark 6:56 states, "And wherever he came, in villages, cities or country..." Matthew has no direct parallel; the author opts instead for phrases incorporating πόλις or phrases such as "and he went about all Galilee" (4:23) or "so his fame spread throughout all Syria" (14:24). Consider also Mark 6:6, which reads, "And he went about among the villages teaching." Matthew 9:35 reads, "And Jesus went about all the *cities* and villages...." This suggests that Matthew incorporates a more urban tone into the text.

In addition, Matthew links the term οἶκος ("house") to πόλις at least five times, again indicating that the community's permanent dwellings were in or near the city.[4] For example, the magi travel to a city (Bethlehem) and enter the house (2:8–11). Furthermore, in Matt 10:11–12 Jesus instructs the disciples, "And whatever town or village you enter, find out who is worthy in it, and stay with him until you depart. As you enter the house, salute it." Jesus resides in the city of Bethany at the house of Simon the leper (26:6). This suggests that the authors of the Matthean Gospel indicated their own community's location.

Yet some scholars, such as Eduard Schweizer, have postulated that this community was a wandering fringe group located somewhere near the border of Galilee and Syria.[5] In other words, the Matthean community could be seen as similar to the Qumran community. As Kingsbury points out, this is quite similar to Gerd Theissen's view of the early Christians as "wandering charismatics" who gave up all of their goods in order to live and follow in the steps of Jesus.[6] Both scholars (Schweizer and Theissen) seem to portray the Matthean community as wandering monastics, unconcerned with city life or permanent dwellings.

Schweizer cites Matt 8:20 as evidence of Jesus' wandering, rural nature.[7] In this passage Jesus states, "Foxes have holes, and birds of the air

---

[4] Michael H. Crosby, *House of Disciples* (New York: Orbis, 1988), 40.

[5] Eduard Schweizer, *The Good News according to Matthew* (trans. David E. Green; Atlanta: John Knox, 1975), 219. There are other instances as well. To be precise, in this case, while explaining 8:20 Schweizer states, "Thus to follow Jesus in fact is to step forth into insecurity, because the one in whom God comes to men has no home among men; they fail to recognize him."

[6] Kingsbury, "Verb Akolouthein," 63.

[7] Eduard Schweizer, *Matthäus und seine Gemeinde* (SBS 71; Stuttgart: KBW Verlag, 1974), 19–20, 61, 67, 147–48.

have nests; but the Son of man has nowhere to lay his head." Yet this can easily be interpreted to mean that Jesus himself was peripatetic.[8] But the passage in no way indicates that the followers of Jesus or the Matthean Christians followed suit and became nomads. So I dismiss this line of reasoning. In fact, Kingsbury believes that when one compares Matthew to Mark and Luke, it becomes clear that Matthew actually downplays any notion of Jesus as an itinerant.[9]

There are additional cogent reasons for arguing that the Matthean community was an urban group. First, scholars have pointed out that the very language of the Gospel indicates an urban setting. The Koine Greek utilized by the New Testament writers was spoken primarily in the cities.[10] William V. Harris notes, for example, that in Syria, Judea, and Arabia Greek was one of the languages of city governments.[11] The rural areas spoke a different Greek dialect. The form of Koine Greek found in Matthew's Gospel suggests that the text, as well as early Christianity itself, was an urban movement.[12]

Other scholars also disagree with Schweizer's views. As noted above, Kingsbury believes that the Matthean community must have been an urban group. To prove this point, he provides textual evidence. Much of his study centers around Matthew's usage of the verb οκολούθειν ("to follow"). He notes that about half of the usages in the Gospel contain no references to "wandering."[13] Other instances of the verb fail to convince him that the Gospel's intent is to show that Jesus and his disciples were nomads. G. D. Kilpatrick also has noted that the Gospel indicates an urban preference. He points out that in Matt 10:23 and 23:34 the disciples flee from city to city, not to the hills, as one would think.[14] The hills, after all, would have provided a better hiding place. Jesus recites in the former passage, "When they persecute you in one town, flee to the next." In the latter passage Jesus cautions that the prophets, wise men, and scribes will persecuted from "town to town." In both instances the Gospel utilizes πόλις.

---

[8] Kingsbury, "Verb Akolouthein," 65. Jesus may have always wished to be "with" his community. See Matt 1:23; 18:20; and 28:20, where Jesus remains close to his followers.

[9] Ibid., 65.

[10] Gerd Theissen, *Social Reality and the Early Christians* (trans. Margaret Kohl; Minneapolis: Fortress, 1992), 54–55.

[11] William V. Harris, *Ancient Literacy* (Cambridge: Harvard University Press, 1989), 187.

[12] See Meeks, *First Urban Christians*, 9.

[13] Kingsbury, "Verb Akolouthein," 64.

[14] G. D. Kilpatrick, *The Origins of the Gospel according to St. Matthew* (Oxford: Clarendon, 1946), 125.

Furthermore, J. Andrew Overman agrees that the Matthean Gospel must have been written in or near a major city.[15] To begin, the community appears to have lived near a major center of Jewish life, where officials would reside. The tone of Matthew bears this out. For example, in the Gospel Jesus spends much time discussing legal debates.[16] Religiously, this is found in 12:1–8, where Jesus debates with the Pharisees about Sabbath laws. Regarding civil laws, 22:15–22 shows Jesus' view regarding imperial taxation. It seems likely, then, that the community was located near a court (which would be located in a city).[17]

At least two Jewish communities must have been in existence where the Matthean community had settled for such debates to be taking place.[18] This suggests that the place where the Gospel was written was large, indicating an urban location.[19] The tone of the Gospel again indicates an awareness of this struggle for power. Chapter 23, for instance, finds Jesus addressing "the scribes and the Pharisees." The Pharisees, of course, were one of the groups struggling to keep Judaism from disappearing following the disastrous revolt against Rome.

It is plausible that this urban location was located within ancient Israel. Consider Matthew's handling of Mark 1:35–39. Portions of Mark 1:35–38 read, "And in the morning ... he rose and went out to a lonely place.... And he said to them, 'Let us go on to the next towns.' ... And he went throughout all Galilee, preaching in their synagogues and casting out demons." In contrast, the Matthean Gospel omits much of Mark's text. Parts of Matt 4:23–25 state, "And he went about all Galilee, teaching in their synagogues and preaching the gospel.... And great crowds followed him from Galilee and the Decapolis and Jerusalem and Judea and from beyond the Jordan." There is no mention here of "lonely places" or "the next towns." The cities within Israel are what is important to Jesus.

The Matthean Gospel therefore emphasizes Jesus' mission only to Israel.[20] He does not wander about, as other scholars suggest. Furthermore, his actions are largely restricted to Galilee, as 4:23; 9:35; and 11:1 show. Jesus only leaves Galilee for brief periods of time (see 3:13–14; 8:23–9:1;

---

[15] J. Andrew Overman, *Church and Community in Crisis: The Gospel according to Matthew* (Valley Forge, Pa.: Trinity Press International, 1996), 18.

[16] Ibid.

[17] J. Andrew Overman, *Matthew's Gospel and Formative Judaism: The Social World of the Matthean Community* (Minneapolis: Fortress, 1990), 159.

[18] Anthony J. Saldarini believes that the Gospel was authored in a setting "with an established Jewish community." See Anthony J. Saldarini, *Matthew's Christian-Jewish Community* (Chicago: The University of Chicago, 1994), 26.

[19] Overman, Matthew's Gospel, 159.

[20] Kingsbury, "Verb Akolouthein," 65.

16:13–20; etc.). On the basis of such evidence Kingsbury concludes, "In reality, a careful consideration of Matthew's treatment of the region of Galilee reveals that it is the wider, not the narrower, setting for Jesus' activity."[21] In other words, Galilee is the main point of reference found in the Matthean Gospel.

The Matthean community must have been located within a Jewish community that also spoke a good deal of Greek.[22] According to Saldarini, many of the cities in Galilee fit this description. They had sizable Jewish populations as well as many Greek-speaking residents. So both populations must have existed in the same urban region. Furthermore, Saldarini states, "Good-sized cities such as Sepphoris, Tiberias, Capernaum, and Bethsaida, would have had the resources to educate and support a leader and writer such as the author of Matthew."[23] These factors lead me to conclude that the Matthean community must have been located in a major city such as Sepphoris.

THE MATTHEAN COMMUNITY'S LOCATION: ANTIOCH VERSUS SEPPHORIS

The Traditional Location of the Matthean Community: The "Myth of Antioch"

In this paper I argue that the Matthean community was located in Lower Galilee in the city of Sepphoris. Textual and modern archaeological evidence support this position. Yet traditionally, scholars have placed the Matthean community in Syria, often in the prominent city of Antioch.[24] This trend continues into the twenty-first century.[25] Scholars have provided four primary arguments for this position. First, the large city of Antioch became

---

[21] Ibid., 66.

[22] Anthony J. Saldarini, "The Gospel of Matthew and Jewish-Christian Conflict in the Galilee," in *The Galilee in Late Antiquity* (ed. Lee I. Levine; Cambridge: Harvard University Press, 1992), 26–27. In this paragraph I am following Saldarini's line of thought.

[23] Ibid., 27.

[24] One of the first scholars to adopt this view was Burntett Hillman Streeter. See *The Four Gospels: A Study of Origins, Treating the Manuscript Traditions, Sources, Authorship, and Dates* (London: Macmillan, 1964), 16, 500–527. Other scholars followed suit. See, for instance, Eduard Schweizer, "Matthew's Church," in *The Interpretation of Matthew,* (ed. Graham Stanton; Issues in Religion and Theology 3; Philadelphia: Fortress, 1983), 129–30; or Kingsbury, *Matthew As Story,* 121. There are numerous other scholars who also adhere to this theory.

[25] See Donald Senior, "Directions in Matthean Studies," in *The Gospel of Matthew in Current Study* (ed. David E. Aune; Grand Rapids: Eerdmans, 2001), 8.

a center of Christianity by the late first century. With the death of James and the destruction of the holy temple in Jerusalem, the conservative Jewish Christian party's hold on Christianity was weakened, and liberal Christian elements that had existed for some time in Antioch began to gain power.[26] Christianity, according to some scholars, had first spread near Antioch. In fact, the first Gentiles were probably converted there.[27] Acts 11:19–26 indicates that Antioch was an early center of Christianity. This has led many scholars to argue that the Matthean community was located there.

Second, the tone of the Gospel suggests that there was friction between the church community and a nearby group of formative Jews. This is evident by Jesus' admonishment of the scribes and Pharisees in chapter 23. This has led some scholars to posit a Syrian location for the Gospel. To support this view, they point to rabbinic literature, which seems to indicate that Syria was involved in Jewish affairs.[28] In fact, the region had a large Jewish population, as Josephus points out.[29] Syria, then, provided an opportunity for Jews and Christians to function alongside one another.

Hans Drijvers notes that even in the smaller Syrian cities such as Edessa, "Gentiles, Jews, and Christians walked along the same streets, did their shopping at the common market-place, suffered from the same diseases, epidemics and wars, and therefore shared a lot of ideas and concepts about which they talked with each other."[30] This mixture of Jews and Christians, though, undoubtedly would have created an atmosphere of tension from time to time. Matthew 23 conveys this tension, according to some scholars. These conflicting traditions would also have provided the setting required for the development of such a prominent Gospel.[31]

---

[26] Raymond E. Brown and John P. Meier, *Antioch and Rome: New Testament Cradles of Catholic Christianity* (New York: Paulist, 1983), 46–47.

[27] Hans Drijvers, "Syrian Christianity and Judaism," in *The Jews among Pagans and Christians in the Roman Empire* (ed. Judith Lieu, John North, and Tessa Rajak; London: Routledge, 1992), 124.

[28] Some scholars also posit a Syrian location but do not necessarily specify a city. See W. D. Davies, *The Setting of the Sermon on the Mount* (Cambridge: Cambridge University Press, 1964), 295–96. See also *m. Hallah* 4:7–8 or *m. Shevi'it* 6:2 for examples of the rabbinic references.

[29] See *Jewish War* 7.3.3. All excerpts from Josephus come from the following translation: William Whiston, trans., *The Complete Works of Josephus* (Grand Rapids: Kregel, 1981).

[30] Drijvers, "Syrian Christianity and Judaism," 128.

[31] Brown and Meier, *Antioch and Rome,* 22. The community probably was well-versed in the Septuagint as well as the Jewish Christian Gospel of Mark. So the Jewish Christian viewpoint of Matthew is appropriate.

Third, scholars such as Seán Freyne look to textual evidence to support the Antioch hypothesis. For example, the Matthean Gospel mentions Syria by name in 4:24.[32] Furthermore, some scholars have discussed the possibility that Igantius of Antioch was utilizing Matthew in some of his early second-century letters, possibly indicating a "hometown bias" toward the text.[33] Peter's place in the Gospel is also quite prominent. After all, in Matt 16:13–20 Jesus gives Peter "the keys of the kingdom of heaven," and the apostle spent much time in Antioch.[34]

Fourth, the Syrian area surrounding Antioch was multilingual. More than one language was spoken there. Greek was widely spoken, and, since the Matthean Gospel was composed in Greek, some scholars cite this as another reason why the Gospel was written from this location.[35] All these factors together have led many scholars to argue that Matthew's Gospel most likely was written in Antioch.

REFUTATION OF THE "MYTH OF ANTIOCH"

Let us first discuss the issue of language. Many scholars posit an urban Syrian location because Greek was spoken there, in contrast to the Aramaic that was allegedly spoken in Palestine. Since Matthew was written in Greek, these scholars eliminate other regions such as Galilee, where Aramaic may have been the colloquial language. They thereby assign the community to a Syrian city such as Antioch.

Is this the case? It is not true that Aramaic was the only language spoken in Palestine. Greek was also widely spoken throughout Palestine.[36]

---

[32] Seán Freyne, *Galilee from Alexander the Great to Hadrian 323 BCE to 135 CE: A Study of Second Temple Judaism* (Edinburgh: T&T Clark, 1980), 364.

[33] For a good discussion of this topic, consult the essay by William R. Schroedel, "Ignatius and the Reception of the Gospel of Matthew in Antioch," in *Social History of the Matthean Community: Cross-Disciplinary Approaches* (ed. David L. Balch; Minneapolis: Fortress, 1991), 154–77. In particular, see Ignatius's *Letter to the Trallians* 9, *Letter to the Philadelphians* 8:2, and *Letter to Polycarp* 2:1–2.

[34] See Gal 2:11.

[35] David E. Garland, *Reading Matthew: A Literary and Theological Commentary on the First Gospel* (New York: Crossroad, 1995), 3. See also John P. Meier, *The Vision of Matthew: Christ, Church and Morality in the First Gospel* (New York: Paulist, 1979), 13–15. In particular, Meier strongly believes that the most prevalent language in Palestine was Aramaic, not Greek. Therefore, a Greek document such as Matthew must have been written elsewhere, most likely a city like Antioch, in Syria. His reasons for an urban location are also language-based. He claims that Aramaic was a rural language; Greek was more urban. On the basis of this he hypothesizes that the Matthean Gospel must have been written in a city.

[36] Freyne, *Galilee from Alexander,* 139.

Textual and archaeological evidence support this assertion, especially concerning Galilee. In Beth Shearim, located near Sepphoris, 196 Jewish Greek inscriptions have been found.[37] Many are connected to burial inscriptions. Some catacombs contain both Hebrew and Greek inscriptions, as the tomb of one Rabbi Gamaliel indicates. One inscription reads: זו של רבי גמליאל מ. A second one reads: ΡΑΒΙ ΓΑΜΑΛΙΗΛ.[38] Also, Greek texts have been found in other cities in Galilee, such as Nazareth.[39] Josephus acknowledges that although Aramaic was the primary spoken language in Palestine, many Jews also knew Greek.[40] Furthermore, Rabbi Yehudah ha-Nasi states, "Why use the Syrian language [Aramaic] in the land of Israel? Either use the holy tongue [Hebrew] or Greek!"[41] This indicates that Jews were encouraged to speak Greek, not Aramaic, in Palestine. In fact, there seems to have been a bias against speaking Aramaic. But was Greek spoken in cities such as Sepphoris?

The answer is yes. First, the above quote from Yehudah ha-Nasi, a Galilean known to frequent the larger cities, provides evidence for this view.[42] Second, a lead market weight found at Sepphoris, dating from the first century C.E., contains Greek writing.[43] Third, Greek writing appears on many first-century Palestinian coins, further attesting to the region's familiarity with the language.[44] Fourth, archaeological evidence from the city of Beth Shearim supports this theory. In particular, one Greek inscription

---

[37] G. Mussies, "Greek in Palestine and the Diaspora," in *The Jewish People in the First Century* (ed. S. Safrai et al.; Philadelphia: Fortress, 1976), 2:1042–43.

[38] Jack Finegan, *The Archeology of the New Testament: The Life of Jesus and the Beginning of the Early Church* (Princeton: Princeton University Press, 1969), 205.

[39] Eric M. Meyers and James F. Strange, *Archaeology, the Rabbis and Early Christianity* (Nashville: Abingdon, 1981), 83–84. Meyers and Strange also contend that Greek was widely used in Palestine, perhaps second only to Aramaic. See pages 77–88 for their complete discussion.

[40] See *Antiquities* 20.11.1ff. See also J. N. Sevenster, *Do You Know Greek? How Much Greek Could the First Jewish Christians Have Known?* (Leiden: Brill, 1968), 65. Sevenster points out this fact regarding Josephus.

[41] *b. Sotah* 49b. Finegan points out this passage (*Archeology of the New Testament*, 204).

[42] In fact, Jewish legend states that the Mishnah was recorded by Yehuda ha-Nasi in Galilee. What is also interesting is that another prominent rabbi cited in the Mishnah was himself believed to have been a product of Sepphoris. See David Aden-Bayewitz, *Common Pottery in Roman Galilee: A Study of Local Trade* (Romat-Gan, Israel: Bar Ilan, 1993), 26. See *b. Sanhedrin* 19a, 32b, 109a, 113a, and *b. Eruvin* 86b for confirmation of the fact.

[43] Jonathan L. Reed, *Archaeology and the Galilean Jesus* (Harrisburg, Pa.: Trinity Press International, 2000), 121.

[44] Sevenster, *Do You Know,* 122.

found on a white marble slab near a mausoleum (by catacomb 11) is worth noting. It is the epitaph of a Jewish man named "Justus." One phrase reads: καὶ γ' ἐλθὼν εἰς "Αδην. The opening usage of καὶ γε is common both in the LXX and the the New Testament but is rarely found elsewhere in Greek literature.[45] Perhaps the author of the inscription was familiar with these Greek biblical texts.

Most compelling, though, is the phrase "and having gone to Hades." The same phrase has also been found in another Jewish inscription (from the first century) in the Egyptian city of Leontopolis. Furthermore, the Greek word "Αδης is used in the LXX, not in the Hebrew texts. The Hebrew authors would have used שׁאוּל. The author here has chosen the Greek term. Two things follow from these assertions. First, the Egyptian find indicates that similar Greek colloquial expressions may have been in use throughout the first-century cities of the world. Second, the author's use of "Hades" suggests a preference for a Greek term, not a Hebrew one. This proves that the Greek language was in use throughout Galilee.

I argue, then, that the Matthean Gospel could have been written in Greek from a Galilean city such as Sepphoris. It has also been suggested that Greek became prevalent following the Jewish revolt of 66–70 C.E., when the Jewish population was forced to scatter across Judea and Galilee and into other regions. If Greek was already in use to some degree, then it would have spread throughout the rest of Palestine and into other places such as Egypt. The above archaeological evidence supports this assertion. Ultimately, then, the Greek language was prevalent in Palestine. The idea that only Aramaic was used in Galilee is false. Evidence indicates otherwise.

Yet some scholars insist that the social situation in Antioch supports the theory that the Matthean Gospel was written in the city. I have already noted that Antioch contained a mixture of Jewish and Christian inhabitants, providing the diverse culture that the Gospel presupposes. The Gospel was likely composed within a city that contained a large Jewish population. Recall, of course, that the Matthean community was rooted in Judaism. On this basis, these scholars have concluded that Antioch is the most logical choice.

Again, this is mere conjecture. As evidence for the Syrian view, scholars often cite the Mishnah and Talmud. Since the rabbis mention Syria, the area must have contained a concentrated Jewish population. Some passages

---

[45] Moshe Schwabe and Baruch Lifshitz, *Beth She'arim, vol. 2: The Greek Inscriptions* (New Brunswick, N.J.: Rutgers University Press, 1974), 103. I am following these authors here. Schwabe and Lifshitz identify this inscription. For a complete discussion, see pages 97–110.

do indeed allude to the rabbis' familiarity with the Syrian region. Yet these citations are few in number when compared to the rabbis' discussion of Jewish Galilean affairs. Galilee is mentioned numerous times by the rabbis. For instance, the Palestinian Talmud discusses the purchase of wheat in Tiberias and Sepphoris. One passage states, "Had you bought [the wheat] in Tiberias, I would have twenty-five modii; now that you bought it in Sepphoris I have only twenty modii.[46] Another passage from the Babylonian Talmud discusses whether slaughtered animals found between Tiberias and Sepphoris may be eaten lawfully by a Jew.[47]

Furthermore, many rabbis such as Yehuda ha-Nasi are mentioned in connection with the region, including the city of Sepphoris. Rabbi Yohanan, for example, discusses whether one can assume that a dead body found between Tiberias and Sepphoris is that of a Jewish person.[48] Therefore, it is not the case that the Matthean community *must* have been located in Syria, since it is obvious from this evidence that a competing group of formative Jews was also located in Galilee. In addition, according to many sources the Mishnah itself was written in Galilee by Yehuda ha-Nasi around the beginning of the third century.[49] Therefore, it is likely that the formative Jewish group in conflict with the Matthean church was Galilean.

In fact, Antioch itself may have been too big to serve as the Matthean community's base of operation. Antioch, one of the largest cities in the Roman empire, might not have contained the intimate atmosphere necessary for the tension indicated in the Gospel. Scholars estimate its population to have been anywhere from 75,000 to 250,000.[50] Yet in a city that big would the two competing groups have occasion to come into contact with one another that often? In other words, a city such as Sepphoris could have provided the intimate atmosphere necessary for this degree of interaction. Antioch could not. In Antioch the two groups could avoid each other; in Sepphoris this would not have been as easy to do. The conservative Jewish population of Sepphoris no doubt would have heard of the heretical teachings of the nearby Matthean community.

---

[46] *y. Bava Qamma* 9:5, 6d–7a. In this section the following passages have been pointed out by Isaiah Gafni in his article, "Daily Life in Galilee and Sepphoris," in *Sepphoris in Galilee: Crosscurrents of Culture* (ed. Rebecca Martin Nagy et al.; Winona Lake, Ind.: Eisenbrauns, 1996), 51–57.

[47] *b. Bava Metzi'a* 24b.

[48] *y. Sanhedrin* 5:1, 22c.

[49] Geza Vermes, *Jesus the Jew: A Historian's Reading of the Gospels* (Philadelphia: Fortress, 1973), 43, 52. Vermes is not alone in this thinking. Other scholars support this view as well.

[50] Meeks, *First Urban Christians,* 28.

Furthermore, scholars claim that because Ignatius of Antioch possibly cites the Matthean Gospel, the text must have been written nearby.[51] There is no concrete evidence that Ignatius was actually writing about Matthew at all. In fact, Ignatius merely mentions "the gospel," a supposed reference to the Matthean Gospel.[52] This hardly proves that he was familiar with Matthew, but even if was, does this necessarily prove that the Gospel itself had to originate in Antioch? Texts could be distributed over wide areas quite rapidly. The same argument from location is made regarding the early Christian writing called the *Didache,* which some scholars also claim was written in Syria.[53] Yet scholars such as R. T. France dispute these claims, noting the weakness of such arguments.[54] Therefore I dismiss such claims.

In addition, the fact that Peter is mentioned in the Matthean Gospel does not prove that it was written in Antioch. Even if Peter was active in Antioch, it does not mean that the authors of Matthew's Gospel favored Peter in any particular way. It could simply be that the authors wished to emphasize their interest in both the church (remember, Jesus gives Peter the "keys" in 16:13–20) and in the observance of the Torah.[55] In other words, the authors of the Gospel were more concerned with theology than with geography. It did not matter where Peter was. What mattered was the message that Peter could convey to the Matthean community.

Consider also how Matthew portrays Jesus. As Overman points out, the authors of Matthew's Gospel are hesitant to have Jesus leave Galilee

---

[51] Streeter was one of the first scholars to support this view. See *Four Gospels,* 505–7.

[52] *Letter to the Philadelphians* 8:2. Other supposed inferences are found in his *Letter to the Trallians* 9:1 and the *Letter to Polycarp* 2:1–2. Yet none of the references are conclusive.

[53] Streeter, *Four Gospels,* 508–11. Again, Streeter brought up this point, and other scholars seemingly followed suit. He alludes to passages such as 8:1–2; 11:3–4, 7, etc. Again, these passages do not prove anything other than the fact that the authors of the *Didache* were familiar with some of the basic principles and sayings circulating throughout the ancient Roman world. The fact, for instance, that the *Didache* teaches that men should reconcile with each other before coming to the assembly (see 14:2) does not prove that the Matthean community was located in Antioch.

[54] R. T. France, *Matthew: Evangelist and Teacher* (Grand Rapids: Academie Books, 1989), 92–93.

[55] Henry Thatcher Fowler, *The History and Literature of the New Testament* (New York: Macmillan, 1925), 317. Even at this early date, Fowler alluded to this possibility. The author of the Gospel surely incorporated his or her own beliefs and traditions into the text. Hence, Peter may have been only a prominent character who served the author's needs.

at all.[56] He states, "We have noted Matthew's unusual concentration on Galilee. Matthew seems to know Galilee quite well and essentially limits the activity of the Jesus movement to Galilee."[57] Passages such as 4:13; 8:5; 9:1; and 17:22 confirm this. In the first passage, the reader learns that Jesus "dwelt" in Capernaum, while in 9:1 the city is referred to as Jesus' "own city." Jesus also enters Capernaum (8:5) and "gathers" the disciples in Galilee (17:22). In fact, Jesus himself may have visited cities such as Sepphoris and Tiberias, considering that Lower Galilee seemed to be his home region.[58]

Further evidence for Galilee is found in Matthew's portrayal of the Pharisees. The Pharisees, Jesus' main adversaries, were a Galilean group, as 9:11 and 15:1 indicate. The former passage, for example, discusses Jesus' debates with the Pharisees (in Galilee) concerning the laws of table fellowship. The lone exception to this is found in 27:62–66, but Overman explains that this passage was probably a unique insertion placed into the story by the Matthean scribes to implicate the Pharisees in the death of Jesus.[59] After all, the authors of the Gospel sought to put the blame on their adversaries. In this case, the opponents are a Galilean Jewish group. It is logical, therefore, to locate the Matthean community in that region rather than in Antioch. Hence, I dismiss the "Myth of Antioch."

SEPPHORIS: THE HOME TO THE MATTHEAN COMMUNITY

Admittedly, one cannot be sure of the Matthean community's exact location. Yet there are compelling reasons to locate the community in or near the city of Sepphoris. Let us begin with a brief overview of the city. Sepphoris was a major Lower Galilean city that thrived from the first century C.E. until the Byzantine era as a major center of trade and commerce.[60] Scholars have estimated its population to be between 25,000 and 30,000, making it the largest city in Galilee.[61] Many factors contributed to this large

---

[56] Overman, *Church and Community*, 17.

[57] Overman, *Matthew's Gospel*, 159.

[58] Eric M. Meyers, "Jesus and His Galilean Context," in *Archaeology and the Galilee: Texts and Context in the Graeco-Roman and Byzantine Periods* (ed. Douglas R. Edwards and C. Thomas McCollough; Atlanta: Scholars Press, 1997), 60–61.

[59] Overman, *Matthew's Gospel*, 156.

[60] Meyers, "Roman Sepphoris in Light of New Archaeological Evidence and Recent Research," in *The Galilee in Late Antiquity* (ed. Lee I. Levine; Cambridge: Harvard University Press, 1992), 321.

[61] Richard A. Batey, *Jesus and the Forgotten City* (Grand Rapids: Baker, 1991), 136. Josephus also calls it the largest city. See *Jewish War* 3.2.4. Recently, however, this population estimate has been challenged. See Reed, *Archaeology and the Galilean Jesus*, 79–80.

number. First, Sepphoris was located near a major road, which would have provided easy access to those who wished to conduct business there.[62] In fact, the city stood near two major roads: a major east-west highway and a main north-south junction.[63] Its cosmopolitan nature has been cited by scholars as one of the main reasons for the city's reluctance to rebel against Rome during the first-century Jewish revolt.[64] The city was prosperous, and its residents had no real reason to fight the Romans.

Second, according to rabbinic texts, Sepphoris was a prominent Galilean fortress.[65] This would place it among the major Jewish cities of the first century. Third, the area surrounding Sepphoris was quite fertile.[66] As one scholar has noted, "The Hebrew phrase, 'a land flowing with milk and honey,' might best express the exceeding fertility and richness of Galilee at the time of Christ."[67] The city itself was located near a high hill that overlooked the Bet Netofa Valley. This particular valley was noted for its lush green landscape and fertile fields, which served as a bread basket for the city.[68] These factors indicate that Sepphoris was a vital center of Jewish life in the first century.

A final factor may have contributed more than the others to the status of Sepphoris as the most important city in Galilee. Its high status may have been due to bureaucratic reasons. First, it was named as a major governmental seat by Gabinius, the proconsul of Syria, in 55 B.C.E., providing the city with additional importance.[69] Therefore, many key institutions were located there, including a royal bank and an archive.[70] This would have made it vital to Jew and Gentile alike, thereby increasing the amount of traffic that would pass through the city.

The status of Sepphoris as a well-to-do first-century city is confirmed through recent archaeological evidence. Luxurious houses have been unearthed, some complete with exquisite mosaic floorings.[71] In fact, some

---

[62] Ernest W. Gurney Masterman, *Studies in Galilee* (Chicago: Chicago University Press, 1909), 134.

[63] Meyers, "Roman Sepphoris," 321.

[64] For instance, see Stuart S. Miller, *Studies in the History and Traditions of Sepphoris* (Leiden: Brill, 1984), 57.

[65] Freyne, *Galilee from Alexander,* 122. Freyne is referring here to *m. Arakhin* 9:6, where "the old castle of Sepphoris" is mentioned.

[66] Freyne, *Galilee from Alexander,* 122.

[67] Selah Merrill, *Galilee in the Time of Christ* (Oxford: Oxford University Press, 1898), 25.

[68] Batey, *Jesus and the Forgotten City,* 136.

[69] Freyne, *Galilee from Alexander,* 122.

[70] Ibid.

[71] Carolyn Osiek and David L. Balch, *Families in the New Testament World: Households and House Churches* (Louisville: Westminster John Knox, 1997), 13.

of the first-century houses contained luxury items such as molded glass cups and cosmetic items.[72] Paved and colonnaded streets have been found, and a public water works exists near the acropolis.[73] Regarding wealth in Sepphoris, Arlene Fradkin states, "Archaeological excavations ... have revealed a sophisticated urban metropolis complete with colonnaded streets, a theater, an aqueduct system, villas, synagogues, and a large public building."[74]

Furthermore, the city's population was overwhelmingly Jewish.[75] This is important, because Matthew's Jewish Christian community was in conflict with a nearby formative Jewish group. Therefore, if I am to locate the Matthean church in Sepphoris, there needs to be evidence that a sizable Jewish population existed there. Josephus supports this view. He points out that the city's Jewish inhabitants acted as traitors in the war against Rome by refusing to side with the rest of the rebels.[76] The city was an active center of Jewish learning during the rabbinic age.[77] In fact, the Sanhedrin was located in Sepphoris at times during the first century.[78]

Following the first revolt, many Jewish leaders settled in Sepphoris.[79] Also, the Jewish population in Sepphoris was traditional in nature. Rabbi Yose ben Halafta, who lived in and after the last half of the first century, reports that priests resided in the city even after the war against Rome.[80] If the Matthean community was in conflict with a surrounding Jewish one, these Jews would also have been quite conservative, much like an

---

[72] Reed, *Archaeology and the Galilean Jesus*, 126.

[73] Mark Chancey and Eric M. Meyers, "How Jewish Was Sepphoris in Jesus' Time?" *Biblical Archaeology Review* 26/4 (2000): 24.

[74] Arlene Fradkin, "Long Distance Trade in the Lower Galilee: New Evidence from Sepphoris," in *Archaeology and the Galilee: Texts and Context in the Graeco-Roman and Byzantine Periods* (ed. Douglas R. Edwards and C. Thomas McCollough; Atlanta: Scholars Press, 1997), 107.

[75] Meyers, "Roman Sepphoris," 324.

[76] *Jewish War* 3.4.1.

[77] Meyers, "Roman Sepphoris," 330. See the Tosefta, where Sepphoris is mentioned in conjunction with the rabbis. In particular, see *t. Bava Batra* 2:10 and *t. Ma'aser Scheni* 1:13.

[78] Overman, *Matthew's Gospel*, 159. Josephus alludes to this as well. See also *b. Rosh HaShanah* 31ab, where the "Great Court" moved ... ומבית שערים לצפורי ומצפורי לטבריא ("and from Beth Shearim to Sepphoris, and from Sepphoris to Tiberias"). For a brief discussion of the Sanhedrin, see Alexander Guttmann, *Rabbinic Judaism in the Making: A Chapter in the History of the Halakhah from Ezra to Judah I* (Detroit: Wayne State University Press, 1970), 27–28.

[79] Ya'akov Meshorer, *City-Coins of Eretz-Israel and the Decapolis in the Roman Period* (Jerusalem: The Israel Museum, 1985), 36.

[80] Miller, *Studies in the History*, 103. See *m. Ta'anit* 2:5 for the complete report.

aristocratic or priestly group that wished to continue practicing a traditional Jewish faith.

Archaeological evidence also supports the theory that Sepphoris was a Jewish city.[81] First, although thousands of animal bones have been found in the city, almost none are pig bones. Pigs, of course, would not have been consumed by a Jewish population; they are not kosher. Second, 114 fragments of stone vessels have been recovered by archaeologists. This is relevant since Jews preferred stone vessels to metal or glass ones because they believed that stone could never become impure. Hence, stone vessels were favored by Jews for storing pure water for hand washing. John's Gospel mentions such stone vessels that were used for "Jewish rites of purification" (2:6).

Third, many Jewish ritual baths, or *mikva'ot,* have been unearthed in the residential areas of Sepphoris, suggesting a strong Jewish presence in the city. Fourth, coins found in the city dating from the Jewish war contain no images of emperors or pagan deities. This indicates that the residents of Sepphoris were concerned with maintaining Jewish law (which prevented any artificial images or idols). Coins minted in the first century also contain a double cornucopia intersected by a staff. These two symbols are indicative of first-century Jewish coinage.[82] Finally, no remains of any pagan temples or cultic objects dating from the first century C.E. have been found. All of this evidence leads to one conclusion: Sepphoris was a Jewish city.

Accordingly, Sepphoris in Galilee is the most plausible location for the Matthean community. Modern archaeological evidence disproves much of the dated literature discussing the city and its inhabitants. The city fits virtually all of the criteria needed for a Jewish Christian population such as Matthew's. Sepphoris was a wealthy Jewish city with an active economy that allowed Matthew's community the means to produce and distribute a Gospel. A city with a wealthy, conservative, aristocratic Jewish population would have provided the perfect setting for the Gospel, since Matthew's own upstart Jewish Christian church appears to have been arguing with just such a Jewish group over the correct interpretation of the Torah and its laws.

Textual evidence supports the assertion that Jews and Jewish Christians continued to live as distinct competing groups within Sepphoris for quite some time after the birth of Christianity. A passage from the Babylonian Talmud discusses an incident in Sepphoris where the famous Rabbi

---

[81] Chaney and Meyers, "How Jewish Was Sepphoris," 25–27. The archaeological evidence cited in this paragraph is taken from this article.

[82] Ibid., 24.

Eliezer agreed with a follower of Jesus on a point of Jewish religious law.[83] This follower of Jesus, named Jacob of Siknin, is referred to as "a healer in Yeshua's name."[84] Matthew's own Jewish Christian orientation was evident in that the Gospel clearly exhibited an intense fervor for the Torah. This zeal for the Torah was important. A large portion of the Matthean Gospel deals with the group's attempts to convince other Jews in the city that they alone were the correct interpreters of the Jewish law.

A Final Note regarding Sepphoris: The Minting of Money

There is one more interesting feature regarding coinage that directly involves the city of Sepphoris. Sepphoris was granted permission to mint its own coins toward the end of the Jewish war, around 67 C.E.[85] This was probably a reward for the city's loyalty to Rome during the war.[86] Coins from this time bear the Greek inscription ΕΙΡΗΝΟΠΟΛΙΣ ("city of peace").[87]

The Matthean Gospel mentions coinage a number of times, particularly where the higher denominations are concerned. Since silver coins were the normative currency in the markets of the ancient world, I am not surprised by Matthew's preference for those coins.[88] This is important for two reasons. First, Matthew's concern for coinage increases the likelihood that the community was wealthy and engaged in commercial activity. Second, the Matthean Gospel depicts the type of coinage that could have easily been struck in the city of Sepphoris. These factors support the possibility that the Gospel was written there.

I acknowledge that my attempts to link the Matthean community to the city of Sepphoris are speculative. Yet there is evidence to support this view. The authors of the Gospel were writing from a wealthy urban setting that contained a large, conservative, Jewish population. Sepphoris certainly fits the criteria. Even if one is hesitant to accept this theory, the argument for Antioch is significantly weaker. Antioch is a good guess at best, but Sepphoris is a logical choice that is supported by archaeological and textual evidence.

---

[83] *b. Avodah Zarah* 16b–17a. For an analysis of this exchange, see Freyne, "Christianity in Sepphoris and Galilee," in *Sepphoris in Galilee: Crosscurrents of Culture*, (ed. Rebecca Martin Nagy et al.; Winona Lake, Ind.: Eisenbrauns, 1996), 67–70.

[84] *t. Hullin* 2:22–23.

[85] Meyers, "Roman Sepphoris," 324.

[86] Shaye J. D. Cohen, *Josephus in Galilee and Rome: His Vita and Development As a Historian* (Leiden: Brill, 1979), 246–47. Cohen notes that Josephus supports the conclusion that Sepphoris was loyal to Rome. See Josephus, *Life,* 8, 9, 25, 45, 65, etc. See also Freyne, *Galilee, Jesus,* 138.

[87] Meyers, "Roman Sepphoris," 324.

[88] Meshorer, *City Coins,* 6.

Blasphemy against the Spirit and the Historical Jesus

Amy M. Donaldson
University of Notre Dame

In recent work on the historical Jesus, one of the topics rarely discussed is the role of the Holy Spirit. Although several references to the Spirit in the Gospels appear to be individual interpretations of Jesus' activity, there is one saying in particular that does have support for being historical. This saying, that blasphemy against the Holy Spirit is unforgivable (Matt 12:31–32 // Mark 3:28–29 // Luke 12:10), has been treated in a variety of ways during the third quest. To name a few examples: John Meier, in three volumes of *A Marginal Jew*, does not address this saying at all.[1] John Dominic Crossan lists it as one of his highest ranking logia, placing it in the earliest stratum of material and claiming four independent sources.[2] Eugene Boring argues that the saying was not spoken by Jesus himself but by an early Christian prophet.[3] James Dunn, who argues a case similar to the one I will present but without applying any criteria of historicity, says that this logion is historical because (1) it is early and (2) it cannot be the saying of a Christian prophet.[4]

This paper proposes to take a first step in filling a lacuna in historical Jesus research by applying the criteria of historicity to this logion about the Spirit. In doing so, we may hope to determine the meaning and

---

[1] J. P. Meier, *A Marginal Jew: Rethinking the Historical Jesus* (3 vols.; New York: Doubleday, 1991–2001).

[2] J. D. Crossan, *The Historical Jesus: The Life of a Mediterranean Jewish Peasant* (New York: HarperCollins, 1991), 257–59, 436.

[3] E. Boring, "How May We Identify Oracles of Christian Prophets in the Synoptic Tradition? Mark 3:28–29 As a Test Case," *JBL* 91 (1972): 501–21.

[4] J. D. G. Dunn, *Jesus and the Spirit: A Study of the Religious and Charismatic Experience of Jesus and the First Christians As Reflected in the New Testament* (Philadelphia: Westminster, 1975), 49–53.

implications of such a statement on the lips of the historical Jesus. We will begin by examining the text to determine the number of independent sources and the nature of the original saying. Then, the relevant criteria will be applied with the inclusion of significant historical information about blasphemy and spirit. After determining the amount of certainty for the historicity of this saying, we will take a look at how this logion should be interpreted. Finally, some brief suggestions will be made regarding the implications of this statement for the historical Jesus.

Before proceeding, it is important to say a word about the criteria. I fully acknowledge that many of the criteria have been disputed and that none is universally accepted or applied. However, there must be a starting point for the discussion of any text. In this study, I will be using the criteria as carefully laid out by John Meier in the first volume of *A Marginal Jew*.[5] I recognize that the persuasiveness of the argument largely rests upon one's acceptance of these criteria. Based on this set of criteria, however, it appears that this logion has arguably one of the better claims for authenticity among the sayings material.

THE TEXT

Matt 12:31–32	Mark 3:28–29	Luke 12:10
Διὰ τοῦτο λέγω ὑμῖν, πᾶσα ἁμαρτία καὶ βλασφημία ἀφεθήσεται τοῖς ἀνθρώποις, ἡ δὲ τοῦ πνεύματος βλασφημία οὐκ ἀφεθήσεται. Καὶ ὃς ἐὰν εἴπῃ λόγον κατὰ τοῦ υἱοῦ τοῦ ἀνθρώπου, ἀφεθήσεται αὐτῷ· ὃς δ' ἂν εἴπῃ κατὰ τοῦ πνεύματος τοῦ ἁγίου, οὐκ ἀφεθήσεται αὐτῷ οὔτε ἐν τούτῳ τῷ αἰῶνι οὔτε ἐν τῷ μέλλοντι.	Ἀμὴν λέγω ὑμῖν ὅτι πάντα ἀφεθήσεται τοῖς υἱοῖς τῶν ἀνθρώπων τὰ ἁμαρτήματα καὶ αἱ βλασφημίαι ὅσα ἐὰν βλασφημήσωσιν· ὃς δ' ἂν βλασφημήσῃ εἰς τὸ πνεῦμα τὸ ἅγιον, οὐκ ἔξει ἄφεσιν εἰς τὸν αἰῶνα, ἀλλὰ ἔνοχός ἐστιν αἰωνίου ἁμαρτήματος.	Καὶ πᾶς ὃς ἐρεῖ λόγον εἰς τὸν υἱὸν τοῦ ἀνθρώπου, ἀφεθήσεται αὐτῷ· τῷ δὲ εἰς τὸ ἅγιον πνεῦμα βλασφημήσαντι οὐκ ἀφεθήσεται.
Because of this, I say to you, "Every sin and	Truly I say to you that all will be forgiven (to) the sons of men, the	

---

[5] Meier, *Marginal Jew*, 1:167–95.

Matthew	Mark	Luke
blasphemy will be forgiven (to) men, but the blasphemy of the spirit will not be forgiven. And whoever speaks a word against the Son of Man, it will be forgiven (to) him; but whoever speaks against the holy spirit, it will not be forgiven (to) him either in this age or in the coming one.	sins and blasphemies whichever they may blaspheme; but whoever blasphemes at the holy spirit, he does not have forgiveness into the age, but he is guilty of eternal sin.	And everyone whoever utters a word at the Son of Man, it will be forgiven (to) him; but (to) the one blaspheming at the holy spirit it will not be forgiven.[6]

Jesus' saying about blasphemy against the Holy Spirit appears in all three Synoptic Gospels. There is also a parallel in the Coptic *Gospel of Thomas,* to which we will return later. The Markan version, coming at the end of the Beelzebul controversy (3:20–30), states that all sins and blasphemies will be forgiven the sons of men, but whoever blasphemes against the Holy Spirit does not have forgiveness. While both Matthew and Luke appear to be influenced by Mark, they also diverge from Mark in similar ways. First, both express this saying as a statement about the Son of Man: whoever speaks a word against the Son of Man, it will be forgiven him; but whoever speaks against the Holy Spirit, it will not be forgiven him. Second, both Matthew and Luke phrase the act of blasphemy in the first half of the saying as "to speak a word against." Third, both versions have a comparable structure that differs significantly from Mark, changing the subject from "all sins and blasphemies" to "whoever speaks a word" and adding the same object of the speech, namely, the Son of Man. Finally, both Evangelists use identical wording in several places (see the underlining in the chart).

Given these correlations, there appears to be a distinct Q version of the saying. The Q saying was likely similar in form to the Lukan version, consisting of two parallel parts contrasting the one speaking against the Son of Man and the one speaking against the Holy Spirit: "And everyone who speaks a word against the Son of Man, it will be forgiven (to) him, but whoever speaks against the Holy Spirit, it will not be forgiven (to) him" (Καὶ πᾶς ὃς ἐὰν εἴπῃ λόγον εἰς τὸν υἱὸν τοῦ ἀνθρώπου, ἀφεθήσεται αὐτῷ· ὃς

---

[6] The Greek synopsis roughly follows that of K. Aland (*Synopsis of the Four Gospels: Greek-English Edition of the Synopsis Quattuor Evangeliorum* [10th ed.; Stuttgart: German Bible Society, 1993], §118). English translations are my own.

δ' ἂν εἴπῃ εἰς τὸ ἅγιον πνεῦμα οὐκ ἀφεθήσεται αὐτῷ).[7] Given this Q form, it is clear that Matthew and Luke appropriate the sources in a slightly different way. Matthew follows the context of Mark (the Beelzebul controversy) but conflates or combines the Markan and Q versions,[8] yielding a double saying: every sin and blasphemy will be forgiven men (rather than "sons of men" in Mark), and the one speaking against the Son of Man will be forgiven. Luke chooses to exclude the logion from this controversy story and instead, possibly following the order of Q, places it with other Son of Man and Spirit sayings. Luke's form of the saying, while similar to Q, appears to be slightly influenced by Mark as well (especially in the use of the verb βλασφημέω). However, Luke also has unique features (such as the participial construction in the second half, similar to Luke 12:9).

Comparing the Markan and Q forms of the blasphemy saying, we can attempt to rediscover the original form. Rather than trying to reconstruct precise wording, we will begin by identifying the common elements. First, the structure of the saying is an adversative bicolon: this is forgiven, but that is not. While Mark and Q disagree at some points about the format of each phrase, this basic bicolon is present in each version. Second, the distinction being made is between human and spirit, between the sons of men/Son of Man and the spirit of holiness. Third, the act for which one will or will not be forgiven is some kind of blasphemy, such as a slanderous word. Fourth, while forgiveness is available for this blasphemy in certain cases, anyone who speaks against the spirit of holiness will not have such forgiveness. This final clause is the one element that is most similar among all three Synoptic versions and the *Gospel of Thomas* (see below).

These common elements having been identified, it is important now to investigate the immediate relationship between the Markan and Q sayings. The "sons of men"/"Son of Man" correspondence between Mark and Q is perhaps the most critical issue in establishing the original form of the saying and will serve well to illustrate the relationship between the versions. First, the mention of forgiveness for all sins in the Markan version already alludes to a previous Son of Man saying in the story of the paralytic (Mark 2:10); the use of "Son of Man" here would further connect the two stories, but Mark does not employ it. Second, it seems more likely that

---

[7] This reconstruction follows *The Critical Edition of Q* (ed. J. M. Robinson, P. Hoffmann, and J. S. Kloppenborg; Hermeneia; Minneapolis: Fortress, 2000).

[8] This is assuming Markan priority and the four-source hypothesis. Regarding Matthew's use of Mark, Robert Holst disagrees with the editorial choices by both Aland and Huck in their synopses and instead argues for a different parallel structure: Matt 12:31 // Mark 3:28–29a rather than Matt 12:31 // Mark 3:28 ("Reexamining Mk 3 28f. and Its Parallels," *ZNW* (1972): 122–24).

the early church would have highlighted rather than obscured a Son of Man saying. Based on these two points, it is unlikely that Mark would have changed "Son of Man" to "sons of men," and therefore more likely that Q or its source interpreted the Semitic "son of man" as a proper title.

One hypothesis seems to offer a reasonable explanation for the emergence of these two divergent renderings: both Mark and Q represent separate translations of the Aramaic. As many scholars have argued, the Aramaic phrase "son of man" (בר נש[א]) could readily yield both translations, "sons of men" and "the Son of Man."[9] Likewise, several other differences between the versions could also easily be explained as distinct interpretations of one Aramaic original. Both versions use πᾶς or πάντα as the subject of the first clause. While Q refers to "every one" speaking and Mark to "all" sins and blasphemies, both could derive from the Aramaic כל. As seen in the Markan saying, if כל were followed immediately by the verb, this could leave "all/every" open to interpretation. After the verb, an Aramaic preposition such as ל or ב could be interpreted either as "to" (Mark) or "against" (Q) a son of man. Reading "Son of Man" requires shifting this figure from the object of forgiveness to the object of blasphemy (whereas a shift in the opposite direction is unnecessary for "human"), which suggests that the Q reading is secondary in this respect. Perhaps most importantly, Aramaic has no exact equivalent for βλασφημέω, so both "blaspheme" and "speak a word against" could be adequate translations of the same Aramaic phrase. Based on this evidence, it seems reasonable that Mark and Q may each represent a separate translation from the Aramaic. Therefore, for this study, it is more valuable for us to focus on the common elements between the two versions (as already enumerated) than to reconstruct a single Greek urtext.[10]

CRITERIA OF AUTHENTICITY

Let us turn now to the criteria. There are two primary criteria of authenticity that may be applied here: multiple attestation and discontinuity. First,

---

[9] For example, see A. J. B. Higgins, *The Son of Man in the Teaching of Jesus* (SNTSMS 39; Cambridge: Cambridge University Press, 1980), 88–90 and the studies cited there. There is no end to the amount of material that has been written on the issue of the title "Son of Man"; I will simply refer the reader to a recent summary of the literature by Delbert Burkett (*The Son of Man Debate: A History and Evaluation* [SNTSMS 107; Cambridge: Cambridge University Press, 1999], esp. 126–61).

[10] Also, rather than attempting to reconstruct the exact wording of a hypothetical original moving from one language back to another, I think it is a more honest task simply to highlight certain qualities. For examples of different attempts to retrovert into Aramaic, see the excursus by Higgins, *Son of Man,* 116–17.

multiple attestation. There are two different forms of the saying that occur in the Synoptic Gospels, a Markan form and a Q form, representing two different sources. This information alone supports multiple attestation. However, there are two additional parallels that are sometimes considered to be independent witnesses: *Gos. Thom.* 44 and *Did.* 11.7.

Gospel of Thomas 44 reads: "Whoever speaks blasphemy against the father will be forgiven, and whoever speaks blasphemy against the son will be forgiven, but whoever speaks blasphemy against the Holy Spirit will not be forgiven, either on earth or in heaven" (ⲡⲉϫⲉ ⲓ̅ⲥ̅ ϫⲉ ⲡⲉⲧⲁϫⲉ ⲟⲩⲁ ⲁⲡⲉⲓⲱⲧ ⲥⲉⲛⲁⲕⲱ ⲉⲃⲟⲗ ⲛⲁϥ ⲁⲩⲱ ⲡⲉⲧⲁϫⲉ ⲟⲩⲁ ⲉⲡϣⲏⲣⲉ ⲥⲉⲛⲁⲕⲱ ⲉⲃⲟⲗ ⲛⲁϥ ⲡⲉⲧⲁϫⲉ ⲟⲩⲁ ⲇⲉ ⲁⲡⲡ̅ⲛ̅ⲁ̅ ⲉⲧⲟⲩⲁⲁⲃ ⲥⲉⲛⲁⲕⲱ ⲁⲛ ⲉⲃⲟⲗ ⲛⲁϥ ⲟⲩⲧⲉ ϩⲙ̅ ⲡⲕⲁϩ ⲟⲩⲧⲉ ϩⲛ̅ ⲧⲡⲉ). Rather than two lines, this version has three, and all three have the same format, most closely resembling the reconstructed Q saying. This three-part structure yields a Trinitarian formula, casting doubt upon the originality of this version. Also, this rendering seems to be dependent on a Greek translation because Son of Man/sons of men has simply become "son" (rather than "man"). Assuming the logion was initially spoken in Aramaic, this then also moves the *Gospel of Thomas* version a step away from the original. Therefore, *Gos. Thom.* 44 yields no concrete evidence for an earlier form of this saying than the Synoptics.

The *Didache* contains a saying that seems to paraphrase rather than quote the Synoptic versions: "For every sin will be forgiven, but this sin will not be forgiven" (πᾶσα γὰρ ἁμαρτία ἀφεθήσεται, αὕτη δὲ ἡ ἁμαρτία οὐκ ἀφεθήσεται). This most closely parallels the Matthean version of the Markan saying, but notably omits blasphemy from either half. Instead, false prophets are discussed; the text commands not to test or examine any prophet speaking in a/the spirit (ἐν πνεύματι), for all sins will be forgiven but this one. If the *Didache* is dependent upon a Gospel, that is most likely Matthew because of similarities in form and context, but the absence of more concrete connections between the two also allows the possibility that the *Didache* attests a version of the saying independent from or prior to the Synoptic Gospels.[11] While a case can be argued that both the *Gospel of Thomas* and the *Didache* are independent of the Synoptics, a case may also be made for the opposite, so the evidence is not conclusive. The result is that there are two independent witnesses (Mark and Q) with a slight possibility of one or two additional witnesses alongside of them.

---

[11] Because the allusion to Matthew is also an allusion to the order of the *Gospel of Thomas*, it is also possible that the *Didache* is depending on this or another sayings source. However, the form of the saying diverges greatly from the *Gospel of Thomas* version.

Blasphemy against the Spirit and the Historical Jesus   163

The second primary criterion, discontinuity, is more controversial. It holds the inherent contradiction of arguing for a historically contextualized Jesus who does not fit his historical context. In other words, it seeks to establish a Jesus who is historically viable, but only by illustrating how he differs from his historical situation. By beginning with an examination of two key aspects of this logion, blasphemy and the Holy Spirit, in first-century Palestinian Judaism, we can attempt to use this criterion without resulting in a paradoxical Jesus.

First, let us look at blasphemy. In the first century and preceding, Hebrew and Aramaic did not have a specific technical term for blasphemy. Rather, a range of terms appears in the literature to represent this idea.[12] In the Masoretic Text, there are four basic Hebrew roots relating to blasphemy: גדף (revile, slander), קלל (curse, revile), חרף (reproach), and נאץ (despise). In the LXX, βλασφημεῖν and its substantival cognates frequently, but not exclusively, translate these four Hebrew roots.[13] Therefore, the LXX does not employ βλασφημεῖν as an absolute technical term for blasphemy, and there is even variation from one Greek recension to another.[14] Through the time of the rabbinic literature, the same range of terminology continues to appear, but in the rabbinic texts and even at Qumran previously, the root גדף shows evidence of emerging as the primary term for blasphemy.

A survey of the biblical, intertestamental, and other contemporary literature yields at least four general categories of blasphemous activity: (1) cursing/speaking against God or his representative; (2) despising/rejecting God or his representative; (3) challenging God's ability or authority; and (4) idolatry or other infidelity to God.[15] The first and second categories

---

[12] For the discussion of terms and sources that follows, I am heavily indebted to the exhaustive work of Darrell Bock on blasphemy in Judaism (*Blasphemy and Exaltation in Judaism and the Final Examination of Jesus* [WUNT 2/106; Tübingen: Mohr Siebeck, 1998], 30–112). See also E. P. Sanders, *Jewish Law from Jesus to the Mishnah: Five Studies* (London: SCM, 1990), 57–67.

[13] For example, the root גדף is translated twice by βλασφημεῖν (4 Kgdms 19), but also by καταλαλεῖν (Ps 43:16 [A, S2]), παραλαλεῖν (Ps 43:16 [B, S1]), παροχύνειν (Num 15:30; Isa 37:23), and παροργίζειν (Ezek 20:27; all references here are for the LXX). For additional examples, see Bock, *Blasphemy and Exaltation,* 46–47.

[14] See the example for Ps 43:16 (LXX) in the previous note. Also, Lev 24:11 uses βλασφημεῖν in the fourth column of the Hexapla but not in other translations (cf. Bock, *Blasphemy and Exaltation,* 47).

[15] Examples of each category: (1) Exod 22:28; Lev 24:10–23; 1 Kgs 21:13; Job 2:9–10; Pss 10:3; 74:10, 18; Isa 8:21; (2) Num 15:30–31; 16:30; Deut 31:20; Isa 1:4; 5:24; (3) 2 Kgs 19 // Isa 37; Ps 10:13; Ezek 35:12; and (4) 2 Sam 12:14; Neh 9:18, 26; Ezek 20:27.

tend to be the speech and action counterparts of one another (respectively), while the third and fourth each encompass both speech and action. In the first two categories, God's representative may be a leader, the law, the covenant, or some other source of authority established by God, indicating that blasphemy extends to any word or action that either directly or indirectly challenges God.[16]

In the interest of brevity, only select examples of key texts will be offered here. The primary text on blasphemy in the Old Testament is Lev 24:10–23. This serves as the foundational legal text describing the punishment for blasphemy. In this case, a man of mixed Israelite and Egyptian birth speaks the Name (of God) in a curse while fighting.[17] As a result, he is sentenced to be taken outside the camp and stoned. In fact, the explanation that follows leads directly from blasphemy to murder and a citation of the *lex talionis* (24:13–22). While the main point of the story is that this man of mixed birth should be punished the same as any Israelite, the implications are that blaspheming God's name is equivalent to murder. Subsequent interpretation of this legal text often centers on the precise act that is committed by this man. For example, Philo understands the offense to include both cursing and naming the divine Name (*Mos.* 2.203–204), and he extends the application of this to foreign deities out of respect for the name "god" (2.205). Later, in the rabbinic material, several rabbis conclude that for the death penalty to apply, blasphemy must involve uttering the Name.[18]

Moving beyond the biblical text, the Dead Sea Scrolls offer a couple of interesting passages. The four references to blasphemy among this material relate to sins of speech (falling into category 1) and require strict punishment. Two of these passages are worth mentioning here. Column 4 of the *Community Rule* opens with the ongoing discussion of the antithetical spirits of light and darkness. This passage lists a blaspheming tongue (לשון גדופים) as one of the traits of those living by the spirit of

---

[16] There are also instances where a human is cursed or despised without any implication that this affects God; but, since most of our texts and legal arguments focus on blasphemy against God, these entirely human instances are being excluded to narrow the scope of this inquiry.

[17] The verbs here can be understood either as two separate actions or one complex action. I am treating them as one action, as J. Weingreen argues ("The Case of the Blasphemer [Leviticus XXIV 10ff.]," *VT* 22 [1972]: 118–23).

[18] One text in which this emerges is *m. Shevu'ot* 4:13, where Rabbi Meir gives the opinion that a wide range of curses that invoke divine names comprise the blasphemy worthy of death, but the sages disagree. Likewise, the Targums *Pseudo-Jonathan* and *Neofiti* on Lev 24:11–13 both indicate that it is the man's blasphemy involving the Name that requires the death penalty.

darkness in contrast to the virtues of those living by the spirit of light. This also provides interesting background for a related text. The *Damascus Document*, column 5, contains a passage describing the sins of the opponents of the community. These people have profaned the temple and committed incest. Moreover, "they defile their holy spirit and open their mouth with a blaspheming tongue against the laws of the Covenant of God saying, 'They are not sure.'"[19] This passage refers to people who should be living by the covenant, but through their unfaithfulness they have committed blasphemy by stating (either by word or action) that it is not authoritative for them, thereby defiling the spirit of holiness by which they should be living. Although this is by no means a direct parallel for the saying in the Gospels, it has interesting similarities to which we will return later.

Philo provides additional turn-of-the-era information. One of the key passages in Philo for this treatment of blasphemy is *Fug.* 84. Philo is discussing the cities of refuge in Exod 21 and asserts that for the guilty to flee to God's protection is to accuse God of causing the offense. Comparing this with the text that follows, regarding the death penalty for assaulting or speaking against a parent, he concludes that this indicates there is no pardon at all for those who blaspheme the Deity, for if those cursing a parent deserve death, certainly those daring to blaspheme the Father and Creator deserve as much. This passage is especially significant because Philo refers to the death penalty in the negative: to be without pardon. Other writings by Philo also show that he considers a human claim for divinelike authority to be blasphemous (for example, *Decal.* 61–69), which would fall into category 3 (a challenge to God's authority).[20]

Several uses of blasphemy in the New Testament exemplify meanings and concerns already discussed. Looking first at those references outside of the Gospels, many seem to indicate blasphemy as disrespectful speech toward God or his representative (such as Moses in Acts 6:11) and would fit into category 1. A number of the occurrences refer to blaspheming the name of God (1 Tim 6:1; Jas 2:7; Rev 13:6; 16:9), highlighting the emphasis from Leviticus. A few texts also mention the concern that impropriety or disobedience on the part of the faithful could cause others to blaspheme God (Rom 2:24; 1 Tim 6:1; cf. Titus 2:5).[21]

---

[19] Translation from Geza Vermes, *The Dead Sea Scrolls in English* (4th ed.; New York: Penguin, 1995), 101.

[20] See Bock for further discussion of *Decal.* 61–65 (*Blasphemy and Exaltation*, 65–66).

[21] A passage from *2 Clement* explains this in more detail. People will be attracted by the words of God that Christians speak, but if the deeds of Christians

Within the Gospels, blasphemy is mentioned in different contexts. In a few cases, Jesus himself is accused of committing blasphemy. When Jesus heals the paralytic and proclaims his sins to be forgiven, the opponents in attendance consider this to be an act of blasphemy because God alone has the authority to forgive sins.[22] The implication is that Jesus is equating himself with the divine by assuming the same authority, an aspect of blasphemy also illustrated by Philo. Similarly, at the trial of Jesus, the high priest asks him to answer charges that he claimed to have the ability to miraculously rebuild the temple and had called himself Messiah and Son of God. Jesus responds enigmatically that they will see the Son of Man seated at the right hand of power and coming on the clouds of heaven, which the high priest understands as blasphemy (Matt 26:61–65 // Mark 14:58–64). Again, the implication in the text is that Jesus has claimed some kind of divine authority, and the immediate judgment passed on this verdict of blasphemy is the death penalty.[23] In John 10:31–39, Jesus has been speaking at the temple, and upon his proclamation that "I and the Father are one," the Jews prepare to stone him. When Jesus questions them, the Jews reply that they are stoning him for blasphemy because he is making himself God, explicitly indicating that they consider equating himself with God to be blasphemous.

One other reference to blasphemy in the Gospels is worth noting. In a dialogue about clean versus unclean food (Matt 15:19 // Mark 7:21–22), Jesus declares that it is not what goes into but what come out of a person that makes one unclean, for out of the heart emerges a slew of sins—among them, blasphemy. Although not all of the sins mentioned are necessarily of equal weight, the list as a whole has overtones of the Decalogue. The language here also recalls the text from column 5 of the *Damascus Document,* referring to defiling oneself. In that text, those

---

are unworthy of their words, people will resort to blasphemy, saying the words are false and deceptive (*2 Clem.* 13).

[22] Matt 9:3 // Mark 2:7 // Luke 5:21. Bruce Malina and Jerome Neyrey explain that to claim for oneself God's power (over forgiveness) would lessen his power and thereby dishonor him ("Honor and Shame in Luke-Acts: Pivotal Values of the Mediterranean World" in *The Social World of Luke-Acts: Models for Interpretation* [ed. J. Neyrey; Peabody, Mass.: Hendrickson, 1991], 59). The same honor-shame language can be applied to the extension of dishonoring God's agent to dishonoring God himself (cf. 59–60).

[23] The charge of blasphemy at the trial is a weighty subject that cannot properly be treated here. For a full discussion, see the monograph by Bock (*Blasphemy and Exaltation*). The significance for the present study is the understanding of blasphemy within the literary context, so issues of historicity need not be decided at this point.

defiling the temple and committing incest are defiling their holy spirit by blaspheming, or despising, the covenant. Although Jesus does not use "spirit of holiness" here, both passages refer to the defiling of the self in some way through sinful acts.[24] Other vice lists in the New Testament epistles include blasphemy, either referring to sins that should not proceed from the people of God—similar to the meaning of Jesus—or indicating activities that will mark the opponents of God's people—similar to the Qumran adversaries who live in darkness.[25]

In summary, blasphemy is often associated with speech, especially cursing, although it may also consist of an action in defiance to God. The speech or action might be against God's representative and by implication dishonor God himself. A direct or indirect challenge to God is also considered blasphemous, for example by assuming divine authority for oneself. Furthermore, showing infidelity to God is considered an insult and therefore blasphemous. In general, blasphemy is punishable by death (specifically by stoning), but such a wide range of blasphemous activities remains open to interpretation in each case. The range of terms encompassing blasphemy also has some variety, but more specific terms are seen to develop under Greek influence and in rabbinic Hebrew. All of this provides the context for Jesus' saying about blasphemy against the spirit in the Synoptic Gospels.

Before continuing with the criterion of discontinuity, let me make a comment about the Spirit in first-century Palestine.[26] The scriptural and intertestamental texts up to this time do not refer to the Spirit as the third person of the Trinity. The Spirit in the Old Testament is most frequently the Spirit of the Lord or Spirit of God and is referred to as the Holy Spirit only three times (twice in Third Isaiah, once in Ps 51). However, according to the Hebrew construction, it would be more accurate to translate this as "spirit of holiness." In the scriptural texts, the Spirit is a divine agent often associated with prophecy and sometimes appears as a kind of raw power, especially in Judges. The spirit of holiness again appears several times among the Dead Sea Scrolls, usually in terms of the contrast between the spirit of light and the spirit of darkness. Among this literature, the spirit is typically an agent of God or even synonymous with God's presence, but

---

[24] Both texts also deal with those who (by implication) should otherwise be holy. Both Jesus and the *Damascus Document* assume that these are people who live under the law and should be concerned with upholding it (if they simply lived in the spirit of darkness, as in 1QS 4, one would naturally expect these evils to flow from them).

[25] See Col 3:8 and 2 Tim 3:2–5.

[26] For an excellent survey of first-century understandings of spirit, see J. R. Levison, *The Spirit in First Century Judaism* (AGAJU 29; Leiden: Brill, 1997).

it is not until Paul that the Holy Spirit is seen to emerge with a distinct personality and can be personified as a third divine person alongside of the Father and Son.

The contextual evidence viewed thus far clearly shows that the blasphemy saying is not entirely discontinuous with either Judaism or early Christianity. However, what is arguably discontinuous with both is this *type* of statement, that blasphemy against the Holy Spirit is unforgivable. Nowhere does the Hebrew Bible make an explicit correlation between blasphemous acts and the Spirit of God. Similarly, the other Jewish literature we have examined speaks of blasphemy against a number of God's representatives and, with increasing frequency, of blasphemy against the Name, but not of blasphemy against the Spirit. The one body of literature that comes closest to this idea is the Dead Sea Scrolls. Both the *Community Rule* and the *Damascus Document* contain passages mentioning a blasphemous tongue in the context of a spirit. Yet in neither instance is the blasphemy said to be directed against the spirit itself. Therefore, while the nature of the saying about blasphemy against the spirit is in line with contemporary Judaism, the way in which this is expressed is not typical of Jewish statements about blasphemy.

Early church writings prove the same point. Of the New Testament references to blasphemy, several speak of blaspheming the name or even the word of God or blaspheming his representatives, but the language about blaspheming the Spirit remains within the Gospels.[27] If the *Gospel of Thomas* and the *Didache* are indeed early interpretations of the Gospels rather than independent witnesses, it is noteworthy that both change the saying rather than accepting it as it stands in any Synoptic context. The *Gospel of Thomas* makes the saying Trinitarian so that the emphasis shifts toward the Holy Spirit in distinction to both the Father and the Son. The *Didache* heads in a different direction and removes any reference to blasphemy, instead applying the saying to the testing of Christian prophets.

Another point of discontinuity within the early church relates to the concept of an eternal sin in the Markan version. Even Matthew avoids this last phrase, perhaps revealing some discomfort with it. In the New Testament and beyond, the early church grappled with the idea of an unforgivable or eternal sin, usually in terms of apostasy.[28] Among the earliest church

---

[27] Perhaps the closest parallel outside of the Gospels is the warning in Ephesians not to grieve the Holy Spirit (μὴ λυπεῖτε τὸ πνεῦμα τὸ ἅγιον τοῦ θεοῦ; 4:30), but this is not treated as serious as blasphemy. Another text with some similarity is 1 Cor 12:3, but in this case it is stated that no one curses *Jesus* when speaking *in* the Spirit of God.

[28] 1 John 5:16–17 makes a distinction between sins that lead unto death and sins that do not. Hebrews 6 similarly discusses believers who had once participated in

fathers, the Shepherd of Hermas deals at length with the issue of apostasy, specifically using the language of blasphemy. Blasphemers fall into the same category as apostates and betrayers of God's servants (Herm. *Sim.* 9.19.1). The Shepherd recognizes that there is no repentance available for these sinners and that their end is death (Herm. *Sim.* 6.2.3). But they are referred to as blaspheming against the Lord, the name of the Lord, or the law, never against the Spirit. In this early Christian context, it is easy to understand how a reference to eternal sin may be interpreted as apostasy, but it is striking that the earliest sources do not refer to apostasy in the same language as this logion, as blasphemy against the Holy Spirit. Based on this discontinuity with specific language about blasphemy but not the broader concept, it is more likely that the saying should be attributed to Jesus than to another Jewish or early Christian source.

Besides the primary criteria, there is also one secondary criterion that, in this case, may contribute additional weight toward authenticity. This is the criterion of traces of Aramaic. As we have seen, some of the variations between Mark and Q may easily be explained as translational differences.[29] This evidence may simply point toward an original Semitic form of the saying and does not prove that Jesus himself was the one to first speak it, but this data could at least lend credence to its historicity once the evidence of the other criteria has been weighed. Based on these criteria of authenticity, therefore, it is highly probable that such a saying was spoken by the historical Jesus.

INTERPRETATION AND IMPLICATIONS OF THE SAYING BY THE HISTORICAL JESUS

While a full investigation of the historical implications is beyond the scope of this paper, we can at least take a step toward interpreting the

---

the Holy Spirit but have now fallen away and compares them to useless soil whose end is burning. However, neither text specifically defines the sin as speech against God or designates the Holy Spirit as the object of that sin.

[29] To summarize the evidence: (1) the sons of men/Son of Man distinction points toward a Semitic origin, as does the shift from "to the son of man" to "against the Son of Man," which could both be interpreted from one Semitic preposition (such as ל or ב); (2) by the first century there was not yet one specific technical term for blasphemy in Hebrew or Aramaic, so "to speak a word against" and "to blaspheme" were both adequate ways to express the same Semitic idea in Greek; (3) the Semitic phrase "spirit of holiness" need not refer to *the* Holy Spirit (as in later Trinitarian understanding), so the Aramaic version of the saying may have sounded more congruent to either a Jewish or Christian context than the Q version that seemingly elevates the Holy Spirit over the Son of Man.

logion in its context. As argued above, the original Aramaic saying consisted of an adversative bicolon, two clauses presenting a contrast. The first clause states, in essence, that every blasphemy will be forgiven to humans. The second clause, which can be established with greater certainty, states: "but whoever speaks a word against the spirit of holiness will not be forgiven." Both "speak a word against" and "blaspheme" bear the same meaning, namely, to speak against God or his representative in an irreverent way that may pose a challenge to God's ability or authority. Although blasphemy may encompass actions as well, speech seems to be highlighted in this saying, which is the interpretation of all three Synoptic contexts. Within these three contexts, the type of blasphemy implied is a challenge to God's authority by slandering his agent (such as in the Beelzebul controversy in Matthew and Mark) or rejecting his agent (in the Lukan context, where denial of Jesus is parallel to blaspheming the Spirit).

While there is some ambiguity as to the object of blasphemy in the first clause, the blasphemy of the second clause is undoubtedly directed against the holy spirit. In light of the evidence that blasphemy against a representative of God is considered just as serious as blasphemy directly against God himself and thus leads to the same punishment (by death, therefore being without pardon), it is most reasonable to understand the holy spirit here as the divine agent. In this reading, the second clause is merely stating the traditional understanding of blasphemy in nontraditional terms, that speaking against God through his agent is without pardon. This stands in contrast to lesser forms of blasphemy for which there is forgiveness. Therefore, Jesus' words are not radically different from those of any other Palestinian Jew at his time, but he phrased this idea in a unique way that has caused Christians, from then until now, many challenges in its interpretation.

Finally, we will now turn to the broader implications of the blasphemy saying for the historical Jesus. First, there is the issue of context. Mark and Luke (or Q) provide two distinct contexts for this saying. Of the two contexts, the saying fits most fluidly with, and is most clearly understood in, the Markan context. It is not necessary to accept the narrative in Mark (or the larger exorcism context in Matthew) as the original, but it is still possible to assert that the saying may well have originated in this type of setting. The historical Jesus was a public figure who came into conflict with the authorities of his day,[30] so it is possible that he may have interpreted challenges to his own work as challenges to God and expressed this by

---

[30] Both of these assertions are represented in E. P. Sanders's list of "indisputable facts" about Jesus (as a public figure: nos. 3 and 7; in conflict with authorities: nos. 5 and 6; *Jesus and Judaism* [Philadelphia: Fortress, 1985], 11).

reminding his Jewish opponents of the seriousness of their blasphemy. If this saying does emerge from a context in which Jesus feels his own ability or authority is being challenged, then this suggests that he understood himself as a prophetic figure somehow enabled by the Spirit of God.[31]

In conclusion, the saying about blasphemy against the Holy Spirit can most likely be traced back to the historical Jesus. Based on the distinct versions preserved by Mark and Q, there is the multiple attestation of at least two sources. The criterion of discontinuity also shows that the concept of such blasphemy may be continuous with the Judaism of the time, but the way in which Jesus described this blasphemy is not familiar either from the Judaism that preceded him or the earliest Christianity that followed. In addition to this, the traces of Aramaic apparent by comparing both forms may also help weigh the evidence in favor of authenticity. If the historical Jesus then indeed did make this statement in some form, what he meant by it was to contrast sins of speech that are forgivable with blasphemy against God's agent, the spirit of holiness, which is not forgivable. The implications of this saying for the historical Jesus are more tenuous and require further research, but it is possible that the saying was spoken during a controversy between Jesus and his opponents and that Jesus understood himself to be acting under the power of the divine spirit.

---

[31] Although I simply propose this as a possibility, requiring further research, James Dunn is quite certain that the original Aramaic saying reveals this self-understanding by Jesus (*Jesus and the Spirit* [Philadelphia: Westminster, 1975], 52–53).

Galilee and Greco-Roman Culture in the Time of Jesus: The Neglected Significance of Chronology

Mark A. Chancey
Southern Methodist University

In much recent New Testament scholarship, Jesus appears to have been recontextualized within late second- or even third-century C.E. Galilee. What I mean by this claim is not that Jesus has literally been redated, of course, but rather that many scholarly constructions of his Galilean context are anachronistic. Too often they rely heavily on archaeological evidence that postdates him, sometimes by centuries. While we have some first-century C.E. archaeological finds that reflect Greco-Roman cultural influence there, we do not have nearly as many as is often supposed. Much of the pertinent evidence is from the second or later centuries. The most important question facing scholars interested in the Greco-Roman milieu of Galilee is whether or not we can use this later evidence to understand what was going on in the early first century. How we deal with this question has implications not only for historical Jesus research but also for Gospel provenance studies, Q research, and any scholarship dealing with the Galilean setting of early Judaism and Christianity.

A few citations from well-respected scholars illustrate the pervasiveness of the view that Galilee was already thoroughly infused with Greco-Roman culture by the early first century C.E. Howard Clark Kee describes Sepphoris in the time of Jesus as a "Greco-Roman-style city" and writes that "all the features of a Hellenistic city were there, including a theater, hippodrome and temples."[1] As examples of Galilee's Greco-Roman

---

[1] Howard Clark Kee, "Early Christianity in the Galilee: Reassessing the Evidence from the Gospels," in *The Galilee in Late Antiquity* (ed. Lee I. Levine; New York and Jerusalem: Jewish Theological Seminary of America, 1992), 15.

culture, Paula Fredkriksen points to "architectural remnants, inscriptions, [and] coins" and refers to "Hellenized public architecture—theaters, baths, stadiums, and the like" at Sepphoris and Tiberias.[2] Marcus Borg writes, "Recent archaeological finds suggest that the use of Greek was much more widespread than we thought, and this creates the very real possibility that Jesus, and perhaps the disciples, were bilingual."[3] The Jesus Seminar's *Five Gospels* claims that "recent archaeological excavations in Galilee indicate that Greek influence was widespread there in the first century of our era."[4]

I cite these particular scholars (or, in the case of the Jesus Seminar, group of scholars) not to single them out for criticism but because their statements are so representative of what is often being said in the field of New Testament studies. I also cite them because they reflect different points along the spectrum of scholarship.[5] The fact that such varied people make such similar claims demonstrates that this view is not limited to one camp of scholars.[6]

In this paper I will present a brief, chronological overview of the published archaeological data from Galilee, an overview that highlights the difference in quantity between first-century C.E. and earlier archaeological finds and those of later centuries. The delineation of the boundaries of Galilee is a matter of debate, but for the present purposes I will rely on the description in Josephus: west of the territory of Hippos, Gadara, and Gaulanitis; south of the territory of Tyre; east of the territory of Ptolemais; north of the territory of Scythopolis and Samaria.[7] My review will focus on three categories of evidence: first, inscriptions; second, Greco-Roman architectural features and urban planning (with a nod to the importance of the information provided by Josephus, as well); and third, Greco-Roman iconography and imagery. Needless to say, these three categories are not

---

[2] Paula Fredriksen, *Jesus of Nazareth: King of the Jews* (New York: Vintage Books, 1999), 160–61.

[3] Marcus J. Borg, "The Palestinian Background for a Life of Jesus," in *Searching for Jesus* (Washington, D.C.: Biblical Archaeology Society, 1994), 46–47.

[4] Robert W. Funk, Roy W. Hoover, and the Jesus Seminar, *The Five Gospels: The Search for the Authentic Words of Jesus* (New York: Macmillan, 1993), 28.

[5] Borg, though a member of the Jesus Seminar, describes a very different Jesus in his own work. See, for example, *Jesus: A New Vision* (San Francisco: HarperSanFrancisco, 1987).

[6] This view plays different roles in the works of different scholars; for some, such characterizations of the region form a vital part of their overall arguments, while for others, they are included as merely passing remarks.

[7] *J.W.* 3.35–44; see discussion in Mark A. Chancey, *The Myth of a Gentile Galilee* (SNTSMS 118; Cambridge: Cambridge University Press, 2002), 9 n. 26.

comprehensive and do not encompass all aspects of Greco-Roman culture. They are nonetheless good starting points for discussion, both because of the frequency with which they are cited in scholarship on Jesus and the Gospels and because they are more easily discernible in the archaeological record than other aspects of Hellenism (for example, philosophy). Furthermore, a brief survey such as the present one can provide only basic information about particular finds and sites, not details.[8] After summarizing the archaeological data, I will argue that it is methodologically problematic to rely on second-century C.E. and later evidence to shed light on the first century C.E.

In emphasizing the importance of chronology for understanding ancient Galilee, I am not attempting to turn back the clock to the pre-Hengel era and to drive a wedge between "Judaism" and "Hellenism."[9] Instead, I am arguing that the interplay of local culture and Greco-Roman culture looked different at different points in time at different places. First-century C.E. Galilee was not the same as third-century C.E. Galilee, and if we are to understood either period, we must be attentive to the particularity of each.

Perhaps no aspect of Galilee's material culture is more misunderstood than its inscriptions. Simply put, we have not recovered that many of them from first-century C.E. and earlier contexts.[10] The ones we have found show that Greek was used for some, particularly governmental, functions, but they do not demonstrate that it was widely spoken.

In the Hellenistic period (late fourth century B.C.E. through the mid-first century B.C.E.), coins with Greek legends are the most common type of inscription uncovered in Galilee. All such coins originated elsewhere, however, having been minted by the Ptolemies, Seleucids, or various cities (usually from the Decapolis or the coast). In addition, the Hasmoneans minted coins (presumably at or near Jerusalem). Many had Hebrew inscriptions; those of Alexander Jannaeus (103–76 B.C.E.) bore both Greek and

---

[8] This paper reflects preliminary research for my forthcoming book, tentatively titled *Greco-Roman Culture and the Galilee of Jesus*. For a site-by-site discussion of Galilee and for interaction with the standard scholarly works on the region (e.g., those by Eric M. Meyers, Sean Freyne, Richard Horsley), see my *Myth of a Gentile Galilee*.

[9] Cf. Martin Hengel, *Judaism and Hellenism: Studies in Their Encounter in Palestine during the Early Hellenistic Period* (trans. John Bowden; 2 vols.; Philadelphia: Fortress, 1974).

[10] My summary of Galilee's inscriptions is based on a review of archaeological journals (*IEJ, Excavations and Surveys in Israel, BASOR,* etc.), the articles and references in archaeological encyclopedias such as *NEAEHL* and OEANE, collections of inscriptions, the volumes of *Supplementum epigraphicum graecum,* and published excavation reports.

Hebrew, as did those of Mattathias Antigonus (40–37 B.C.E.).[11] Amphora handles with Greek inscriptions are also occasional finds, but, as imports, their inscriptions reflect the linguistic milieus of their places of origin, not their places of discovery. Within Galilee itself, I have found only one other inscription from the Hellenistic period, an ostracon from Sepphoris. This sherd is probably from the mid-second century B.C.E., and excavators interpret some of its seven Semitic characters (אפמלסלש) as a Greek loanword, epimeletes, or "manager," a civic official.[12] Between the coins, amphora handles, and the ostracon, this is a rather meager number of inscriptions, certainly not enough to demonstrate that Greek was widely used in Galilee in the Hellenistic era.

Despite frequent claims to the contrary, we have very, very few inscriptions from first-century C.E. Galilee, either. Most are numismatic inscriptions from old Hasmonean coins (Greek and Hebrew), more recent Herodian coins (Greek), and civic coinage (Greek), the latter mostly from non-Galilean cities.[13] In fact, of the known inscriptions produced in Galilee during the lifetime of Jesus—the first 30 years C.E. or so—all but one are on the coins of Herod Antipas (4 B.C.E.–39 C.E.). The other is a market weight from Tiberias, also with a Greek inscription.[14]

Indeed, numismatic inscriptions dominate the epigraphic corpus for the rest of the first century as well. The use of Greek on coins reflects the cultural values of the minting authorities.[15] It is clear that the Herods wanted their currency to look like—and thus compare favorably with—other coinage emanating out of the eastern Mediterranean. Their coins' Greek inscriptions thus attest to their Hellenizing aspirations. Similarly, the use of Greek on city coins throughout the Levant reflects the openness of the civic elites to Greco-Roman culture.

Do numismatic inscriptions tell us what the masses were speaking? When considering this question, we sometimes make what I think is a mistake: we imagine that most people were actually reading the legends on

---

[11] Yaakov Meshorer, *Ancient Jewish Coinage* (2 vols.; Dix Hills, N.Y.: Amphora Books, 1982), 1:118–34, 155–59.

[12] See comments by Joseph Naveh in *Sepphoris in Galilee: Crosscurrents of Culture* (ed. Rebecca Martin Nagy et al.; Winona Lake, Ind.: Eisenbrauns, 1996), 170.

[13] Meshorer, *Ancient Jewish Coinage;* Yaakov Meshorer, *City-Coins of Eretz-Israel and the Decapolis in the Roman Period* (Jerusalem: Israel Museum, 1985).

[14] Shraga Qedar, "Two Lead Weights of Herod Antipas and Agrippa II and the Early History of Tiberias," *Israel Numismatic Journal* 9 (1986–87): 29–35.

[15] Mark A. Chancey, "City Coins and Roman Power in Palestine: From Pompey to the Great Revolt," in *Religion and Society in Roman Palestine: Old Problems, New Approaches* (ed. Douglas R. Edwards and C. Thomas McCollough; London: Routledge Press, in press).

coins. If literacy rates are as low in the Roman Empire as recent studies suggest—William Harris suggests 10 percent, perhaps higher in the cities—then who was reading these inscriptions?[16] If most of the population could not read at even a basic level, then we cannot assume that the language chosen for governmental inscriptions reflects what was actually spoken by the common people. Just because the masses were exposed to Greek letters on coins does not mean they could speak Greek. (This latter point also holds true for other governmental inscriptions, such as the market weight from Tiberias.)

We have only a few inscriptions from the rest of the century (ca. 30–100 C.E.), mostly in Greek. The most famous is an imperial edict prohibiting tomb robbing, probably from the mid-first century. This inscription was shipped from Nazareth to Europe in the late nineteenth century, but its original provenance is unknown. It may be from Galilee, but it could have been brought to Nazareth from elsewhere because of the city's heavy involvement in the European antiquities trade.[17] In 53 C.E., Tiberias issued several denominations of coins, all with Greek inscriptions, and another coin with the city's name on it was probably minted later under Agrippa II.[18] During the first revolt, Sepphoris minted two pro-Roman coins, both with Greek inscriptions. In addition, one had the Latin letters "SC"—an abbreviation for *senatus consulto*.[19] We have an ostracon with Semitic letters (אב) from Jotapata, exact date unknown, but definitely prior to the Revolt.[20] A second market weight, perhaps also from Tiberias, is from late in the century.[21]

Other inscriptions may be from the first-century, but their exact dates are unclear. One is a pottery fragment from Gischala with the Greek letters ARIST on it;[22] the other is a mosaic at Magdala with the words KAI

---

[16] William V. Harris, *Ancient Literacy* (Cambridge: Harvard University Press, 1989), 22.

[17] See discussion in Eric M. Meyers and James F. Strange, *Archaeology, the Rabbis, and Early Christianity* (Nashville: Abingdon, 1981), 83–84, and in *SEG* 8.13, 13.596, 16.828, 20.452.

[18] Meshorer, *Ancient Jewish Coinage*, 2:166–67, 279; Ya'akov Meshorer, "Ancient Jewish Coinage Addendum I," *Israel Numismatics Journal* 11 (1990–91): 104–32.

[19] See comments by Yaakov Meshorer in Nagy et al., *Sepphoris*, 195–196; see also Yaakov Meshorer, "Sepphoris and Rome," *Greek Numismatics and Archaeology: Essays in Honor of Margaret Thompson* (ed. O. Mørkholm and N. M. Waggoner; Belgium: Cultura Press, 1979), 159–171.

[20] David Adan-Bayewitz and Mordechai Aviam, "Iotapata, Josephus, and the Siege of 67: Preliminary Report on the 1992–1994 Seasons," *Journal of Roman Archaeology* 10 (1997): 131–65, esp. 152.

[21] Qedar, "Two Lead Weights."

[22] Eric M. Meyers, Carol L. Meyers, and James F. Strange, Excavations at the Ancient Synagogue of Gush Halav (Winona Lake, Ind.: Eisenbrauns, 1990), 126; cf. Eric M.

SU.²³ In addition, there are three inscriptions that could come from either the first or second century: a Greek ossuary inscription at Qiryat Tiv'on, on the southwest edge of Galilee;²⁴ graffiti (two Greek letters) in a cave at Gush Halav;²⁵ and a fragmentary (three characters), unpublished Latin inscription found at Sepphoris.²⁶ The range of dates for these last three inscriptions—first or second century—is significant, because of the evolution of Galilean culture between 50 C.E. and 150 C.E.

As with the earlier materials, this very limited amount of first-century C.E. epigraphic evidence is an insufficient basis from which to conclude that Greek was widely spoken. We are largely in the dark about how extensively, and by whom, it was used. At the same time, it is worth noting that not only do have very few Greek inscriptions, but we do not have many inscriptions of any language at all. Theoretically, one could argue that the sole Semitic inscription from Jotapata is insufficient evidence to conclude that Aramaic was spoken, either. No one, to my knowledge, has made this absurd argument, since literary and other evidence for the use of Aramaic throughout the Jewish parts of Palestine is quite strong. Ultimately, though, whether one regards Aramaic or Greek as the dominant language in Galilee depends less on epigraphic evidence, which is lacking for both, than on presuppositions about the extent and nature of Hellenization.

What is indisputable is that the number of inscriptions steadily increases in later centuries, as the following inventory makes clear:

- coins with Greek inscriptions (second-third century; mostly civic issues from Sepphoris, Tiberias, and the surrounding cities; occasionally from imperial mints)²⁷
- market weight with a Greek inscription identifying the *agoranomos* (mid-second century, Sepphoris)²⁸
- milestones with Latin inscriptions naming the emperor under which the roads were built or renovated and (often) Greek

---

Meyers, James F. Strange, Carol L. Meyers, Richard S. Hanson, "Preliminary Report on the 1977 and 1978 Seasons at Gush Halav (El Jish)," *BASOR* 233 (1979): 56.

²³ *SEG* 38.1590.

²⁴ Fanny Vitto, "Qiryat Tiv'on," *IEJ* 24 (1974): 279; and idem, "Kiriat Tiv'on," *RB* 9 (1972): 574–76.

²⁵ *SEG* 43.1055.

²⁶ James F. Strange, "Josephus on Galilee and Sepphoris" (paper presented at the Josephus Seminar of the Annual Meeting of the Society of Biblical Literature, Denver, Colorado, 19 November 2001).

²⁷ Meshorer, *City-Coins*.

²⁸ See comments by Meshorer in Nagy et al., *Sepphoris*, 201 and in his "The Lead Weight: Preliminary Report," *BA* 49 (1986): 16–17.

Galilee and Grecco-Roman Culture in the Time of Jesus 179

inscriptions providing the distance to the nearest city (post-120 C.E., various locations)[29]
- roof tiles with the stamp of the VI Ferrata legion (post-120 C.E., various sites)[30]
- a Greek honorific inscription to Septimus Severus (ca. 197 C.E., Khirbet Qision [Upper Galilee])[31]
- Greek funerary inscription (second century, Tiberias)[32]
- a Greek burial inscription (second or third century, Horvat Asaf [Upper Galilee])[33]
- Greek inscriptions on mosaic depicting Dionysos, Hercules, and related figures; nearby mosaic inscription reads "Hygeia" (early third century, Sepphoris)[34]
- Greek inscription from mosaic depicting Orpheus (late third or fourth century, Sepphoris)[35]
- Greek inscription on an amphora (second or third century, Sepphoris)[36]
- Greek mortarium inscription (Late Roman period [250–360 C.E.], Sepphoris)[37]
- Greek inscription reading "Good Luck" (pre-fourth century basilical building, Sepphoris)[38]
- one Greek burial inscription and two Latin burial inscriptions, all of Roman soldiers (second to fourth century, Tiberias)[39]

---

[29] Benjamin Isaac and Israel Roll, *Roman Roads in Judaea 1: The Legio-Scythopolis Road* (Oxford: B.A.R., 1982).

[30] E.g., David Adan-Bayewitz, "Kefar Hanania," *IEJ* 37 (1986): 178–79; D. Bahat, "A Roof Tile of the Legio VI Ferrata and Pottery Vessels from Horvat Hazon," *IEJ* 24 (1974): 160–69.

[31] *CIJ* 2:972.

[32] Yossi Stepanski, "Greek Funerary Inscriptions from Eastern Galilee," *Excavations and Surveys in Israel* 9 (1989/1990): 79.

[33] Ibid.

[34] Carol L. Meyers, Eric M. Meyers, Ehud Netzer, and Zeev Weiss, "The Dionysos Mosaic," in Nagy et al., *Sepphoris*, 111–16; Eric M. Meyers, Ehud Netzer, and Carol L. Meyers, *Sepphoris* (Winona Lake, Ind: Eisenbrauns, 1992).

[35] "The Mosaic Pavements of Roman and Byzantine Zippori." Cited 27 August 2003. Online: http://www.hum.huji.ac.il/archaeology/zippori/mosaic.htm.

[36] Meyers, Netzer, and Meyers, *Sepphoris*, 22.

[37] B. Lifshitz, "Notes d'épigraphique Grecque," *RB* 77 (1970): 76–83, no. 14; L. Y. Rahmani, "Miscellanea—Roman to Medieval," *Atiqot* 14 (1980): 103–13, esp. 104.

[38] James F. Strange, "The Eastern Basilical Building," in Nagy et al., *Sepphoris*, 117–21.

[39] *IGRP* 3:1204; M. Avi-Yonah, "Newly Discovered Latin and Greek Inscriptions," *QDAP* 12 (1946): 88–91, nos. 5 and 7.

- two sarcophagi with Greek inscriptions (possibly third or fourth century, Tiberias)[40]
- Latin funerary inscription (second to fourth century, Gabara)[41]
- nearly 280 inscriptions, with approximately 80 percent in Greek, 16 percent in Hebrew, and the rest in Aramaic or Palmyrene (late second to early fourth century, the catacombs of Beth She'arim)[42]
- a Semitic inscription on a proposed "chair of Moses" (fourth century or later, Chorazin)[43]
- two ostraca, one Semitic and one Greek (possibly third or fourth century, Meiron)[44]
- an inscribed ring (date is uncertain, but probably Roman period, Gush Halav)[45]
- a sarcophagus with a Greek inscription (date uncertain, but probably Roman period, Selame [Upper Galilee])[46]
- Greek grave inscription (date uncertain, but probably Roman period, Dibl [Upper Galilee])[47]

The proliferation of inscriptions in Galilee and the surrounding areas continues into the post-Constantinian era.

A clear trajectory is visible when one looks at Galilee's epigraphic corpus through this lens: the later the period, the more numerous the Greek inscriptions. Understanding the linguistic milieu of a region is admittedly more complicated than counting inscriptions, but it is difficult to escape the impression that Greek enjoyed considerably wider usage in the second and

---

[40] Chester C. McCown, "Epigraphic Gleanings," *AASOR* 2–3 (1922–23): 109–15; *SEG* 8:9–10.

[41] Avi-Yonah, " Newly Discovered Latin and Greek Inscriptions," 88 no. 4.

[42] Moshe Schwabe and Baruch Lifshitz, *The Greek Inscriptions* (vol. 2 of *Beth She'arim*; New Brunswick, N.J.: Rutgers University Press, 1974); Nahman Avigad, *The Excavations, 1953–1958* (vol. 3 of *Beth She'arim*; New Brunswick, N.J: Rutgers University Press, 1976). The statistics are from Lee I. Levine, "Beth She'arim," *OEANE* 2:309–11.

[43] Zeev Yeivin, "Chorazin," *NEAEHL* 1:301–4.

[44] Eric M. Meyers, James F. Strange, and Carol L. Meyers, *Excavations at Ancient Meiron, Upper Galilee, Israel 1971–1972, 1974–1975, 1977* (Cambridge, Mass.: American Schools of Oriental Research, 1981), 66; cf. the critique of Gideon Foerster, "Excavations at Ancient Meron (Review Article)," *IEJ* 37 (1987): 262–69.

[45] Meyers, Meyers, and Strange, *Excavations at the Ancient Synagogue of Gush Halav*, 125.

[46] *SEG* 32.1515.

[47] Leah Di Segni, "A Dated Inscription from Beth Shean and the Cult of Dionysos Ktistes in Roman Scythopolis," *Scripta classica Israelica* 16 (1997): 141 n. 5.

later centuries than it had had in the first. A more detailed analysis of the inscriptions of the sites in neighboring areas (e.g., Beth Yerah [Philoteria],[48] Gaba,[49] Qeren Naftali,[50] Kedesh,[51] and Scythopolis[52]) would reveal the same basic trajectory, though with more Hellenistic-period and first-century C.E. examples.

Architectural developments in Galilee display a similar pattern. Sepphoris, perhaps the best known site in Galilee, provides a good example of this phenomenon.[53] As early as Antipas, at least a few of the streets appear to have been on a grid pattern. Both an aqueduct system and the earliest phase of a basilical building date to the first century C.E., though most of the remains of the latter structure are dated later. Though some scholars have argued that the theater at Sepphoris is from the early first century C.E., this now seems to be a minority view among archaeologists, most of whom date it to the end of the first century or early in the next century. Indeed, a considerable amount of construction took place in the late first and early second centuries. Ultimately, two bathhouses were built, as well as a second aqueduct system and peristyle residences. An orthogonal plan for the city streets became even more pronounced. It is no surprise that post-Hadrianic rabbis refer to Greco-Roman urban structures at Sepphoris.[54] In short, Sepphoris is more typical of Greco-Roman cities in the eastern Mediterranean in the second and later centuries, not the first. Even so, a number of buildings typical of such cities have not yet been discovered at Sepphoris, such as an amphitheater, a stadium, a hippodrome, a nymphaeum, a gymnasium, or pagan temples.

---

[48] L. Sukenik, "The Ancient City of Philoteria (Beth Yerah)," *JPOS* 2 (1922): 101–7.

[49] For four Greek inscriptions, see Z. Safrai and M. Lin, "Mishmar Ha'Emeq," *Excavations and Surveys in Israel* 6 (1987–88): 11; Raphael Giveon, "Geva, A New Fortress City: From Tuthmosis to Herod," *BAIAS* 3 (1983–84): 45–46; Ayriel Siegelmann, "The Identification of Gaba Hippeon," *PEQ* 116 (1984–85): 89–93; Götz Schmitt, "Gaba, Getta und Gintikirmil," *ZDPV* 103 (1987): 22–48.

[50] E. W. G. Masterman, "Two Greek Inscriptions from Khurbet Harrawi," *PEQ* 20 (1908): 155–57.

[51] Moshe Fischer, Asher Ovadiah, and Israel Roll, "The Epigraphic Finds from the Roman Temple at Kedesh in the Upper Galilee," *Tel Aviv* 13 (1986): 60–66; McCown, "Epigraphic Gleanings," 114–15 (the other Kedesh inscription on 113 is included in the Fischer, Ovadiah, and Roll article).

[52] E.g., *SEG* 20.455, 457, 458, 546; 27.1446; 37.1529, 1530, 1531/40.1509; 41.1575; 46.2047, 2048; 47.2057.

[53] See the sources cited in Chancey, *Myth of a Gentile Galilee*, 69–83; Mark A. Chancey, "The Cultural Milieu of Ancient Sepphoris," *NTS* 47 (2001): 127–45; and Mark Chancey and Eric M. Meyers, "How Jewish Was Sepphoris in Jesus' Time?" *BAR* 26/4 (2000): 18–33, 61.

[54] For the citations, see James F. Strange, "Sepphoris," *ABD* 5:1090–93.

Such buildings are equally rare elsewhere in Galilee, especially in the first century. At Tiberias, because the modern city makes extensive excavation impossible, sizeable first-century remains are limited to a gate complex with towers and a paved road leading into the city.[55] More recently, an ancient stadium, presumably the one to which Josephus refers,[56] has been discovered, though it is not yet published. Two structures elsewhere are also notable. A rectangular building at Hammath Tiberias from the first or second century was initially identified as either a gymnasium or a palaestra, but very few people accepted this interpretation and the building's excavator himself eventually moved away from it, acknowledging that the remains could have been from an early synagogue.[57] More recently, at et-Tell, possibly Bethsaida, excavators have claimed that a rectangular basalt building was a temple of the imperial cult. Several arguments undergird this proposal: the renaming of Bethsaida by Philip as Julias, in honor of either Augustus's daughter or wife (probably the latter);[58] the identification of a female figurine with a veil and curly hair as Julia; the suggestion that a carving of an eagle found several miles away at Chorazin is from this temple; and the discovery nearby of a bronze incense shovel. The excavation team has not yet, however, found any statues, dedicatory inscriptions, votive gifts, animal bones, altars, or other artifacts that would confirm their theory about the building's identity. The jury is still out on the nature and use of this building.[59]

When discussing the first century C.E., it is also important to consider the information provided by Josephus, who mentions several notable buildings in the vicinity of the Sea of Galilee at the time of the first revolt. At Tiberias, there was a lavishly decorated palace, a *proseuche,* and the

---

[55] Yizhar Hirschfeld, "Tiberias," *OEANE* 5:203–6; Yizhar Hirschfeld, "Tiberias," *NEAEHL* 4:1464–70; Gideon Foerster, "Tiberias: Excavations in the South of the City," *NEAEHL* 4:1470–73

[56] *J.W.* 2.618 and 3.539–540.

[57] Moshe Dothan, *Hammath Tiberias: Early Synagogues and the Hellenistic and Roman Remains* (Jerusalem: Israel Exploration Society, 1983), 15–19; and idem, "Hammath-Tiberias," *NEAEHL* 2:575.

[58] See Fred Strickert, *Bethsaida: Home of the Apostles* (Collegeville, Minn.: Michael Glazier, Liturgical Press, 1998), 91–107 for discussion of this issue.

[59] Rami Arav, "Bethsaida Excavations: Preliminary Report, 1994–1996," in *Bethsaida: A City by the North Shore of the Sea of Galilee* (ed. Rami Arav and Richard A. Freund; Kirksville, Mo.: Truman State University Press, 1999), 2:3–113, esp. 19–24; Rami Arav, "An Incense Shovel from Bethsaida," *BAR* 23/1 (1997): 32; Rami Arav, Richard A. Freund, and John F. Shroder Jr., "Bethsaida Rediscovered," *BAR* 26/1 (2000): 44–56; Strickert, *Bethsaida,* 103–5.

afore-mentioned stadium.⁶⁰ Josephus also refers to a hippodrome at Taricheae/Magdala.⁶¹ When were this stadium and hippodrome, in particular, built? In the time of Antipas? Agrippa I? the period of direct Roman administration that began in 44 C.E.? during the reign of Agrippa II, who received Tiberias and Taricheae in 61 C.E.? For those of us whose primary concern is understanding the Galilee of Jesus, the date of construction makes a huge difference.

Later, we see the same type of development elsewhere in Galilee that we saw at Sepphoris. At Tiberias, in the second century, the main cardo was built, demonstrating the presence of orthogonal planning. Epiphanius refers to the beginning of the construction of a temple to Hadrian there, though he does not mention its completion.⁶² In the second or third century, a theater was constructed,⁶³ and in the fourth, a bathhouse. Bathhouses were also built at Capernaum in the second or third century⁶⁴ and at Rama, in Upper Galilee, in the third or fourth century.⁶⁵ The most significant architectural development from the third and following centuries is the appearance of synagogues with features that clearly reflect Greco-Roman influence.⁶⁶ Most of the remains visible in Galilee today should be attributed to even later centuries, in the Byzantine, not the Roman, period.

The communities surrounding Galilee underwent similar development. At Scythopolis, the closest city of the Decapolis, the whole array of new buildings emerged in the second century: streets on a grid pattern, an amphitheater, a bathhouse, a palaestra, another temple, and possibly a nymphaeum.⁶⁷ Other examples can be found at Kedesh, where a temple was built in the second century,⁶⁸ and at Beth Yerah, where a bathhouse was constructed in the third or fourth century.⁶⁹

The third and final category under review includes various kinds of finds that illustrate Greco-Roman artistic influence, such as statues, figurines,

---

⁶⁰ *Life* 276–303; *Life* 65, 68; *Life* 331; and *J.W.* 2.618 and 3.539–540.

⁶¹ *J.W.* 2.599; *Life* 132, 138.

⁶² Epiphanius, *Adv. Haereses* 30.12.1.

⁶³ Yizhar Hirschfeld and Gideon Foerster, "Tiberias," *NEAEHL* 4:1464–73; Yizhar Hirschfeld, "Tiberias," *OEANE* 5:203–6.

⁶⁴ John C. H. Laughlin, "Capernaum: From Jesus' Time and After," *BAR* 19/5 (1993): 54–61.

⁶⁵ Vassilios Tzaferis, "A Roman Bath at Rama," *Atiqot* 14 (1980): 66–75.

⁶⁶ Lee I. Levine, "Synagogues," *NEAEHL* 4:1421–24.

⁶⁷ Gaby Mazor and Rachel Bar-Hathan, "The Beth She'an Excavation Project, 1992–1994," *Excavations and Surveys in Israel* 17 (1998): 7–38.

⁶⁸ Moshe Fischer, Asher Ovadiah, and Israel Roll, "The Roman Temple at Kedesh, Upper Galilee: A Preliminary Study," *Tel Aviv* 11 (1984): 146–72.

⁶⁹ B. Maisler, M. Stekelis, and M. Avi-Yonah, "The Excavations at Beth Yerah (Khirbet el-Kerak) 1944–1946," *IEJ* 2 (1952): 165–73, 218–29.

numismatic images, frescoes, mosaics, funerary art, and lamps. Despite the breadth of this category, it includes relatively few artifacts from the first century C.E. As for statues, not a single one from this period has been discovered. Figurines include the previously mentioned curly headed figurine at et-Tell/Bethsaida and a bone figurine of a female at Tiberias, from the first or second century.[70]

Galilee's numismatic evidence clearly reflects Greco-Roman conventions, employing the types of symbols found on other coins of the Roman world and, especially, of the eastern Mediterranean. The coins of Antipas are decorated with designs such as wreaths, palm branches, and reeds. The coins issued by Tiberias around 53 C.E. and the other one issued there, probably by Agrippa II, also depict palm branches and inscriptions enclosed by wreaths. Both of the coins of Sepphoris, issued during the Revolt, have wreath-surrounded inscriptions; one also depicts a double cornucopia, with a cadeucus between them. In a striking departure from numismatic norms, however, all of these Galilean coins are void of images of rulers, other political figures, deities, or pagan temples, omissions that presumably reflect the region's Jewish ethos. These coins thus clearly reflect Greco-Roman influence, but they do so in a relatively conservative way. Galileans would have encountered pagan imagery on coins minted elsewhere, not locally.

What about frescoes and mosaics in the first century C.E.? At Sepphoris we have simple mosaics, often of black and white, and frescoes with basic geometric patterns: lines, dots, blocks of color. Similar designs are found at other sites, such as the frescoes at Jotapata.[71] Such frescoes are sometimes compared to those of Pompeii, a comparison that, while correct, needs clarification. The simple patterns mentioned above are indeed found at Pompeii, but that city's frescoes also depict deities; mythological figures; individuals of everyday occupations, such as a baker or scribe; and animals. Nothing like this has yet been discovered in first-century Galilean contexts;[72] the closest parallel is a first-century mosaic at Magdala depicting a fish, a ship, and a kantharos.[73] In addition, Josephus notes representations of animals (whether in frescoes, mosaics, or statues is unclear) at the

---

[70] Yizhar Hirschfeld, "Tiberias," *Excavations and Surveys in Israel* 9 (1989/1990): 107–9.

[71] Peter Richardson, "Jewish Galilee, Its Hellenization, Romanization, and Commercialization," in *New Views of First-Century Jewish and Christian Self-Definition* (ed. Fabian Udoh, Susannah Heschel, Gregory Tatum, and Mark Chancey; forthcoming).

[72] On the aniconic nature of the findings at Yodefat, see Adan-Bayewitz and Aviam, "Iotapata," 165.

[73] *SEG* 38.1590.

royal palace at Tiberias, but his passing reference suggests that such art was the exception, not the norm, and mobs destroyed these images at the start of the Revolt.[74] A final example of representative art comes not from a fresco or a mosaic, but from a bronze plaque at Sepphoris, dating to either the first century B.C.E. or the first century C.E., that depicts a winged figure standing in front of a table or altar.[75]

The now familiar pattern repeats itself: once again, there is much more evidence from the second and later centuries. A few marble statue fragments, exact date unknown, were found at Sepphoris;[76] at nearby Beth Yerah, a marble head of Tyche, date unknown, has been discovered;[77] and at Gaba, just southwest of Galilee, a head of Athena (date unknown) and a masklike spout from a jug (third century) have been discovered.[78] Several figurines have also been found at Sepphoris, including one of Pan and another of Prometheus, from the second or third century, and a bull, incense altar, and bowl from the fourth century. Additional figurines from Bethsaida may also date to this period.[79] Coins from Sepphoris as well as Tiberias begin depicting the emperor, gods (or at least, cult statues), and temples. As for Galilee's mosaics, most of the well-known ones are from the Byzantine period, but at Sepphoris one third-century mosaic depicts Dionysos, Heracles, and associated figures, while one from the third or fourth century depicts Orpheus. At Beth She'arim, both the catacombs themselves and the sarcophagi within are decorated with carvings of animals, people, and mythological figures, such as the famous sarcophagus fragment depicting Leda and the Swan.[80] In addition, lamps bear new symbols, some distinctly Jewish (e.g., menorah), others decidedly atypical for Jewish settings (e.g., Helios, erotic scenes).[81] At Chorazin, a basalt block from the third–sixth century C.E. synagogue depicts a carving of either a medusa or Helios, the date of which is unknown.[82] At Khirbet Shema, a gem with an image of Athena engraved on it was discovered in fourth-century fill but is probably earlier.[83]

---

[74] *Life* 65–67.

[75] See sources cited in notes 52 and 53 above.

[76] Zeev Weiss, "Greco-Roman Influences on the Art and Architecture of the Jewish City in Roman Palestine," in *Religious and Ethnic Communities in Late Roman Palestine* (ed. Hayim Lapin; Baltimore: University Press of Maryland, 1998), 245.

[77] Sukenik, "Ancient City."

[78] Safrai and Lin, "Mishmar Ha'Emeq," 11; Giveon, "Geva," 45–46.

[79] Arav, "Bethsaida Excavations," 22.

[80] Nahman Avigad and Benjamin Mazar, "Beth She'arim," *NEAEHL* 1:236–48.

[81] See comments by Eric C. Lapp in Nagy et al., *Sepphoris in Galilee,* 220–22.

[82] Yeivin, "Chorazin."

[83] Eric M. Meyers, A. Thomas Kraabel, and James F. Strange, *Ancient Synagogue Excavations at Khirbet Shema' Upper Galilee, Israel, 1970–1972* (Durham, N.C.: Duke University Press, 1976), 250–53.

Even a brief overview such as the present one makes the chronological dimension of the archaeological record quite clear: evidence for Greco-Roman culture is present in first-century C.E. contexts, but in relatively limited quantities; it is much more common in later contexts. The numerous first-century finds often vaguely alluded to in New Testament scholarship are difficult to locate in the archaeological publications. Discussions of Galilee's Greco-Roman milieu that emphasize the abundance of evidence seem to be based on synchronic generalizations that lump together artifacts and buildings from all centuries of the Roman period and perhaps the Byzantine period as well, not on a familiarity with the published evidence.

This chronological pattern poses a question that has too often been neglected: To what extent can we use later evidence to shed light on the cultural atmosphere of the first century C.E.? How one answers this question is related to how one treats a related one: Is the pattern due to accidents of survival and discovery or to ancient social realities?

I would argue that evidence from the second through fourth centuries should be used only with the greatest of caution, if at all, to understand the first century, especially the early part of that century during the time of Jesus and Antipas. In my opinion, the pattern in the evidence does correspond to ancient social realities. Greco-Roman culture was indisputably making inroads into Galilee at the turn of the era, as seen in the building projects of Antipas, but the Hellenization and Romanization of the region were processes that took time. Their full flowering took place in the second and subsequent centuries. The eventual increase in Greco-Roman culture can be attributed to two main developments. The first was the influx of Judean refugees from the south, in the wake of each of the two Jewish revolts. Many of these new arrivals were from Jerusalem and its vicinity, which we know was quite Hellenized in the late Second Temple period. They would have brought their southern, more Hellenized culture with them to their new home. The second event occurred in the early second century, when large numbers of Roman troops were permanently stationed in Galilee for the first time, arriving by 120 C.E.[84] The VI Ferrata legion was the main garrison in the area, establishing its headquarters south of Galilee in the Jezreel Valley and sending patrols and outposts throughout the region. It can hardly be coincidental that evidence for Greco-Roman culture dramatically increases after its arrival. These tremendous changes in

---

[84] Baruch Lifshitz, "Sur la date du transfert de la Legio VI Ferrata en Palestine," *Latomus* 19 (1960): 109–11; cf. also Zeev Safrai, "The Roman Army in Galilee" in Levine, *Galilee in Late Antiquity*4 103–114; Benjamin Isaac and Israel Roll, "Judea in the Early Years of Hadrian's Reign," *Latomus* 39 (1979): 54–66.

Galilee make it impossible to simply retroject conclusions drawn from later finds into the pre-70 C.E. era.

Some might argue that this emphasis on the relatively limited amount of early findings reflects a minimalist stance, since so much from antiquity has been lost forever or not yet found. We are better off, however, taking seriously the patterns in the evidence we do have than basing our arguments too heavily on evidence that we do not have. Furthermore, our present data is probably representative of what will be discovered in the future. If so, then those finds will reflect the same basic chronological pattern that the currently available evidence does.

This overview also suggests that we should pay more attention to regional variations in the extent of Greco-Roman influence. Other parts of Palestine—Jerusalem, some of the coastal cities, certain members of the Decapolis—reflect a more Hellenized milieu than does Galilee. My point is not that Galilee was uniquely isolated from the cultural trends of the larger Roman Empire but rather that we should be sensitive to the various ways in which Greco-Roman and local cultures interacted, rather than assuming that such interaction was uniform across regions and centuries.

Too often, our discussions in New Testament scholarship of Galilee's Hellenization and Romanization have skirted issues like these. We have too rarely noted the paucity of first-century evidence or the significance of the changes at the end of the first and the beginning of the second century. These topics merit far more attention than they have thus far received. If Jesus is to be properly put in his place—first-century Galilee, not third-century Galilee—then many of our characterizations of the Greco-Roman culture there need clarification, moderation, and perhaps even correction.

Josephus's Caesarian *Acta*:
History of a Dossier

Claude Eilers
McMaster University

The documents that Josephus has included in book 14 of the *Jewish Antiquities* have long attracted the attention of historians interested in Diaspora Jewry. They give us a unique glimpse into their condition, the Greek cities in which they lived, and the Romans who governed them. Without them we would be much more poorly informed about the history of the Diaspora in the Roman provinces.

These documents not only reveal an interesting history, but they also have an interesting history of their own, a history that is mostly invisible to us, but about which some things can be said. Each document will have been composed under individual circumstances and, for reasons that we shall discuss shortly, were copied and recopied until they came into the hands of Josephus. The process by which these documents came together is a question that is fundamental to their interpretation, as is the question of what role Josephus played in that process.

These questions are hardly new, and various answers have been offered over the last 130 years. One approach has been to suppose that Josephus found the documents in some literary work, usually that of Nicolaus of Damascus.[1] Serious objections to this view have been raised,[2] and these need not be repeated here, except perhaps to add the observation that Josephus' Caesarian *acta*—by which I mean all the documents that he has inserted into his narrative of Hyrcanus's encounter with Caesar (14.145–55, 190–264)—seem half-digested (if that). Indeed, insofar as the earlier history of this dossier have left any traces, it points in a rather different, nonliterary direction.

---

[1] The suggestion was first made by Niese 1876: 477–83.
[2] For a full discussion of this and similar theories, see Pucci Ben Zeev 1998: 388–89, with full bibliography.

1. SOME ARCHIVED DOCUMENTS

A more likely suggestion, which has had its fullest exploration in Pucci Ben Zeev's recent monograph, supposes Josephus's dossier was derived, directly or indirectly, from an archive or archives. The idea has been around for some time. An old (and unsatisfactory) version of it supposes that Josephus collected his material in Rome.[3] This, however, is unlikely given the state of Roman archives in Josephus's day and the significant practical challenges that such research would entail. There is in any case no reason to suppose that Josephus would have been allowed access.[4]

Moreover, one can point to places in the *acta* where archival processes have left traces, and mostly point away from Rome. One of these is a letter that Dolabella wrote to Ephesus in January 43 B.C. (14.225–227):

ἐπὶ πρυτάνεως Ἀρτέμωνος μηνὸς Ληναιῶνος προτέρᾳ. Δολαβέλλας αὐτοκράτωρ Ἐφεσίων ἄρχουσι βουλῇ δήμῳ χαίρειν. (226) Ἀλέξανδρος Θεοδώρου, πρευβευτὴς Ὑρκανοῦ τοῦ Ἀλεξάνδρου υἱοῦ ἀρχιερέως καὶ ἐθνάρχου τῶν Ἰουδαίων, ἐνεφάνισέ μοι περὶ τοῦ μὴ δύνασθαι στρατεύεσθαι τοὺς πολίτας αὐτοῦ, κτλ.

In the prytany of Artemon, on the first of the month Lenaion. Dolabella, imperator, to the magistrates, council, and people of Ephesus, greetings. (226) Alexander son of Theodoros, ambassador of Hyrcanus son of Alexander, high priest and ethnarch of the Jews, made clear to me that his fellow citizens were unable to serve in the military, etc.

Dolabella goes on to confirm the already-existing Jewish exemption from military service. The dating formula is noteworthy. Dating by eponymous magistrate was typical in the Greco-Roman world, and in Ephesus the eponym was a *prytanis*. Here, however, the eponymous formula was not part of Dolabella's original letter: he would have no reason to date his letter by the local system of its recipient, and his own words begin with the salutation. The date must have been added on its receipt in Ephesus, probably as an aid to filing[5]—what I call an "archival tag"—material that is neither part of the original document nor part of Josephus's commentary and has been added to help organize the material. The presence of this "archival tag," however, requires that our version be a descendent of the copy deposited in Ephesus, and not of a copy (say) that Dolabella had

---

[3] Laqueur 1920: 222–28; Thackery 1929: 70–71, 100.
[4] Pucci Ben Zeev 1998: 394–99.
[5] Other Roman documents to which local dates have been added: *Syll.*[3] 684 = *RDGE* 43; *Syll.*[3] 674 = *RDGE* 9; *Syll.*[3] 780 = *RDGE* 67; *Syll.*[3] 810.

kept for his own purposes. Insofar as archives were involved, then, we must suppose that they were not Roman.

The same point can be made about another document, a decree of Athens praising the high priest Hyrcanus (14.149–151):[6]

ἐπὶ πρυτάνεως καὶ ἱερέως Διονυσίου τοῦ Ἀσκληπιάδου, μηνὸς Πανέμου πέμπτῃ ἀπιόντος, ἀπεδόθη τοῖς στρατηγοῖς ψήφισμα Ἀθηναίων. (150) ἐπὶ Ἀγαθοκλέους ἄρχοντος· Εὐκλῆς <Ξ>ενάνδρου Α<ἰθαλίδη>ς[7] ἐγραμμάτευε· ... ἔδοξε τῷ δήμῳ, Διονύσιος Διονυσίου εἶπεν· (151) ἐπειδὴ Ὑρκανὸς {Ἀλεξάνδρου} ἀρχιερεὺς {καὶ ἐθνάρχης}[8] τῶν Ἰουδαίων, κτλ.

<u>When Dionysius the son of Asclepiades was the prytanis and priest, on the fifth day before the end of the month of Panemus, the decree of the Athenians was delivered to the magistrates</u>. (150) When Agathocles was archon, Eukles, son of <X>enander, of (deme) A<ithalide>s was secretary, ... resolved by the people; Dionysios son of Dionysios said: (151) whereas Hyrcanus {son of Alexander}, the high priest {and ethnarch} of the Jews, etc.

The decree proper begins, as all Athenian decrees do, with the eponymous formula ἐπὶ Ἀγαθοκλέους ἄρχοντος, which dates the document with certainty to spring 105 B.C.[9] In the immediately preceding line is another "archival tag" with a local dating formula (underlined here). The formula is clearly not Athenian—Athens did not use an eponymous prytanis and the month Panemos was not in its calendar.[10] The "archival tag" records the moment when the Athenian decree was delivered to some other city,[11] analogous with the deposit of Dolabella's letter, above. Two more details appear than in the Dolabella-"tag" (both redundant in the latter case because they are communicated in his salutation): that what follows is a ψήφισμα Ἀθηναίων and that it was delivered to the στρατηγοί of some city.

The eponymous formulas differ from one Greek city to the next: some use *prytaneis,* some priests, some archons, and so forth. Previous attempts to identify the city have failed because of a failure to recognize the unique combination in the eponym.[12] Only in Pergamum is the formula ἐπὶ

---

[6] This document is often left out of discussions of Josephus's documents (cf., e.g., Rajak 1984: 110).
[7] Μενάνδρου Ἁλιμούσιος codd.; Ξενάνδρου Αἰθαλίδης cf. IG ii2 1011.
[8] MSS Ὑρκανὸς Ἀλεξάνδρου ἀρχιερεὺς καὶ ἐθνάρχης. See below.
[9] Agathocles was archon in 106/105; the decree was passed in the tenth month: thus, no earlier than early April 105.
[10] Sherk 1990: 269–79; Samuel 1972: 57–58.
[11] Niese 1876: 481–82; Marcus 1943: 527 note c.
[12] Reinach 1904: 230 n. 2 opted for Ascalon; Niese 1876: 481–82, for Ephesus.

πρυτάνεως καὶ ἱερέως attested,[13] a fact that is consistent with the use of the month of Panemos[14] and delivery to the *strategoi*, who were Pergamum's chief magistrates.[15]

The delivery of the decree to Pergamum is a significant new fact, one that yet again undermines the idea that Roman archives were involved in the history of the dossier: this document at least came to Josephus via Pergamum (perhaps many times removed), not Rome. This Pergamum connection, however, is significant for another reason: Josephus's *acta* include another document from Pergamum of roughly the same period, a decree that is introduced with its own truncated archival tag (14.247–248):

Ψήφισμα Περγαμηνῶν. ἐπὶ πρυτάνεως Κρατίππου μηνὸς Δαισίου πρώτῃ γνώμη στρατηγῶν. ἐπεὶ οἱ Ῥωμαῖοι κατακολουθοῦντες τῇ τῶν προγόνων ἀγωγῇ τοὺς ὑπὲρ τῆς κοινῆς ἁπάντων ἀνθρώπων ἀσφαλείας κινδύνους ἀναδέχονται καὶ φιλοτιμοῦνται τοὺς συμμάχους καὶ φίλους ἐν εὐδαιμονίᾳ καὶ βεβαίᾳ καταστῆσαι εἰρήνῃ, (248) πέμψαντος πρὸς αὐτοὺς τοῦ ἔθνους τοῦ Ἰουδαίων καὶ Ὑρκανοῦ τοῦ ἀρχιερέως αὐτῶν πρέσβεις Στράτωνα Θεοδότου Ἀπολλώνιον Ἀλεξάνδρου Αἰνείαν Ἀντιπάτρου Ἀριστόβουλον Ἀμύντου Σωσίπατρον Φιλίππου ἄνδρας καλοὺς καὶ ἀγαθούς, κτλ.

> Decree of the people of Pergamum. In the prytany of Kratippos, on the first of the month of Daisios, a proposal of the magistrates. Whereas the Romans follow the practice of their ancestors by undertaking dangerous risks for the common safety of all mankind and strive to keep their allies and friends in a state of happiness and lasting peace; (248) and (whereas) the Jewish nation and their high priest Hyrcanus have sent as envoys to them Straton son of Theodotos, Apollonios son of Alexander, Aeneas son of Antipater, Aristobulos son of Amyntas, and Sosipatros son of Philip, worthy and excellent men, etc.

The decree, which seems to be the second in the city concerning these matters,[16] reflects Roman concern regarding news that had been brought to them by ambassadors from Judaea. The Roman senate passed a decree that instructed "King Antiochus, son of Antiochus" (Ἀντίοχος ὁ βασιλεὺς Ἀντιόχου υἱός) to cease harassing the Jewish state and return certain of its territories. The Seleucid king must be Antiochus IX Cyzicenus

---

[13] For parallels, see *Pergamum* viii/2.258, 323. Sometimes the formula is shortened to ἐπὶ ἱερέως or ἐπὶ πρυτάνεως (Sherk 1992: 238–39).

[14] Samuel 1972: 125–26.

[15] Allen 1983: 165–67: only *strategoi* could introduce public business in Pergamum, which makes it appropriate that the documents be delivered to them.

[16] The decree refers to an earlier decree at 14.253.

(114–95),[17] and Hyrcanus is therefore John Hyrcanus I, high priest from 135–104.

The Pergamum decree falls within the years 114–104, a decade in which we know that Athens also had diplomatic exchanges with Hyrcanus. Until now, the rough coincidence in the date of these decrees has not attracted attention. Now that we know that the Athenian decree was actually delivered to Pergamum, the inevitable question is whether the two documents are related: both being reactions to the arrival of a delegation from Judaea. It was the arrival of the Judaean delegation that prompted Pergamum to enthusiastically endorse Roman policy. It also praised Hyrcanus "because he is generous to all men generally and in particular upon those who come to him."[18] In Athens, the language is similar: Hyrcanus is praised for having shown goodwill toward the Athenians, for having hospitably received Athenian ambassadors and private citizens and arranging for their safe return.[19] Pergamum, like Athens, was impressed by the high priest's hospitality. Connecting the two documents would nicely explain the Athenian decree and why Hyrcanus became topical in the spring of 105. Connecting the two documents would also date the Pergamum decree to around 105.

2. THREE QUESTIONS

There are other reasons to suppose that the decrees belong together, though my thoughts on this front are still immature enough[20]—and space here in short enough supply—that I pass over them to consider three questions: (1) How did these two documents come to be included among Josephus's Caesarian *acta*? (2) Are there other early documents here? (3) What does this imply about the history of the dossier?

---

[17] Ritschl 1873: 610–11 n. 31 emended the text to <Δημητρί>ου υἱός and identified the monarch as Antiochus VII Sidetes; several scholars have followed him (Marcus 1943: 582 nn. a–d; {Schürer, 1973 #83@205–6 n. 7}; Rajak 1981: 78–79; etc.). See below n. 18.

[18] 14.252–253: καὶ ὅτι κοινῇ πάντας εὐεργετεῖ καὶ κατ' ἰδίαν τοὺς πρὸς αὐτὸν ἀφικομένους. The reference rules out the early date for the Pergamum decree (above, n. 17): Sidetes besieged Jerusalem in the first year of Hyrcanus's reign; hospitality was out of the question, much less a reputation for such.

[19] 14.151: τοὺς παραγινομένους Ἀθηναίων ἢ κατὰ πρεσβείαν ἢ κατ' ἰδίαν πρόφασιν ὡς αὐτὸν ὑποδέχεται φιλοφρόνως καὶ προπέμπει, τῆς ἀσφαλοῦς αὐτῶν ἐπανόδου προνοούμενος.

[20] I intend to explore this connection more fully in ch. 6 of a monograph with the tentative title *Josephus and the Evolution of Jewish Privileges* (in progress).

2.1. Why Are These Cocuments Included Here?

The answer to the first question is fairly straightforward. These documents appear in a narrative in which Hyrcanus II (high priest 63–43) plays a major role. They are introduced at the points in the narrative where, respectively, Caesar confirmed Hyrcanus's position (14.143–145) and (slightly later) received his ambassadors in Rome (14.185); documents concerning Hyrcanus II occupy a prominent place within the dossier (14.190–212); and Josephus introduces the main dossier with the claim that he was providing Roman measures concerning him (14.189). Clearly Josephus assumed that the Hyrcanus honoured in Athens and Pergamum was Caesar's contemporary. Unfortunately, he had the wrong Hyrcanus.

It is even worse, however. Josephus's mistake about Hyrcanus's identity has led him into an even more serious false step: he has altered his text.[21] The Athenian decree calls its honorand Hyrcanus, son of Alexander, high priest and ethnarch. This is the name and title of the grandson, the grandfather was a son of Simon and was never ethnarch. Clearly the name has been tampered with, which is in itself unsettling. Even more disturbing, however, is the fact that Athens is the only city in the Greek world where the eponyms are known well enough to expose such an error. Had the decree come from anywhere else, we would have assumed that the honours were for Hyrcanus II.

2.2. Are There Other Early Documents?

That Josephus is capable of errors will surprise no one, especially in light of four early documents within his Caesarian *acta*.[22] That he has included these documents, however, raises the question of what else is here. Are there other early documents within Josephus's Caesarian acta?

2.2.1. The Decree of Rabirius

One document that is worthy of further attention is a letter of the city Laodicea to the governor (14.241–243):

Λαοδικέων ἄρχοντες ⌜Γαίῳ Ῥαβ<ηρ>ίῳ²³ ⌜Γαίου υἱῷ <ἀνθ>υπάτῳ χαίρειν.
Σώπατρος Ὑρκανοῦ τοῦ ἀρχιερέως πρεσβευτὴς ἀπέδωκεν ἡμῖν τὴν παρὰ

---

[21] I assume the tampering is Josephus's, since the result makes the text fit *his* narrative.

[22] The two others are a letter of C. Fannius (cos. 161) to Cos arranging for safe passage for the Jewish ambassadors who had negotiated the first treaty between Rome and the Jews (14.233 with Niese 1906) and a renewal of the treaty in ca. 139 B.C. (14.145–148).

[23] Ῥαβελλίῳ (or sim.) codd.; Ῥαβηρίῳ Homolle on the basis of *I. Délos* 1859 (quoted below).

σοῦ ἐπιστολήν, δι' ἧς ἐδήλου<ς> ἡμῖν παρὰ Ὑρκανοῦ τοῦ Ἰουδαίων ἀρχιερέως ἐληλυθότας τινὰς γράμματα κομίσαι περὶ τοῦ ἔθνους αὐτῶν γεγραμμένα, (242) ἵνα τά τε σάββατα αὐτοῖς ἐξῇ ἄγειν καὶ τὰ λοιπὰ ἱερὰ ἐπιτελεῖν κατὰ τοὺς πατρίους νόμους, ὅπως τε μηδεὶς αὐτοῖς ἐπιτάσσῃ διὰ τὸ φίλους αὐτοὺς ἡμετέρους εἶναι καὶ συμμάχους, ἀδικήσῃ τε μηδεὶς αὐτοὺς ἐν τῇ ἡμετέρᾳ ἐπαρχίᾳ, κτλ.

The magistrates of Laodicea to Gaius Rab<er>ius, son of Gaius, <pro>consul, greetings. Sopatros, ambassador of the high priest Hyrcanus, gave us your letter, in which you made clear to us that some men had come from Hyrcanus, the high priest of the Jews, with documents concerning their people—(242) that they be free to observe their Sabbaths and perform their other sacred rites in accordance with their ancestral customs, and that no one impose orders on them, because they are our friends and allies, and that no one in our province injure them, etc.

The governor's name, like so many in Josephus, is corrupt but can be corrected on the basis of a bilingual inscription from Delos:[24]

[C. Rabeirium C.f.] | pro cos. | ⌜Γ⌝άιον Ῥαβήριον ⌜Γ⌝αίου | υἱὸν ἀνθύπατον | Ῥωμαίων.

The two documents clearly belong together, but their date has proven controversial. Some have identified the governor as Rabirius Postumus, an officer of Caesar, and dated his proconsulship (and this document) to the year 47; the Jewish high priest in the letter would therefore be Hyrcanus II Jannaeus.[25] Others have argued that the high priest is John Hyrcanus I, dating the document before 104 B.C., identifying the proconsul as Rabirius Postumus's maternal grandfather.[26] The primary argument for the Caesarian date is the fact that Josephus has included the document among his Caesarian *acta*. It is clear, however, that Josephus was unable to exclude documents pertaining to the first Hyrcanus, and there are reasons to suppose that this is so here.

2.2.1.1. Rabirius could not have been proconsul of Asia under Caesar. It is worth emphasizing how complete our knowledge of the governors of Asia is. In fact, it is sufficient to exclude Rabirius from all the years that

---

[24] Homolle 1882; *I. Délos* 1859 = *CIL* 12 773 = *ILLRP* 399.
[25] Broughton 1986: 181; Pucci Ben Zeev 1998: 194 (with full bibliography); Siani-Davies 2001: 56–62; Gruen 2002: 89.
[26] Reinach 1899: 165; Reinach 1904: 250 n. 1; Syme 1967: 262–63 = Syme 1979–91: ii.639–41; Champlin 1989: 54; Brennan 2000: 548.

Hyrcanus II was high priest,[27] including the years of Caesar's dictatorship, where Rabirius is sometimes placed. The Caesarian years are the most relevant, since this is where his proconsulship is sometimes placed, so these will receive the most attention. After Pharsalus, Caesar entrusted Asia to one of his most senior supporters, Cn. Domitius Calvinus (cos. 53).[28] According to the *Bellum Alexandrinum* (34.1), before becoming embroiled in Egypt, "Caesar had handed over to Domitius Calvinus Asia and the provinces bordering it for him to govern" ("Domitium Calvinum, cui Caesar Asiam finitimasque provincias administrandas tradiderat"), a point confirmed by Dio.[29] This places Asia under Calvinus in 48/47, and while he was in charge of Asia, Rabirius could not be.

Provincial governors held their positions from summer to summer. Calvinus had completed one term (48/47) when he was reconfirmed by Caesar following the Battle of Zela (August 47) and entrusted with resettlement of the region.[30] Sometime in the subsequent months an altar was erected to him near Zela,[31] which both confirms his presence and implies his success in it. Calvinus did not stay in Asia for the whole of 47/46 but was recalled westward to command a wing at the Battle of Thapsus (April 46).[32] A proquaestor, Appuleius, is the next official attested in the province.[33] Standard practice on the early departure of a governor was to delegate authority to a subordinate,[34] which implies that Appuleius was Calvinus's replacement, governing *pro praetore*. He was replaced by P. Servilius Isauricus (cos. 48), who governed the province as proconsul until mid-44.[35] Isauricus was succeeded in turn by C. Trebonius (suff. 45), who had been designated before Caesar's assassination and proceeded to his province shortly thereafter.[36] Thus, Caesar's governors are:

---

[27] For the years down to 50 B.C., see Brennan 2000: 566–70; some uncertainty remains about the years 53/52 and 52/51, but these can be excluded for Rabirius on the grounds that Laodicea and Tralles were in different provinces for the years 56–49: Syme 1939: 305–6 = Syme 1979–91: i.125.
[28] *MRR* ii.277; MRR iii.181.
[29] Dio 42.46.1: "[Caesar] sent Cn. Domitius Calvinus and put Asia under his command" (Γναῖον δὲ Δομίτιον Καλουῖνον ἔπεμψε, τήν τε ᾿Ασίαν οἱ ... προστάξας). Cf. Dio 42.47.1.
[30] Dio 42.49.1: "After completing these things he ordered Domitius to settle other matters" (πράξας δὲ ταῦτα, καὶ τὰ λοιπὰ τῷ Δομιτίῳ καταστήσασθαι κελεύσας) .
[31] *Studia Pontica* iii.260 = IGR iii.10: Καλουείνῳ θεῷ Φίλων.
[32] *B. Afr.* 86, 93.
[33] Cic. *Fam.* 13.45–46 (= SB 271–72), with Shackleton Bailey 1977: ii.438. For the date of the letter, Syme 1939: 315–17 = Syme 1979–91: i.133–35.
[34] Cf. Marshall 1972: 907.
[35] Syme 1939: 307–8 = Syme 1979–91: i.127–8; *MRR* ii.298, 310.
[36] App. *BC* 3.2.4–5; see also the references collected at *MRR* ii.330.

48/47	Cn. Domitius Calvinus (cos. 53)
47/46	" " (early departure) / Appuleius, proq.
46/45	P. Servilius Isauricus, procos. (cos. 48)
45/44	" "
44/43	C. Trebonius, procos. (suff. 45)

The notion that Rabirius was proconsul of Asia under Caesar, then, is precluded by the fact that we already know who Caesar's proconsuls were. Some have suggested that Calvinus had a general command over the region and that Rabirius was (in effect) his subordinate.[37] Day-to-day jurisdiction may indeed have been left to subordinates while Calvinus concentrated on the military challenge presented by Pharnaces.[38] The Rabirius of Josephus and *I. Délos* 1859, however, was a proconsul, and by definition a proconsul was no one's subordinate, so Rabirius could not have served *under* Calvinus. A date following Calvinus's withdrawal from the province, but before the arrival of Isauricus, is no less difficult. Such a successor, holding an *imperium* that had been delegated by the departing governor, will have governed *pro praetore* rather than *pro consule,* as Appuleius did, whose presence in any case blocks Rabirius. Finally, this is one of the few moments in Rabirius's career where his exact whereabouts are actually known: on 1 January 46 he delivered a shipload of supplies to the African coast and was sent by Caesar for more,[39] a task suitable to Rabirius's equestrian background, but surely beneath a potential governor of Asia. (Caesar's proconsuls of Asia, it should be noted, were all consulars. There is no clear evidence that Rabirius was even a senator.[40]) The prosopography, then, is very much against a Caesarian date.

2.2.1.2. Hyrcanus's titulature. The letter of Laodicea refers to the arrival of an ambassador from "Hyrcanus, high priest of the Jews" (Ὑρκανοῦ τοῦ Ἰουδαίων ἀρχιερέως). In mid-47, however, Caesar bestowed on Hyrcanus II the additional title "ethnarch."[41] That "ethnarch" was considered a necessary part of the second Hyrcanus's title is well illustrated by the fact

---

[37] So, explicitly, Siani-Davies 2001: 59; implicitly, it seems, in Broughton 1986: 181.
[38] For the details, see *B. Alex.* 34 with Freber 1993: 81 n. 387.
[39] *B. Afr.* 8; for the date, cf. *B. Afr.* 7, 9.
[40] Rabirius was an equestrian when Cicero defended him in December 54 or January 53 (for the date, see Alexander 1990: no. 305).
[41] See esp. 14.194: Ὑρκανὸν Ἀλεξάνδρου καὶ τὰ τέκνα αὐτοῦ ἐθνάρχας Ἰουδαίων εἶναι.

that Josephus saw fit to add it to Athenian decree discussed above.[42] Contemporary documents in Josephus's Caesarian acta refer to Hyrcanus II as "ethnarch":

191 Ὑρκανὸν υἱὸν Ἀλεξάνδρου ἀρχιερέα καὶ ἐθνάρχην Ἰουδαίων
196 ὁ ἀρχιερεὺς αὐτὸς καὶ ἐθνάρχης τῶν Ἰουδαίων
200 Ὑρκανὸν Ἀλεξάνδρου ἀρχιερέα Ἰουδαίων καὶ ἐθνάρχην
209 Ὑρκανὸν τὸν ἐθνάρχην
211 Ὑρκανοῦ τοῦ Ἀλεξάνδρου ἀρχιερέως Ἰουδαίων καὶ ἐθνάρχου
226 Ὑρκανοῦ τοῦ Ἀλεξάνδρου υἱοῦ ἀρχιερέως καὶ ἐθνάρχου τῶν Ἰουδαίων
306 Ὑρκανῷ ἀρχιερεῖ καὶ ἐθνάρχῃ
314 Ὑρκανοῦ τοῦ ἀρχιερέως καὶ ἐθνάρχου
317 Ὑρκανοῦ τοῦ ἐθνάρχου Ἰουδαίων

In the letter to Rabirius, by contrast, Hyrcanus is called high priest, but not ethnarch—not once, but twice. This is the correct title for Hyrcanus I and identical to his title in the decrees of Pergamum and (it seems) Athens.[43] The titulature again confirms the second century date.

2.2.1.3. *I. Délos* 1859 fits a second-century context better. There are two pieces of evidence for Rabirius's proconsulship: the letter of Laodicea and *I. Délos* 1859. The inscription also fits better in the second century. The most secure dates for inscriptions come from prosopography, the identification of someone in the inscription that we know from another dated context. Other dating criteria include style, the development of institutions, the evolution of language, or the historical context. In the case of Rabirius, prosopographical considerations point toward the late second century, as we have seen, and other criteria confirm that date. In *I. Délos* 1859 Rabirius is called the "proconsul of the Romans" (ἀνθύπατον Ῥωμαίων), which is a typical way to refer to an official in the second century. (Rome was originally only one power among many—its officials were thus identified as Roman.) Over seventy cases of magistrates "of the Romans" survive in Greek inscriptions; almost all belong to the second century, and only one comes after Sulla.[44] The changing usage is not difficult to explain: as Roman rule became entrenched, magistrates' Romanness was implicit. The

---

[42] 14.153 with n. 8 above.

[43] Pergamum (14.248): Ὑρκανοῦ τοῦ ἀρχιερέως αὐτῶν (sc. Ἰουδαίων); Athens (14.149): Ὑρκανὸς ἀρχιερεὺς τῶν Ἰουδαίων (as emended above).

[44] *F. Delphes* iii/4.254 (55/54 B.C.). The same usage is found at 14.213 (Ἰούλιος Γάιος στρατηγὸς <ἀνθ>ύπατος Ῥωμαίων). In ch. 8 of the work mentioned above (n. 20) I will argue that this document dates to 62 B.C.

appearance of Ῥωμαίων in *I. Délos* 1859, then, is consistent with what the prosopography and Hyrcanus's titulature demand: a late second-century date.

2.2.1.4. Dating the older Rabirius. Various considerations converge, then, to place Rabirius's proconsulship in the late second century, and nothing about these two documents argues against it. The recipient of the letter of Laodicea will be maternal grandfather of Caesar's officer,[45] and it will be worthwhile to pull together what we know about him. He must be the father of C. Rabeirius C.f. Gal., a *tribunus militum* who appears in the *consilium* of Pompeius Stabo in 89 B.C.[46] The son will have been born in around 121,[47] implying roughly 151 as a birth year for the father and a praetorship in approximately 110 (give or take a decade). The letter to him, which refers to Hyrcanus I, requires a date before 104.

The date roughly coincides with decrees of 105 from Athens and Pergamum, and there is reason to suspect that it was related to the Pergamum decree. As was noted long ago by Reinach,[48] Rabirius had sent his letter to Laodicea through the agency of "Sopatros, the ambassador of Hyrcanus the high priest" (Σώπατρος Ὑρκανοῦ τοῦ ἀρχιερέως πρεσβευτής; 14.241). One of Hyrcanus's ambassadors in Pergamum was named "Sosipatros son of Philip" (Σωσίπατρον Φιλίππου; 14.248). The name is strikingly similar; a simple error of a kind so common in Josephus's manuscripts could explain the difference, and the similarities go beyond the name. The date is about right; both men served as ambassador of Hyrcanus "the high priest" (but not ethnarch); both were part of larger delegations—four other envoys are named in the Pergamum decree, while the Laodicean letter refers to "certain persons" coming from Hyrcanus to the proconsul;[49] both brought documents pertaining to the Jews;[50] and presumably both came from Rome.[51] This means, however, that instead of

---

[45] Syme 1967: 263 = Syme 1979–91: ii.640; Brennan 2000: 548.
[46] *ILLRP* 415 = *ILS* 8888 with Broughton 1951–52: ii.35.
[47] Among the other military tribunes listed in the *consilium* are a praetor of 81 and a consul of 78, both born no later than 121.
[48] Reinach 1899: 165–66.
[49] 14.241, where Rabirius had written to Laodicea that "certain men came from Hycanus, high priest of the Jews, and brought documents written concerning their nation" (παρὰ Ὑρκανοῦ τοῦ Ἰουδαίων ἀρχιερέως ἐληλυθότας τινὰς γράμματα κομίσαι περὶ τοῦ ἔθνους αὐτῶν γεγραμμένα).
[50] For Laodicea, see 14.241 (n. 49 above); the Pergamum decree summarizes a senate decree concerning the Jewish state (14.249–250) and accepts delivery of a letter and this senate decree (252), which are deposited in the archives (253).
[51] The documents to which Rabirius referred (n. 49) were presumably Roman.

having two documents of 105 in Josephus's Caesarian *acta*, we probably have three.

2.2.2. The Decree of Halicarnassus

There may be a fourth. Toward the end of his dossier, Josephus includes a decree of Halicarnassus (14.256–258):

Ψήφισμα Ἁλικαρνασέων. ἐπὶ ἱερέως Μέμνονος τοῦ Ἀριστείδου, κατὰ δὲ ποίησιν Εὐωνύμου, Ἀνθεστηριῶνος[52] ἔδοξε τῷ δήμῳ εἰσηγησαμένου Μάρκου Ἀλεξάνδρου. (257) ἐπεὶ τὸ πρὸς τὸ θεῖον εὐσεβές τε καὶ ὅσιον ἐν ἅπαντι καιρῷ διὰ σπουδῆς ἔχομεν κατακολουθοῦντες τῷ δήμῳ τῶν Ῥωμαίων πάντων ἀνθρώπων ὄντι εὐεργέτῃ καὶ οἷς περὶ τῆς Ἰουδαίων φιλίας καὶ συμμαχίας ***[53] πρὸς τὴν πόλιν ἔγραψεν, ὅπως συντελῶνται αὐτοῖς αἱ εἰς τὸν θεὸν ἱεροποιίαι καὶ ἑορταὶ αἱ εἰθισμέναι καὶ σύνοδοι, (258) δεδόχθαι {καὶ ἡμῖν}[54] Ἰουδαίων τοὺς βουλομένους ἄνδρας τε καὶ γυναῖκας τά τε σάββατα ἄγειν καὶ τὰ ἱερὰ συντελεῖν κατὰ τοὺς Ἰουδαίων νόμους καὶ τὰς προσευχὰς ποιεῖσθαι πρὸς τῇ θαλάττῃ κατὰ τὸ πάτριον ἔθος, κτλ.

Decree of the people of Halicarnassus. In the priesthood of Memnon, son of Aristeides and of Euonymos by adoption, in (the month of) Anthesterion, on the motion of Marcus son of Alexander, the people resolved the following. (257) Whereas in every circumstance we are earnestly pious toward the divine and holiness, and we follow the example of the Roman people, who are the benefactors of all men, even in the things that *** wrote to our city concerning their friendship and alliance with the Jews— (258) that they should perform their sacred rites towards their god and their accustomed festivals and gatherings—it was resolved {by us} that those Jews who wish, both men and women, can observe the Sabbath and perform their sacred rites according to the laws of the Jews and build synagogues near the sea in their ancestral fashion, etc.

Within Halicarnassus the decree was dated by an eponymous priest. Outside of the city, however, the decree would have been undateable, as indeed it is for us. Reinach noted the similarity between this document and the letter to Rabirius and proposed that it, too, is early.[55] The people of Halicarnassus grant to the Jews several rights, including that they be allowed (1) to observe the Sabbath (τά τε σάββατα ἄγειν) and (2) to per-

---

[52] The lacuna proposed here by Niese (ad loc.) and Marcus (ad loc.) is unnecessary: decrees of Halicarnassus are often dated by month alone.

[53] There is probably a lacuna here or after πρὸς τὴν πόλιν: a subject is required for ἔγραψεν (presumably the name of a Roman official).

[54] καὶ ἡμῖν codd.; delevi.

[55] Reinach 1904: 250 nn. 1–3.

form their sacred rights according to their customs (τὰ ἱερὰ συντελεῖν κατὰ τοὺς Ἰουδαίων νόμους).[56] In their letter to Rabirius, Laodicea repeats his instructions to them: that the Jews be free (1) to observe their Sabbath (τά τε σάββατα αὐτοῖς ἐξῆ ἄγειν), and (2) to perform their other sacred rites according to their ancestral customs (τὰ λοιπὰ ἱερὰ ἐπιτελεῖν κατὰ τοὺς πατρίους νόμους).

The close parallel between the documents, both in content and in wording, is easiest to explain if they were reacting to the same measure and are both reflecting the language of the original ruling, though by itself it cannot be decisive. A connection to the letter to Rabirius seems likely for other reasons. Not only does Halicarnassus move to implement the same Jewish privileges as were introduced in Laodicea (and with virtually identical wording), but they do so as a result of the same impetus, a letter that instructs them to do so: Laodicea responds to a letter of Rabirius; Halicarnassus claims to be following what had been *written* (ἔγραψεν) to them concerning the Jews. (The letter writer's name has unfortunately fallen out of the text; presumably he was a provincial official.) In addition, both cities justify their measures by reference to a Jewish-Roman alliance.[57]

The decree of Halicarnassus also has points of contact with the decree of Pergamum, one of the other documents of 105. Pergamum also mentions a letter concerning the Jews[58] and a Jewish alliance with Rome.[59] The decrees of Pergamum and Halicarnassus also share diplomatic language typical of the second century. Halicarnassus claims that, by pursuing a policy of toleration toward the Jews, they are following the example of the Roman people, who are described as "the benefactors of all men" (τῷ δήμῳ τῶν Ῥωμαίων πάντων ἀνθρώπων ὄντι εὐεργέτῃ); Pergamum praises the Romans for undertaking dangers in the interest of the common safety. The sentiment that the Roman *populus,* collectively, benefactor or saviour of the Greeks is reasonably well attested in Greek epigraphy and has attracted the attention of several scholars of note.[60] The slogan reflects something in the political climate in the Greek East following Rome's first arrival there

---

[56] They also (uniquely) grant the right to make "προσευχαί near the sea," but that may have reflected local priorities.

[57] Laodicea: 14.242; Halicarnassus 14.257.

[58] A letter and a senate decree were delivered to the city (14.252) and deposited in the city's archives (253).

[59] Pergamum: 14.249: ὅπως μηδὲν ἀδικῇ Ἀντίοχος ὁ βασιλεὺς Ἀντιόχου υἱὸς Ἰουδαίους συμμάχους Ῥωμαίων.

[60] Robert 1969: 57–61; Gruen 1984: 196–97; Ferrary 1988: 124–32; Erskine 1994: 70–87.

in the second century: Rome is seen to be impartial and benevolent.[61] The phrase disappeared during the first century, however: only a single extant example comes after Sulla.[62]

The slogan was passing from diplomatic usage. Why? One reason was surely that perceptions of Roman benevolence had been undermined by Roman rule. The end was surely near when Mithridates turned the phrase back at the Romans by calling them "the common enemy" (τοὺς κοινοὺς πολεμίους) during his occupation of Asia Minor.[63] The changing language is reflective of a changing dynamic in Roman-provincial relations. Insofar as provincials looked toward the Romans for salvation, it was less and less toward the Roman people as a collective and more and more for individual Romans. In the last decades of the Roman Republic, it was Pompey, Caesar, and other notables who were called "the common benefactor of the Greeks."[64]

Most commentators have dated the Halicarnassus decree to the age of Caesar.[65] It is more likely, however, that it is yet another early document. The parallels between it and the letter to Rabirius point in such a direction, as does its use of diplomatic language that is typical of the second century. Nothing in the document itself is inconsistent with such a date, and its presence among Josephus's Caesarian *acta* cannot argue one way or the other.

2.2.3. The Jews of Sardis

Given the presence of the other early documents in Josephus's Caesarian narrative, adding two more—the letter to Rabirius and the Halicarnassus decree—should cause no great surprise. The surprise, if there is one, will come with the references in these two documents to the establishment of Jewish religious freedom, specifically the right to observe the Sabbath and perform Jewish rites—a measure that is usually attributed to Caesar.[66] This attribution, however, is based on these very documents, and the primary

---

[61] Erskine 1994: 82–87.

[62] Robert 1969: 52–53 (62 B.C.). The words appear in honours for Cn. Pompeius Theophanes, who is praised for having used his friendship with Pompey to regain his city's liberty, lost following the Mithridatic war, from the Romans, "benefactors of all." The wording is nostalgic and excessive, presumably intentionally so.

[63] *Syll.*³ 741, ll. 32–33.

[64] Pompey (c. 62): *ILS* 9459; Q. Cicero (c. 60): Ferrary 2000b: 351–53 no. 6; Caesar (c. 48): Raubitschek 1954: docs. "B" (Athenians on Delos), "H" (Karatheia), "K" (Pergamum), "M" (Samos), "N" (Chios).

[65] E.g., Smallwood 1976: 135 and n. 53; Schürer et al. 1973–87: iii/1.117 n. 37; Pucci Ben Zeev 1998: 214–15; Saulnier 1981: 189, hesitates between a Caesarian and Augustan date.

[66] Rajak 1984; Rajak 1985: 24–25; Gruen 2002: 89–92.

justification for dating them to the time of Caesar is the fact that Josephus has inserted them into his narrative of 47. It is worth noting, however, that the Jews of at least one Greek city had significant privileges before Caesar's dictatorship. We know this from a letter of L. Antonius to Sardis (14.235):

Λούκιος Ἀντώνιος Μάρκου υἱὸς ἀντιταμίας καὶ ἀντιστράτηγος Σαρδιανῶν ἄρχουσι βουλῇ δήμῳ χαίρειν. Ἰουδαῖοι πολῖται ὑμέτεροι προσελθόντες μοι ἐπέδειξαν αὐτοὺς σύνοδον ἔχειν ἰδίαν κατὰ τοὺς πατρίους νόμους ἀπ' ἀρχῆς καὶ τόπον ἴδιον, ἐν ᾧ τά τε πράγματα καὶ τὰς πρὸς ἀλλήλους ἀντιλογίας κρίνουσι, τοῦτό τε αἰτησαμένοις ἵν' ἐξῇ ποιεῖν αὐτοῖς τηρῆσαι καὶ ἐπιτρέψαι ἔκρινα.

L. Antonius, son of Marcus, *proquaestor pro praetore*, to the magistrates, council, and people of Sardis, greetings. Jewish citizens of yours have come to me and pointed out that from the earliest times they have had an association of their own in accordance with their native laws and a place of their own, in which they decide their affairs and controversies with one another; and upon their request that they be free to do these things, I decided to preserve and allow it.

This letter belongs to 49,[67] and in it Antonius mentions several important Jewish privileges: freedom to associate (as is implied by the mention of their synod) and a degree of internal autonomy (they decide on controversies among themselves). Clearly *some* privileges already existed in early 49 B.C., at least in Sardis. In addition these had existed (according to Antonius) "from the earliest times" (ἀπ' ἀρχῆς): Caesar's decisions as dictator had nothing to do with them.

As it happens, we have other evidence from Sardis, a decree that also appears among Josephus's Caesarian *acta* (14.259–266):

Ψήφισμα Σαρδιανῶν. ἔδοξε τῇ βουλῇ καὶ τῷ δήμῳ στρατηγῶν εἰσηγησαμένων. ἐπεὶ οἱ κατοικοῦντες ἡμῶν ἐν τῇ πόλει ἀπ' ἀρχῆς Ἰουδαῖοι πολῖται πολλὰ καὶ μεγάλα φιλάνθρωπα ἐσχηκότες διὰ παντὸς παρὰ τοῦ δήμου καὶ νῦν εἰσελθόντες ἐπὶ τὴν βουλὴν καὶ τὸν δῆμον παρεκάλεσαν, (260) ἀποκαθισταμένων αὐτοῖς τῶν νόμων καὶ τῆς ἐλευθερίας ὑπὸ τῆς συγκλήτου καὶ τοῦ δήμου τοῦ Ῥωμαίων ἵνα κατὰ τὰ νομιζόμενα ἔθη συνάγωνται καὶ πολιτεύωνται καὶ διαδικάζωνται πρὸς αὐτούς, δοθῇ τε καὶ τόπος αὐτοῖς, εἰς ὃν συλλεγόμενοι μετὰ γυναικῶν καὶ τέκνων ἐπιτελῶσιν τὰς πατρίους εὐχὰς καὶ θυσίας τῷ θεῷ· (261) δεδόχθαι τῇ βουλῇ καὶ τῷ δήμῳ συγκεχωρῆσθαι αὐτοῖς συνερχομένοις ἐν ταῖς προαποδεδειγμέναις ἡμέραις πράσσειν τὰ κατὰ τοὺς αὐτῶν νόμους, ἀφορισθῆναι δ' αὐτοῖς καὶ τόπον ὑπὸ

---

[67] For the date, Eilers 1995.

τῶν στρατηγῶν εἰς οἰκοδομίαν καὶ οἴκησιν αὐτῶν, ὃν ἂν ὑπολάβωσιν πρὸς
τοῦτ᾽ ἐπιτήδειον εἶναι, ὅπως τε τοῖς τῆς πόλεως ἀγορανόμοις ἐπιμελὲς ᾖ
καὶ τὰ ἐκείνοις πρὸς τροφὴν ἐπιτήδεια ποιεῖν εἰσάγεσθαι.

Decree of the people of Sardis. The council and people passed this motion after the magistrates introduced it. Our Jewish citizens, who have lived in our city since ancient times, have continually enjoyed many great privileges from the people and now have come before the council and people. They have requested that, since their customs and freedom have been restored by the senate and people of the Romans, in keeping with their customary traditions they might gather together, have a communal life, and have jurisdiction in cases among themselves, and that a place be given to them, in which they can gather with their wives and children to fulfill their ancestral prayers and sacrifices to their god. Because of this, the council and people have decreed to permit them to come together on the designated days and perform what is required by their laws, and also that the magistrates set aside a place for them to build and use which they consider suitable for this purpose, and that the city's market officials take care that they import provisions suitable for them to eat.

There are many interesting things in this document, including a possible mismatch between what the Jews of Sardis requested and what they actually got.[68] For now I want to consider only the document's date: specifically whether it comes before or after Antonius's letter.

A comparison of the two documents suggests that the decree is earlier. In the first place, in the decree the Jews are reported to have asked their city for the right of self-adjudication (διαδικάζωνται). To judge from Antonius's letter, they not only already have this right but also have a special place for performing it (τόπον ἴδιον, ἐν ᾧ τά τε πράγματα καὶ τὰς πρὸς ἀλλήλους ἀντιλογίας κρίνουσι). Their request to keep this privilege is granted. Since they cannot ask to keep what they do not already have, the decree must come first.

Second, the decree reports that Jews asked for a place where they could gather with their families to worship, a request that Sardis seems to grant: they are given a τόπος "to build and use." In Antonius's letter, however, the Jews are said already to have a place in which they conduct their business. The Jews possessed communal property—a synagogue—in 49 but had to ask for such property at the time of the decree. Again, the decree should come first—surely the property that they had won from Sardis was the property that they boasted of before Antonius.

Finally, in the Sardis decree, the Jews request the right to "gather together and associate" (συνάγωνται καὶ πολιτεύωνται). The decree does

---

[68] See Pucci Ben Zeev 1998: 223.

not state that their request was granted. However, the Jews who approach L. Antonius claim to have an association (σύνοδος) and ask that it be preserved, which seems to assume their request was granted either immediately or in the interim. Yet again, however, the decree comes first.

The natural order of the documents, then, would be to date the decree before the letter. A consensus has emerged, however, that asserts the opposite, that L. Antonius's decision comes before the decree. This in part draws on a widely held conviction that the decree was inspired by the measures of Caesar.[69] Caesar, however, is nowhere mentioned, an unthinkable omission had his rulings really laid behind it. Moreover, the narrative implied by Caesar's involvement is problematic. If the decree comes after Antonius's letter, the narrative must be as follows. (1) Before 49, the Jews had freedom of association, a degree of autonomy in community affairs, and a place to meet (i.e., a synagogue), as is acknowledged in L. Antonius's letter. (2) Early in 49, L. Antonius confirmed these privileges. (3) Between 49 and circa 47, the Jews of Sardis lost these privileges, as well as their synagogue. (4) Shortly after 47, in response to Caesar's measures in Palestine of that year, a civic decree returns to the Jews all the rights that they had lost.

The *order* of events is not completely unbelievable: the Jews in Asia Minor seem to have suffered their share of setbacks. The chronology, however, is exceedingly tight. It requires, for example, that the Jews lost all their privileges in the city (step 3) within a year or two of a Roman official's explicit confirmation of these privileges. It also requires what must have been sweeping anti-Semitic measures in Sardis. The synagogue that the Jews had possessed in 49 must have been expropriated and their community structures forcibly dissolved. But nothing in the decree suggests such tumult. Quite the opposite: Sardis can proudly claim that their Jewish citizens had enjoyed significant privileges "continually" (διὰ παντός). Could this be said only a year or two after the Jews had been stripped of their rights and deprived of their synagogue?

Placing the Sardis decree before L. Antonius's letter causes no such difficulty. (1) Long before 49, the Jews approached the city and, citing Roman favour, asked for an expansion of their existing privileges and were granted freedom of association, a degree of internal autonomy, and a meeting place. (2) Early in 49, the Jews approach L. Antonius and inform him of their privileged position in Sardis, mentioning their association, internal autonomy, and meeting place. He confirms their privileges.

On this arrangement, the Sardis decree comes earlier in the development of Jewish rights in that city, and L. Antonius's role is diminished to

---

[69] Smallwood 1976: 139; Pucci Ben Zeev 1998: 225.

acknowledging and preserving what already existed. This means, of course, that the Sardis decree is another early document within the larger dossier.

The specific historical context for the decree is not immediately obvious. One hint may lie in what the decree says about its own background. The Sardian Jews were emboldened to request an expansion of their privileges on the grounds that "their νόμοι and freedom" had been restored by the *senatus populusque Romanus*. What does this refer to? The words are usually interpreted as a reference to Caesar's measures confirming Hyrcanus II (14.190–212). It is difficult to imagine, however, that Caesar would have been unmentioned if he had been involved, and such a late date can in any case be ruled out, as has been demonstrated above.

It is in any case not clear that the restoration refers to Judaean affairs. It is also possible that the reference is to the recent rulings that allowed the Jews of Laodicea to live κατὰ τοὺς πατρίους νόμους; of Halicarnassus, κατὰ τοὺς Ἰουδαίων νόμους; and Ephesus (to which we shall turn shortly), κατὰ τοὺς ἰδίους αὐτῶν νόμους. In all these cities the Jews were given the freedom to observe the Sabbath and to perform Jewish rites. In Sardis, however, the Jews may have already enjoyed these rights. Some of the background to their community there is known: they were presumably some of the two thousand families of Jewish colonists from Babylon who were transferred under Antiochus III. They were to be settled, according to a royal letter, in the "most strategic places" (τοὺς ἀςναγκαιοτάτους τόπους) of Lydia and Phrygia,[70] a description that could hardly exclude Sardis. Among the privileges bestowed on them was the right to "enjoy their own νόμοις (νόμοις αὐτοὺς χρῆσθαι τοῖς ἰδίοις). This puts the request of the Sardian Jews in a different light. They probably already possessed what the Jews of the other Asian cities lacked, the right to live according to their νόμοι—hence the allusion of the Sardians to "the many great privileges they have always possessed" (πολλὰ καὶ μεγάλα φιλάνθρωπα ἐσχηκότες διὰ παντός). The recent Roman ruling in favour of Diaspora Jews gave the Sardian community the opportunity to request an expansion of their privileges. The Sardis decree, then, fits well with the documents considered above.

2.2.4. The Decree of Ephesus

Most of the documents discussed thus far are clustered together at the end of Josephus's Caesarian *acta*. The last in the series is a ψήφισμα Ἐφεσίων, "a decree of Ephesus." Like the documents considered above, it

---

[70] 12.148–150.

grants the Jews the right to observe the Sabbath and perform their rituals. Again the Romans were involved: the Jews, we are told, had approached the Roman proconsul. His name, like so many in the *acta,* is corrupt. In some manuscripts it appears as M. Iulius Pompeius, son of Brutus (Μάρκῳ Ἰουλίῳ Πομπηίῳ υἱῷ Βρούτου) and in one as M. Iulius, son of Pontius, Brutus (Μάρκῳ Ἰουλίῳ Ποντίου υἱῷ Βρούτῳ). One approach, first proposed 150 years ago,[71] identifies the official as the famous Brutus, Caesar's assassin, and emends the name to read M. Iu<n>ius Brutus. The identification is widely accepted[72] but is not possible. In 59, the young man who had been born M. Iunius Brutus was adopted by a maternal uncle and (as Roman practice required) took his name, becoming Q. Servilius Caepio Brutus. Thereafter his name appears in several ways. Sometimes in personal contexts he was "Brutus" or "M. Brutus"; in official contexts, however, he is always Q. (Servilius) Caepio Brutus,[73] as he appears in documents from the Greek East while it was under his control in 43–42.[74] This becomes a substantial historical and onomastic obstacle to identifying the proconsul mentioned in the Ephesus decree as Caesar's assassin: hundreds of contemporary documents refer to Brutus, but "Iunius" is nowhere attested as part of Brutus's name after his adoption. Thus even if we could be sure that the name "M. Iunius Brutus" were sound, it could not refer to Caesar's assassin, unless we assume that the name has been tampered with in the way Hyrcanus's was in the Athenian decree.[75]

A date depends on identifying the proconsul, who seems to be a M. Iunius. The proconsuls of Asia, almost all of whom are known for the last decades of the Republic, do not produce many candidates. The mid-70s offer two reasonable possibilities: M. Iunius D.f. Silanus (pr. by 77), whose term included the year 76, and his successor M. Iunius Iuncus (pr. 76). Another possibility is a M. (Iunius) Silanus, governor of Asia in circa 100.[76] This would place the Ephesus decree together with the documents considered above. Given the similarity of their contents, that date is on balance to be preferred.

---

[71] Bergmann 1847: 687 n. 364.
[72] E.g., Broughton 1951–52: ii.361; Saulnier 1981: 108 n. 92; Pucci Ben Zeev 1998: 228.
[73] See esp. Geiger 1973: 148–50 and Shackleton Bailey 1991: 83–84.
[74] *IG* vii.383 (Oropus): Κόϊντον Καιπίωνα Κοΐν[του] υἱὸν Βροῦτον; *SEG* xvii.75 (Athens): [Κόϊντον Σερουίλι]ον Κοΐντου [υἱὸν Καιπίωνα] Βροῦτον; *I. Délos* 1622 (Delos): Καιπίωνος (twice).
[75] Cf. section 2.1 (p. 6), above.
[76] *I. Priene* 121 with the interpretation of Eilers 1996; accepted by Ferrary 2000a: 172–75; Brennan 2000: 558 remains unconvinced.

2.2.5. The placement of the early documents

It is time to review. I have argued above to redate several documents. These documents, it should be noted, appear together at the end of Josephus's Caesarian *acta,* the final six documents of which are:

> A letter of Laodicea to the governor, Rabirius (241–243), mentioning Roman rules about Sabbath observance and the performance of Jewish rites.

> (Not discussed here.[77]) A letter of the governor P. Servilius Γάλβας to Miletus (244–246) criticizing the city for preventing the Jews from observing the Sabbath and performing their rites.

> A decree of Pergamum (247–255), probably dating to 105 B.C. No Jewish privileges are mentioned.

> A decree of Halicarnassus (256–258), dealing with Sabbath observance and the performance of Jewish rites.

> A decree of Sardis (259–261), establishing several privileges that were long-standing when L. Antonius reconfirmed them in early 49.

> A decree of Ephesus (262–264), again dealing with Sabbath observance and the performance of Jewish rites.

For each of these five documents I have argued for an early date. Inevitably, of course, some of these arguments are stronger than others. The fact that these documents appear as a group, however, invites further reflection. Their proximity to one another, and the fact that they share certain issues in common, surely becomes another reason to suppose an early date for each of them. Moreover, it provedes a clue about the history of the dossier.

2.3 What Does This Tell Us about the History of the Dossier?

These conclusions have important implications. One is that the history of the Jews of Asia Minor has to be rewritten: their rights, which have been viewed as especially the result of decisions of Caesar, began to evolve long before that; exploration of that theme will have to be left for another venue. My chief interest here lies in a different direction, not so much in

---

[77] I will argue for a date of 63/62 in ch. 7 of my book (n. 20); in ch. 8 I assign to the same date the letter of Ἰούλιος Γάιος to Parium (213–216).

the history that the dossier reveals as in the fact that the dossier has a history of its own.

So let us return to the question of archives and the possibility that our documents have been subject to archival processes. We considered two places above where traces of such processes can be detected. One of these was a decree of Athens of 105 B.C. to which, on its delivery to Pergamum, an "archival tag" was attached (underlining what is "archival"):

14.149: ἐπὶ πρυτάνεως καὶ ἱερέως Διονυσίου τοῦ ᾿Ασκληπιάδου, μηνὸς Πανέμου πέμπτῃ ἀπιόντος, ἀπεδόθη τοῖς στρατηγοῖς ψήφισμα ᾿Αθηναίων. ἐπὶ ᾿Αγαθοκλέους ἄρχοντος κτλ

We have seen, however, that this decree is probably to be connected with the decree of Pergamum, which also has an what may be an archival tag, as do the decrees that follow it:

14.247: ψήφισμα Περγαμηνῶν. ἐπὶ πρυτάνεως Κρατίππου κτλ
14.256: ψήφισμα ᾿Αλικαρνασέων. ἐπὶ ἱερέως Μέμνονος κτλ
14.259: ψήφισμα Σαρδιανῶν. ἔδοξε τῇ βουλῇ καὶ τῷ δήμῳ κτλ
14.256: ψήφισμα ᾿Εφεσίων. ἐπὶ πρυτάνεως Μηνοφίλου κτλ

Are the repeated rubrics "ψήφισμα of..." also "archival"? Very probably yes—they are not part of the original decrees,[78] and they are not likely to be Josephan—without them he would have known to which city each decree belonged.[79] They lack, however, what was surely the main feature of an "archival tag," a date. Why? It is at least theoretically possible that the a date has been excised from each. But if these documents existed as a small dossier—and, considering what has been argued above and the repeated archival rubric, it is difficult to believe that they are unrelated—only the first decree in the series would need a date. This is, in fact, what we have: the Athenian decree offers a full "archival tag" that ends, significantly, with the rubric ψήφισμα ᾿Αθηναίων, which becomes the motif that reintroduces each subsequent document. The archival tag at 14.149, then, could record the delivery not merely of the Athenian decree to the στρατηγοί of Pergamum, but of a small dossier. This means that within Josephus's Caesarian dossier can be identified a proto-dossier. Given the

---

[78] See the comments of Pucci Ben Zeev 1998: 207, 219, 227.
[79] The one place that he has tried to imitate this organizational device he has bungled badly: 14.231–232 purports to be a ψήφισμα Δηλίων of 49 B.C. It cannot come from Delos, however, since the (Athenian) archon of that year was not Boiotos (as at 14.231), but Demochares (Meritt 1977: 191). Nor is it a ψήφισμα, but a χρηματισμός of the στρατηγοί of some city.

content and dating of its parts, a guess can be made about its purpose: to argue, with documentary support, that Rome favoured the Jews and that Jewish privileges within the city should be expanded.[80]

3. HISTORY OF A DOSSIER: A HYPOTHESIS

Such was probably the origin of the dossier. It did not, as might be expected, disappear into a bureaucrat's waste bin. Whoever prepared it—surely the Jewish community itself—kept a copy and shared it with communities in other cities. Mostly it sat; occasionally it was used to serve the apologetical purpose for which it had originally been created. Over time, it grew larger. A local backlash against the Jews brought appeals, and resolution created new documents that were duly added to the dossier. Cross-fertilization with other similar dossiers, some quite far away, added new documents from elsewhere and new versions of old ones. New issues arose: Could Roman Jews be compelled to serve in the legions? Could the temple tax be sent to Jerusalem? Could Jews be summoned to court on the Sabbath? These were added where there was free space or on a new sheet added to the outside of the papyrus roll. Occasionally, the whole roll had to be recopied. Care was taken, of a sort, at least for important passages. But what harm could there be if overly long names were truncated? or if meaningless lists of names, arcane bureaucratic formulas, or tedious repetitions were cut?

Through all this the dossier grew—incrementally, organically, chaotically. To a user, it must have seemed disorganized, which it was. From which end of the scroll did it start? Anyway, one had ever organized it, least of all the historian into whose hands a copy somehow came. He was a failed politician living in exile and, like so many others disappointed by politics, turned to writing history. His people had its own historiographical traditions, one of which was the quoting of documents, and these new documents nicely illustrated an apologetical point that he was keen to make: Roman favour toward the Jews. He carved the dossier up for his narrative; a few documents were moved to where they seemed more useful; explanatory comments were inserted; introductions and conclusions added. Instead of dossier there were now several smaller ones. And, for the first time in its history, the dossier existed within a narrative—more often than not anachronistic. However, despite its dismemberment, the dossier's survival was guaranteed in its new context, where it baffled its users ever since.

---

[80] For its size, cf. Cic. *Flacc.* 68.

BIBLIOGRAPHY

Alexander, M. C. 1990. *Trials in the Late Roman Republic: 149 BC TO 50 BC*. Phoenix Supplementary volume 26. Toronto.
Allen, R. E. 1983. *The Attalid Kingdom: A Constitutional History*. Oxford.
Bergmann, R. 1847. De Asiae Romanorum provinciae praesidibus. *Philologus* 2:639–90.
Brennan, T. C. 2000. *The Praetorship in the Roman Republic*. Oxford.
Broughton, T. R. S. 1951–52. *The Magistrates of the Roman Republic*. Philological Monographs published by the American Philological Association 15. Cleveland.
———. 1986. *The Magistrates of the Roman Republic,* iii. Atlanta.
Champlin, E. 1989. "Magisterial Revisions. *CPh* 84:51–59.
Eilers, C. 1995. L. Antonius, Artemis and Ephesus. *Epigraphica Anatolica* 25:77–82.
———. 1996. Silanus <and> Murena (*I. Priene* 121). *CQ* 46:175–82.
Erskine, A. 1994. The Romans As Common Benefactors. *Historia* 43:70–87.
Ferrary, J.-L. 1988. *Philhellénisme et impérialisme: aspects idéologiques de la conquête romaine du monde hellénistique*. Bibliothèque des Écoles françaises d'Athènes et de Rome 271. Rome.
———. 2000a. Les gouverneurs des provinces romaines d'Asie Mineure (Asie et Cilicie), depuis l'organisation de la province d'Asie jusqu'à la première guerre de Mithridate (126–88 av. J.-C.). *Chiron* 30:161–93.
———. 2000b. Les inscriptions du sanctuaire de Claros en l'honneur de Romains. *BCH* 124:331–76.
Freber, P.-S. G. 1993. *Der hellenistische Osten und das Illyricum unter Caesar*. Palingenesia: Monographien und Texte zur klassischen Altertumswissenschaft 42. Stuttgart.
Geiger, J. 1973. The Last Servilii Caepiones of the Republic. *Ancient Society* 4:143–56.
Gruen, E. S. 1984. *The Hellenistic World and the Coming of Rome*. Berkeley.
———. 2002. *Diaspora: Jews amidst Greeks and Romans*. Cambridge, Mass.
Homolle, T. 1882. Le proconsul Rabirius: Correction au texte de Josèphe. *BCH* 6:608–12.
Laqueur, R. 1920. *Der jüdische Historiker Flavius Josephus: Ein biographischer Versuch auf neuer quellenkritischer Grundlage*. Giessen.
Marcus, R. 1943. *Josephus, Jewish Antiquities, vii: Books XII–XIV*. Loeb Classical Library 365. London and Cambridge, Mass.
Marshall, A. J. 1972. The Lex Pompeia de provinciis (52 B.C.) and Cicero's Imperium in 51–50 B.C.: Constitutional Aspects. *ANRW* i/1:887–921.
Meritt, B. D. 1977. Athenian Archons, 347/46–48/47 B.C. *Historia* 26:161–91.

Niese, B. 1876. Bermerkungen über die Urkunden bei Josephus Archaeol. B. XIII. XIV. XVI. *Hermes* 11:466–88.

———. 1906. Eine Urkunde aus der Makkabäerzeit. Pages 817–29 in *Orientalische Studien Theodor Nöldeke zum siebzigsten Geburtstag (2. März 1906.* Edited by C. Bezold. Giessen.

Pucci Ben Zeev, M. 1998. *Jewish Rights in the Roman World: The Greek and Roman Documents Quoted by Josephus Flavius.* Texts and Studies in Ancient Judaism 74. Tübingen.

Rajak, T. 1981. Roman Intervention in a Seleucid Siege of Jerusalem? *GRBS* 22:65–81.

———. 1984. Was There a Roman Charter for the Jews? *JRS* 74:107–23.

———. 1985. Jewish Rights in the Greek Cities under Roman Rule: A New Approach. Pages 19–35 in *Approaches to Ancient Judaism V: Studies in Judaism and Its Greco-Roman Context.* Edited by W. S. Green. Brown Judaic Studies 32. Atlanta.

Raubitschek, A. E. 1954. Epigraphical Notes on Julius Caesar. *JRS* 44: 65–75.

Reinach, T. 1899. Antiochus Cyzicène et les Juifs. *REJ* 38:161–71.

———, ed. 1904. *Oeuvres complètes de Flavius Josèphe, iii: Antiquités Judaïques livres XI–XV.* Paris.

Ritschl, F. 1873. Eine Berichtigung der republikanischen Consularfasten: Zugleich als Beitrag zur Geschichte der römisch-jüdischen internationalen Beziehungen. *RhM* 28:586–614.

Robert, L. 1969. 'Théophanes de Mytilène à Constantinople. *CRAI:* 42–64.

Samuel, A. E. 1972. *Greek and Roman Chronology: Calendars and Years in Classical Antiquity.* Handbuch der Altertumswissenschaft i/7. Munich.

Saulnier, C. 1981. Lois romaines sur les Juifs selon Flavius Josèphe. *RB* 88: 161–98.

Schürer, E., et al. 1973–87. *The History of the Jewish People in the Age of Jesus Christ.* Edinburgh.

Shackleton Bailey, D. R., ed. 1977. *Cicero, Epistulae ad Familiares.* Cambridge Classical Texts and Commentaries 16–17. Cambridge.

———. 1991. *Two Studies in Roman Nomenclature.* Atlanta.

Sherk, R. K. 1990. The Eponymous Officials of Greek Cities: I. *ZPE* 83: 249–288.

———. 1992. The Eponymous Officials of Greek Cities: IV. *ZPE* 93:223–72.

Siani-Davies, M., ed. 2001. *Marcus Tullius Cicero, Pro Rabirio Postumo* (Oxford).

Smallwood, E. M. 1976. *The Jews under Roman Rule: From Pompey to Diocletian.* Studies in Judaism in Late Antiquity 20. Leiden.

Syme, R. 1939. Observations on the Province of Cilicia. Pages 299–332 in *Anatolian Studies Presented to William Hepburn Buckler.* Edited by W. M. Calder and J. Keil. Manchester. Reprint = Roman Papers 1:120–48.

———. 1967. Review of A. Degrassi, *Inscriptiones Latinae Liberae Rei Publicae*. *JRS* 57: 262–63.
———. 1979–91. *Roman Papers*. Oxford.
Thackery, H. S. J. 1929. *Josephus: The Man and the Historian*. New York.

When Israel Loses Its Meaning: The Reconstitution of Language and Community in Ezekiel's Prophecy

David Casson
Emory University

"As for you, mortal ... I will make your tongue cling to the roof of your mouth, so that you will be speechless and unable to reprove them; for they are a rebellious house. But when I speak with you, I will open your mouth, and you shall say to them 'Thus says the LORD God'; let those who will hear, hear; and let those who refuse to hear, refuse; for they are a rebellious house." (Ezekiel 3:25–27)

In his 1984 book *When Words Lose Their Meaning,* James Boyd White engages a number of familiar Western texts with two questions: "What kind of cultural action is this writing?" and "What kind of social action is it?"[1] White is a rare combination of legal scholar and literary critic. He merges these two callings to explore the peculiar way literary texts do what all human utterance does: constantly create and reconstitute the possibility of human community through language. For White every spoken or written word, whether it intends to be or not, is performative, it does something. What it does is in some way to participate in the forming and reforming of a given society's language. Language is not something stable, says White, but "is perpetually remade by its speakers, who are themselves remade, both as individuals and as communities, in what they say" (preface, x).

White is especially interested in one particular response to this instability of language: the *act* of writing a literary text. In a series of essays he looks at eight seemingly unrelated classic works, spread over thousands

---

[1] James Boyd White, *When Words Lose Their Meaning: Constitutions and Reconstitutions of Language, Character, and Community* (Chicago: University of Chicago Press, 1984), 6. Subsequent references will be parenthetical and in the text.

of years, to ask how each sets out—using the language its culture has provided—to remake that very language. This intentional action results in words "losing their meaning" and taking on new ones. For White this is not primarily a lexical phenomenon, although dictionary definitions may well change as a result. Instead, since words only "mean" in relation to other words, it is in reorganizing the complex connections a given culture makes between words that these texts do their real work of transformation. Nor is language, for White, really just about grammar and syntax. Language includes all the resources available to a given society at a given time for making meaning, determining value, establishing identity, and reasoning about the world. Language is, for White, a very near synonym for culture itself. As such, the resources language provides are both "given" and for the most part unnoticeable. Because of that, any writer is as much a product of her language as a transformer of it, and this "reciprocal" relationship makes writing at the same time both political and personal. In making a text, an author endeavors to somehow reconstitute both the conditions of human community and the possibilities for her own life and character within that community.

White's two questions, then, are questions about two sets, or two levels, of human relations at work in any text. The first question, "What kind of cultural action is this text?" asks how an author portrays relationships between people *within* the text. The question requires of the reader what White calls "imaginary participation" in the text, an acceptance of an author's invitation to provisionally inhabit the world of the text and adopt that world's "language," the words it uses to structure its relationship to nature, its social roles, its terms of value, and its own way of reasoning (9–11). The question goes further, however, and probes the author's appraisal of that language he has been given; how adequate he finds the conceptual resources of his society to create human culture; how well the culture's words are able to create a framework for meaningful and livable relationships. As White imagines his way into the inherited language of each of his wide range of authors—including the poet Homer, the historian Thucydides, the essayist Samuel Johnson, the novelist Jane Austen, and the framers of the U.S. Constitution—he clarifies the kind of cultural action the text represents by asking "What is this author's relationship to his or her language?"

The second question, "What kind of social action is this text?" focuses not on the relationship between people within the text but on the relationship the author is creating with the *reader* of the text. White claims an author invites a reader into his world but also invites the reader to stand with him outside that world, as a textual "community of two" (13). In this relationship the author offers the reader "a place to stand, a place from which she can observe and judge the characters and events of the world he creates, indeed the world itself" (17). In doing so, the author invites a reader to become a certain sort of person, to take on a certain character. In fact, claims White, a text is largely about *how* "its reader will be changed by reading it" (19). The way the author goes about creating this relationship, the trust and respect he invests in his reader, and the ultimate intention he has for her can make this an act of profound human friendship—or of betrayal. In creating this "community of two" the author either models, or he contradicts, the character of relationship he envisions for his culture. White probes the quality of the social act writing involves by asking of each text: "What is the author's relationship to the reader?"

THE LANGUAGE OF SEVENTH-CENTURY JUDAH

The Ezekiel scroll purports to be a first-person memoir of a Hebrew prophet who finds himself among the Judean families taken to Babylon in the first exile. If we accept this, as do a growing consensus of trained readers, here is a text that even in its basic plot structure is all about contested language—or better yet contested constructions of the same language. In the opening chapters, Ezekiel narrates how, in terrible grandeur, Yahweh himself appeared to him in Babylon and recruited him to deliver *Yahweh's* words, כֹּה אָמַר אֲדֹנָי, to a people who already have books full of them. These new words are, of course, in the same basic language as the old. Not just that they are in Hebrew, but they share most of the cultural assumptions, structures of meaning, and terms of value (in fact, this very similarity will prove an early problem for Ezekiel). Yet, by the time Ezekiel is finished with his mission, for those who listen carefully these very words will have changed their meaning.

The first task, then, is to try and describe the cultural resources both he and his first readers together inherit. With each of his chosen texts, James Boyd White repeats this theme of the reciprocity of writer and language. It is not just that writers must use a language to appraise and transform it, but they are themselves products of it. Ezekiel is no different. To communicate at all, he must use the language of his first audience. Moreover, as a Hebrew priest his very identity and worldview are formed by that language he is now called to judge. Although his immediate audience is now in exile, the language they share with Ezekiel is still the one they all knew in Judah only a few years before and share with those still in the land. The political and cultural crisis facing the Hebrew people as Ezekiel writes is stark, but it has been a fairly swift and recent development. Barely more than a decade has passed since the optimistic and culturally robust days of the long Josian monarchy. The language, the system of resources available to the culture for making meaning and creating human community, is the one learned in more stable, confident times.

Describing that language is no easy task. In its more narrow syntactical definition, it is not impossible to reconstruct the grammar of a language. But in the way White uses the word *language,* almost as a synonym for culture, it becomes much more difficult. Because all of the members of a culture are "acculturated," the characteristic features of their shared language are usually hidden—and if pointed out seem absurdly obvious (8). This kind of language contains the mostly invisible presuppositions lying beneath all the community is and does. It creates the possibility for civilization by providing terms of identity, relationship, and discourse. In his first essay on the *Iliad,* for instance, White describes the language of ancient Greek heroic culture, the adequacy of which Homer sets out to question.

To draft a quick "grammar" of the cultural language of seventh-century Judah, I will borrow four analytical questions that White suggests and that he uses in each of his essays (9–11). I will attempt to answer these in a general way from the biblical sources, confident that even if the historical books were still works in progress at this time, any exilic editors would at least be of the same generation. The first of White's questions concerns how a language defines and presents the world of *nature.* It is highly significant that Hebrew thought at the time knew no such independent realm as nature. Instead, all of life, natural or social, was seen as radically contingent on the reality of God, and for Judah, specifically Yahweh (at least in culturally dominant circles). In ways we can probably not fully appreciate, the culture of seventh-century Judah was anchored not only in a conscious awareness of God's reality but in an assurance in their God's ongoing activity among and clear favor toward Israel. Without this assurance national life was incomprehensible. Along with this went a confidence in Yahweh's special presence in the Jerusalem temple. While Judah shared most of these assumptions with her neighbors, she had also developed a more characteristic set of liturgical and theological themes that had by the seventh century been subsumed into the community's "language." The oldest of these concerned Yahweh's mercy and slowness to anger. Another was an elaborate historicized saga of Yahweh's specific unfolding of promises to the Hebrew people. Two more recent elements of this language were a metaphor of covenant, in which Judah saw itself as an independent, though not equal, treaty partner with Yahweh, and an explicit doctrine of the inviolability of Jerusalem.

Most of the other resources Judah had for creating human culture in the seventh century grew up from this bedrock awareness of the reality of Yahweh in their midst. Nearly all of the possible social roles and identities, the topic of the second analytical question White suggests, were in Judah related back to the nation's religious life. At the top, most of the elite received their identities from the closely linked religious institutions of temple and palace. Their place in the Yahwistic faith told them who they were and how they were to function in society. Outside the capital, religious rationale provided the form and boundaries to family and clan relations, land use and interactions with people of other cultures. Even the lives of peasants were given structure by religious calendars of feasts and pilgrimages and by centralized sacrificial slaughter and were protected by legal provisions in codes putatively dictated by God (e.g., gleaning, debt remission).

The third question White provides to understand the grammar of a cultural language is, What are the central terms of meaning and value, and how do they function with one another to create patterns of motive and significance? (11). Although, with some exceptions, alternative discourses about meaning have been left out of the Hebrew canon, it is still remarkable the number of different voices within that canon that use similar terms. And nearly all of these primary terms of value—such as righteousness, justice, steadfast love, and their opposites—receive their meaning and warrant from their place in the very character of Yahweh. Yahweh's own righteousness, justice, and the like are the archetypes that give content and meaning to Judah's ethical discourse. What Yahweh is said to prefer (e.g., the poor, *shalom*, mercy) becomes a cultural value. Every person receives intrinsic worth from his or her created imprint of the image of God. Meaning is also derived from Israel's own experience with God. Their merciful rescue from slavery forbids them from mistreating their own slaves. Again and again, Judah's language links its values and motives to the reality of God. Even in the less "theological" wisdom traditions, fear of the Lord serves as a compelling motive.

White's final question concerns the resources for *reasoning* that a language furnishes a given culture. For Judah, the pattern observed in the first three questions holds here as well. Though there are some exceptions, reasoning in Judah begins and proceeds on the assumption of the reality of God. God's will and God's intention inform not just discourse about proper worship but public deliberation on such things as the acceptable uses of violence, social and economic relations, and the treatment of sojourners and the poor. This reasoning, like most cultural reasoning, is not abstractly theoretical or linear. It does not, as White notes in the discourse of Edmund Burke, seek mere "intellectual assent to the truth of certain propositions" but appeals for "active belief, commitment, and participation" (193). To engage both imagination and intellect, such reasoning relies on metaphor and poetry as much as cold logic (135, 205).

It is apparent that in its awareness of God at the center of its natural world, in its social roles and identities, in its terms of value and meaning, and in its form of reasoning, Judah was a culture whose resources for creating community rested heavily on its perception of God's reality. This central act of imagination allowed an integration of various aspects of the self—religious, personal, and social—that made cultural life possible. What would happen if that center should fade from immediate awareness?

HOW WORDS LOSE THEIR MEANING

To ask about Ezekiel's relationship to his inherited language is not so much to ask about his appraisal of it in the abstract as to probe his sense of its current health as it was actually functioning in his concrete community. Throughout his book, White returns to a refrain about language's tendency to shift and change as people use it ... and abuse it. Judah had used these linguistic resources to constitute its cultural life for many decades. God's decision to commission Ezekiel as a prophet, not as a systematic theologian, means Ezekiel must engage the way Judah had continually *reconstituted* this language in this very process of living it out. It is not a theoretical engagement but a concrete rhetorical act within a real community.

A significant clue to Ezekiel's relationship to Judah's current, reconstituted language occurs in the midst of his commissioning as a prophet. As God gives Ezekiel the "antipep talk" almost obligatory to a prophet's call genre—*they won't listen to you*—God lets slip an intriguing aside: "Now I am not sending you to a people of obscure speech and difficult language, but to the house of Israel ... not to a people of obscure speech; if I sent you to *them* they would listen to you" (3:5–6). The problem, apparently, is not that the people do not know the language Ezekiel is speaking but that they know it *too well*. As they have used this language to continually constitute and reconstitute their culture over many years, they have become *acculturated* to it. What was at one point so starkly contingent, surprising, remarkable, and real has become obvious and invisible to perception. The language is still there, but through its very familiarity it has lost its meaning. Having been dulled into commonplaces and slogans, it no longer has the vitality to do the best things that language does: form and regulate human relationships, serve as the glue that holds people together in community, or provide the sanctions that limit people's abuse of each other. In this vacuum, individual autonomy and selfishness have emerged unchallenged, and community has begun to disintegrate. Ezekiel's relationship to his inherited language is defined by his certainty that through use (and abuse), Judah's language has lost its vital center. The conscious, immediate awareness of the reality of God—that central element that funds at least this particular language's ability to create community—has disappeared. With it has gone this language's capacity to integrate the self. In condemning opponents for various acts he considers religiously reckless or socially callous, Ezekiel repeatedly "quotes" them as saying "God does not see!" (e.g., 8:12). In this bald assertion, they describe the disintegration of their various selves: the severing of their creature self in relationship to God from their social self in relationship to others. The language has lost its meaning. Ezekiel is estranged from his own words. He cannot simply repeat them to his fellow Judeans. The words may not be obscure—but they are empty. Whatever we make of God's puzzling announcement about rendering Ezekiel mute in chapter 3, it has something to do with Ezekiel's estrangement from his own language.

This dulling of the vitality of Judah's language shows up in many different ways as Ezekiel scans the Judean culture. The most obvious of these are religious, as cohesive and shared understandings of who God is give way to experimentation and syncretism (at least from this priest's perspective). But Ezekiel also sees the social costs to this loss of a theological center. Some of these would have been apparent to him even before the recent political disaster. As familiarity tamed the awareness of a present and attentive Yahweh, people of means and ability found little to counter their own ambition and sense of entitlement. "If this city is pot of soup," they have apparently been telling themselves, "we are the meat!" (11:3). These leaders of Judah, in Ezekiel's eyes, have lost all concern but for their own their own "abundance ... their wealth ... and their preeminence" (7:11). Their confidence lies in their silver (7:19) and their land, a divinely guaranteed patrimony of Abraham (33:23). They have acquitted themselves of any responsibility for knowing or doing what is right by an ingenious game of generational blameshifting, epitomized in their proverb about the sour grapes.[2] With neither conscience nor fear of God to curb greed, those who were supposed to be the nation's shepherds, protecting the poor and powerless, have instead become their predators, growing fat on their own flock (34:1–24). Oblivious to any claim their own cultural language might have on their behavior, Judah's leaders—as Ezekiel tells them again and again—have become intoxicated with violence, bloodshed, and economic exploitation. Listen to him describe the dissolving bonds of human community:

> The princes of Israel in you, everyone according to his power, have been bent on shedding blood. Father and mother are treated with contempt in you; the alien residing within you suffers extortion; the orphan and the widow are wronged in you.... you ... take bribes to shed blood; you take both advance interest and accrued interest, and make gain of your neighbors by extortion; and you have forgotten me, says the Lord GOD. (22:6–12)

---

[2] Ezekiel hammers on this ethical evasion again and again (chs. 3; 18; and 33).

Did you catch that final clause? Ezekiel is making the claim that this religious culture, which speaks this religious language, has nonetheless forgotten what their own words mean. They have prophets, but they prophesy out of their own imaginations. Unafraid of the same domesticated God the other elites invoke, these prophets, in Ezekiel's words, "smear whitewash" on anything unsettling and say "peace, when there is no peace" (13:1–16).

As long as the culture is up and running, sick as it might be, this flow of meaningless words keeps going. White says that a culture's language appears so obvious and natural to its members that no one inside the culture can see what a contingent, manufactured—and fragile—thing it is ... until a crisis (277). For Judah this crisis comes with the Babylonian armies in 598. Pounded out of their daydream, the leaders of Judah suddenly find that their language, at least as it had developed, is unable to make sense of the end of Judean statehood. Some habitually assume things will continue, but most are stunned into silence. As "disaster comes upon disaster," they desperately sift their religious language for adequate words. In vain they "keep seeking a vision from the prophet"; instruction has "perished from the priest, and counsel from the elders" (7:26).

RECONSTITUTING LANGUAGE: A SCROLL BITTER AND SWEET

The task to which God recruits Ezekiel during that bleak, suspended decade between the two exiles is more than anything a high-stakes struggle about language. "Do not be afraid of their words," God tells him: "You shall speak my words" (2:6–7). Lined up side by side, these two sets of words would look almost indistinguishable. Yet the crucial claim of the text is that one of these has lost its meaning. The question is whether and how—by delivering God's words—Ezekiel might reconstitute this language, and by doing so reconstitute the possibility for culture among his people. One option is immediately ruled out: the reciprocity of language and speaker means there is no possibility for some wholesale alternative, some entirely new language. Ezekiel and his listeners are created by this language and must work toward its re-creation not by starting over but by rearranging and reconnecting the pieces already there. Nor will this reconstitution of language rely primarily on linear or logical argument. Ezekiel must repair not the definitions and abstractions in the language but the way the language is imagined and felt and experienced. Ezekiel's task will require as much use of image and metaphor, then, as structured argument. His challenge will be to use the language itself to show the inadequacy of what the language has become and to reconnect its parts in a way that will make it again fresh and real and alive.

Ezekiel believes that it is the very familiarity of Judah's language that has robbed it of meaning and its effectiveness. His rhetorical task, therefore, is to re-create the language's *surprise*—the ongoing awareness that any claims it makes are contingent and unexpected, not obvious or natural. Needing to accomplish this using the resources of the language itself, he employs two opposite rhetorical strategies, two imaginary "what ifs." In the one he *intensifies* the claims of Judah's language; in the other he *contradicts* them.

Ezekiel begins his book by yanking his reader, almost without warning, into a scene unprecedented in Hebrew scripture: a dazzling, overwhelming, face-to-face encounter with God's very throne chariot. By taking the "obvious" but unremarkable fact of God's existence and displaying it before the reader with such awful force, Ezekiel is asking the unexpected question, "What would it be like if God were real?" He is reaching deep into the cultural language of Judah and grabbing its central presupposition, rending it out of its comfortable neglect, and putting it awkwardly but powerfully right in their faces. *What if God is real!?* Throughout his book, in chapters 1–3, 8–11, 37, and culminating in the temple vision in 40–48, Ezekiel presents to the cultural imagination of his people this intensified version of their own language. He even suggests an appropriate response: "When I saw it," he tells them, "I fell on my face" (1:28)

Ezekiel employs another strategy of surprise that is equally jarring. He takes cultural premises that simply cannot be contradicted ... and contradicts them. He dares to ask his people, "What if God is *not* for us?" What if, for instance, Jerusalem is not inviolable but doomed (ch. 5)? What if her leading citizens *are* the meat in the pot and God is about to pick out these morsels and devour them (chs. 11 and 24)? What if God is not, as your proverbs say, slow to anger, but swift in bringing about your end (chs. 7 and 12)? What if your cherished event of Passover happened again, in Jerusalem, and this time *you* were the firstborn (ch. 9)? What if your solid claim to Abraham's land is simply void (33:25–26)? What if Yahweh's presence isn't even *in* the Jerusalem temple any more but has moved out (ch. 11)? Perhaps most significantly, what if your proud history with Yahweh is nothing like you remember it—what if it is really a story of you letting God down from the word go (ch. 20)? What if even the best you've had, Noah, Daniel, and Job, wouldn't be enough to save you now (14:14)? By relentlessly posing these unsettling questions, by composing a mock dirge for King Zedekiah (ch. 19) and the astonishingly brutal song of the sword (ch. 21), Ezekiel is snatching from his Judean audience their confidence in the naturalness of their own language.

These two rhetorical strategies, either intensifying or contradicting most of the central elements of Judah's language, give Ezekiel's book a well-earned reputation as both bizarre and harsh. There is obvious risk to both approaches. While offending his audience is a calculated part of his method, he treads dangerously close to overwhelming their ability to listen altogether. In fact, the call narrative seems to make this a foregone conclusion. Yet if he succeeds, if some genuinely experience the surprise he intends, Ezekiel will have used Judah's language to show how it has lost its own meaning. Judah, in her religious language, had attempted to generalize and abstract its own words about God into timeless, natural truths. In doing so it had lost the awareness of these truths as contingent and remarkable gifts that cannot be taken for granted. By aggressively *defamiliarizing* these words, on the one hand by making them astonishingly visible, and on the other by making them dramatically contingent through the possibility of their opposite, Ezekiel reconstitutes Judah's language. In this act he hopes—even in the midst of an appalling national crisis—to reconstitute the possibility of Judean culture. Ezekiel is not, of course, returning the language to some pristine state. That old world is falling apart around him, and any language that promises to fund a vigorous culture must in some ways be a new language for this new age, yet created out of the language that made Judah and Ezekiel. So in fulfilling his prophetic mission, Ezekiel sees to it that the words that had lost their meaning, again lose their meaning ... by taking on a new meaning in a strange new land. Only from such hindsight can we understand what Ezekiel already knew when the bitter scroll he is given to eat, "words of lamentation and mourning and woe," became on his lips "as sweet as honey" (2:10; 3:3).

EZEKIEL AND HIS READER: A COMMUNITY OF TWO

All of Ezekiel's encounters with the personalities of Judean culture—the elders who visit him, the prophets he denounces, the leaders he accuses, the crowds that watch his strange sign-acts in the public square, and even the dazzling throne chariot of Yahweh—are encounters that take place in a narrative Ezekiel has written. Although as a Judean exile living through a particular political crisis, Ezekiel writes a text with undeniable real-world referents, he has nonetheless chosen to render that text in the form of a story. Whatever sort of "cultural action" this text is, to use James Boyd White's term, that action takes place *in* the text. The encounters in which Ezekiel employs his twin rhetorical strategies of intensifying and contradicting Judah's language are narrated, plotted into a story world that for all its realism is still presented to the reader as a literary construction.

That act, that offer by a writer to a reader of an object of mutual consideration, in this case a story, is what White means as the "social" action of writing a text. In doing so the writer invites the reader to become, if only momentarily, a "community of two" outside the text (13). White claims that "whenever you speak, you define a character for yourself and for at least one other" (preface, xi). In his relationship to his reader, what sort of character does Ezekiel take on, and perhaps more importantly, what sort of character does he invite his reader to become? To ask the same question a different way—a way that most interests White—is this relationship a genuine friendship?

This is not to ask if Ezekiel is a "friendly" text. It is clearly not. The prophet's rhetorical strategy of shock and defamiliarization makes that perhaps impossible. And it can certainly be argued—and increasingly is—that Ezekiel goes too far, even for that goal. His decision, in the pursuit of shock value, to employ images of domestic abuse, divine violence, and, some have argued, pornography may result in language too toxic for its goal of reconstituting human community. Even without these objections, Ezekiel is not a friendly text; it is difficult and disturbing. Yet perhaps Ezekiel's own subtle acknowledgment of this truth provide the first glimpse into his literary act of friendship.

Lurking around the edges of the literary character Ezekiel creates for himself is a certain unspoken reluctance to his role as God's companion. He only comes out and says it once at the beginning (3:14), but throughout the text one gets the impression Ezekiel is not enjoying himself. It is not just how he is repeatedly picked up and dragged through the air around the whole ancient Near East, nor the awkward and embarrassing sign-acts he is commanded to perform. It comes through in a certain aloofness suggested by the tone of dialogue: the persistence with which God repeats phrases such as "Do you see this? ... But you will see still greater abominations" (e.g., 8:6); or Ezekiel's weary reply in the valley of dry bones "Oh Lord, you know" (37:3). This distance is reinforced most clearly in God's relentless term of address for Ezekiel, "mortal one." Even while in the text he aggressively pursues the project of reconstituting Judah's language about God, Ezekiel, *as a text,* addresses the reader out of a character subtly distanced from God. In an imaginary triangle between Ezekiel, God and the reader, Ezekiel signals that he occupies a place closer to the reader. He bolsters this act of conspiratorial friendship by sharing with the reader a series of secret views: of hidden blasphemy in Jerusalem, but more dramatically of Yahweh's dazzling throne chariot and of the heavenly temple destined for the new city. In defining for himself such a character, Ezekiel first gives himself to his reader not so much as instructor but as fellow creature similarly unsure of this God he must follow.

But if this friendship has a moment of solidarity with the reader, it also has an equally conspiratorial moment of invitation. *Within* the text, the most remarkable feature of Ezekiel's message is that God has given up hope that Judah will choose obedience. There will be obedience, God says through Ezekiel, but it will be imposed, not chosen. "I will put my spirit within you and *cause* you to walk in my statutes," God says bluntly (36:37). Within the world of the text, there is not much to do but to wait for God to do what God will do. But the very fact that this is a text, a communication event between writer and reader, ironically undercuts the possibility that such fatalism can be what Ezekiel intends. If no change of behavior, no growth and development of character is possible, the writer would save his energy. Instead, the act of writing itself is an act of confidence in the possibility of persuasion. The fact that Ezekiel trusts his reader to catch his literary *wink*—that while the texts *says* there is no way to choose obedience, the experience of reading the book is to learn one way of doing just that—is ample evidence of a textual community of two.

Ezekiel's friendship is, then, the sort that White recognizes in his texts, one that trusts and invites the reader to become a better self. Bidding the reader to look at the world through his text, Ezekiel offers to train the reader in rediscovering the language of humble contingency. That language is unapologetically Yahwist, and it would be inaccurate to portray it in the humanist categories White employs. A reader who assents to learning from Ezekiel, however, will at the very least learn what it takes to keep language fresh and surprising. The reader will also find a friend who is himself trying to put together what culture so often severs: our identity as individuals and our lives in community. Ezekiel does, in words White uses about Edmund Burke, hope to "affect his culture by affecting his readers, to work changes in individuals that will lead to changes in the community" (209). His final eight chapters foresee a world of restored human community, where balances are fair (45:10), where unjust evictions do not happen (45:9) and where the power of the king is restrained (46:16–18). And though the reader may not make this crucial move, the prophet offers it in friendship: Ezekiel cannot imagine such a world anywhere else but in a city whose very name reflects the center of his reconstituted language: *Yahweh is There* (48:35).

www.ingramcontent.com/pod-product-compliance
Lightning Source LLC
Chambersburg PA
CBHW031311150426
43191CB00005B/185